Strategic
Planning
for
Human
Resources
Management

Strategic Planning for Human Resources Management

Robert E. Sibson

amacom

American Management Association

*This book is available at a special
discount when ordered in bulk quantities.
For information, contact Special Sales Department,
AMACOM, a division of American Management Association, 135 West 50th Street, New York, NY 10020.*

Library of Congress Cataloging-in-Publication Data

Sibson, Robert Earl, 1925–
    Strategic planning for human resources management /
Robert E. Sibson.
        p.   cm.
    Includes index.
    ISBN 0-8144-5040-7
    1.   Personnel management.   2. Strategic plan-
ning.   I. Title.
HF5549.S5854   1992
658.3'01—dc20   91-43749
                                                          CIP

Printing number

10 9 8 7 6 5 4 3

Contents

Preface

This is a book about strategic planning in human resources management work. It is a practical book which identifies the major strategic human resources management issues and provides ideas and recommendations for dealing with these matters.

I am not advocating anything in this book. Those who know me would tell you that I have never been reluctant to express opinions, but opinions must be restrained in planning work, so I have tried to keep my philosophy, thinking, and biases out of this book.

And I am not selling anything. While I am still very active with worknetworking clients, *The Sibson Report*, and consulting consultants, I no longer do project consulting work, and haven't for the past six years.

I think that some background information about personnel work is helpful in considering human resources management planning activities. Most of this Preface has to do with such background information and contains the few personal comments that are typical of a preface.

Many good things have been done in human resources management during the thirty-two years that I have been a consultant in the field. Partly because of this good work and partly because people problems have increasingly become a central part of the general management job, the human resources management function has grown and prospered during that period.

For the thirty-year period from 1960 to 1990, personnel was a growth area of work. The average personnel ratio in companies with more than five hundred employees increased from 0.5 in 1960 to 1.2 in 1990. Furthermore, in companies with more than five hundred employees, the percentage of those with personnel departments headed by a professional in the field grew from less than one-third to almost 100 percent during that thirty-year period.

The pay of personnel people also increased rapidly. In the 1960s, 1970s, and 1980s, the average pay of those in personnel work grew more rapidly than in any other work group as far as we can tell from available data. Since 1960, the pay of those in personnel work increased, on average, almost twice as much a year as the pay of workers in general in this country.

As a symbol of the growth and the importance of the personnel field, it became fashionable in the 1980s to call the employee-employer relations function the human resources management department rather than the personnel department. This was done mostly to symbolize a new status for those in the field. The change in name symbolized the fact that the personnel function had become an integral part of the management of more and more companies.

In that period, many businesspeople thought that human resources management was more important, partly because of the great growth in technology. In fact, I am one of those who argue that people are now the *only* unique assets in this country. Such thinking should mean that the human resources management function is not only an integral part of the management of the company but that it is becoming *the* critical support function for executive management.

With these developments in mind, a section titled "The Evolution of the Personnel Function" was published in *The Sibson Report* in the late 1970s. This section traced the distinct stages in the development of the personnel function from its early beginnings to what many of us thought at the time was the fourth and final step in the evolution of the function. The section described the ascent of personnel professionals to the point where human resources management was an integral part of the management of the firm.

More recent developments show that the fourth phase in the evolution of the personnel function was not the last phase. A fifth phase has evolved, and it is affecting substantially the role of those who work in personnel.

Some think that the role of human resources management has diminished in the fifth phase in the evolution of the personnel function. I think that it has just changed.

I think it is very important that human resources management professionals and operating managers understand these changes. These changes are a critical issue for those who work in the field. I think these changes also suggest that strategic human resources thinking and planning are much more important now to successful work in the field.

In large part, the fifth phase of the personnel function is due to external forces. For example, more companies are becoming high-tech. In high-tech businesses, people are clearly the company's only producing asset. Because of this, operating managers personally do more professional personnel work. In effect, the personnel department is shifting in part to the office of the chief executive officer, and that necessarily affects the role of those who work in personnel.

The changing role of human resources management is also being influenced by perceived deficiencies in personnel work in many companies, particularly in the past ten years. These perceptions are widespread, and they relate mostly to failures in the initiative, innovation, and intelligence of personnel work done.

There have been a number of important business issues in the past decade that have essentially been human resources management issues, and executives in many companies have been disappointed in the work done by those in personnel in these areas. Examples would be downsizing, health-care cost containment, the need for more delegative management, and failures in planning. Human resources management professionals rarely took the initiative in such basic issues. In fact, too often key human resources management people resisted downsizing, were ineffective with respect to health-care cost containment, and ignored the real issues of delegative management—often clinging to obsolete programs and the bureaucratic practices of the past. Few in personnel work did any organized planning work at all.

If human resources management was to be an integral part of the management of companies, then key personnel people had to take initiatives in all areas where key problems were essentially personnel issues. This would mean initiative in identifying issues and initiative in evolving appropriate answers. The executive management perception that is held widely in many companies is that human resources management people have failed greatly in taking management initiatives.

In a changing world, innovative answers are needed from time to time. There is a clear need, for example, for a new pay-for-performance system that works, and there is a need for the effective use of computer technology in personnel work. Yet, partly because of poor planning information, many key human resources management people have typically persisted in defending obsolete "merit pay" programs and practices, and many still have not adopted a system of computer-aided personnel.

There is great pure intelligence among human resources management people today. But some think there has been a failure in the *use* of that intelligence. The absence of human resources management planning may be the main reason, due to the lack of planning information.

Those in the personnel function have forgotten too often who they are and the mission of their work. Rather than supporting operating management in the management of personnel and in the more effective management of people, key personnel people in many operations focused too much on technical work and became preoccupied with rules, power, and bureaucracy. A better view of the past and the future should be helpful in dealing with this issue.

The field has become full of canned gimmicks and administrative trivia, and that has become a frustration and disappointment to many operating managers. Many managers think that we in personnel have concentrated too much on professional standards of excellence in developing programs and practices rather than on operating needs.

The current generation of human resources management professionals knows a lot about plans, programs, laws, regulations, and administrative methods. But they generally have less knowledge about the businesses they are in and the operating people who do the work. There is almost always more know-how but sometimes less intelligence about the proper use of knowledge. It is common, in fact, to find human resources management professionals in the corporate office and even in consulting firms who have never done any hands-on personnel work at all.

Perhaps the personnel field just grew too fast. Perhaps because of that growth there are too many good people with insufficient experience. Perhaps personnel has once again become a dumping ground for people who are not good enough.

Strategic human resources management planning is essential to correct many of these deficiencies in initiative, innovation, and intelligence. With the knowledge that comes from strategic planning, human resources management professionals will be more intelligent; they will know about the needs for innovation; and they will have much more confidence to take the initiative on important matters.

There is another important reason for the changing role of human resources management. This involves work on compliance matters by human resources management professionals.

Over the past two decades, personnel people have been doing more and more compliance work. In order to do this work, a lot of technical information must be acquired that is really not a part of employee relations and that is certainly not related to employee capability and productivity.

This compliance role is essentially negative—in many cases preventing management from doing things that are clearly in the interest of the business and its employees. Sometimes colleagues with compliance responsibilities sound like lawyers, or some combination of a lawyer and a union representative.

The cumulative effect is that this work has become more distant from the management of the business, and managers increasingly think of those in human resources management as not being "one of us."

I'm not arguing here about the need for compliance in any way or taking a position on anything. But the compliance work done by personnel people is not part of management; it often does not serve the interests of the company or its employees; and it has most assuredly changed the role of the human resources management function in business.

We should be aware of these concerns about the role of personnel in business and the fact that the role of human resources management is changing. Human resources management planning work will help to identify such issues and provide information that will enhance the ability of those in the field to take proper initiatives and develop innovative answers to such issues. At this point in the history of human resources management and in the evolution of the fifth phase of the personnel function, planning has special importance.

Clearly, the answer is not just to do human resources management planning. Done well, however, the intelligence and information from a sound planning activity will contribute a great deal to the business and to establishing the proper role of the personnel function.

Reflect on these fundamental issues. As I thought about these things, I did more and more work on strategic human resources management planning, and this book is the result.

It is customary to give proper credits and thanks in published material, and I have done a lot of that over the years.

I dedicated a couple of books to Sally, but the fact of the matter is that if I dedicated every day of the rest of my life to her, it would not be sufficient. I dedicated books to our two boys, to colleagues in the field, and my associates. But enough is enough, so I stopped giving credits a few books ago.

I recently realized, however, that there is a whole class of people who were so important in my life and in my work that I would like to dedicate this book to them. They are my teachers.

First, let me thank all the teachers in the public school system of the City of Philadelphia, particularly those at Germantown High School from 1941 to 1943. They taught me to strive for initiative, innovation, and intelligence. They also prepared me to be academically competitive when I went to Yale.

I owe a lot to the administration and faculty at Yale. I remember so well my first day on campus, wondering what a poor kid from the streets of Philadelphia was doing at a place like Yale. It took me only a few days to realize that Yale took highly motivated achievers who were from many different places and who were raised under many different conditions and made them much better when they left than when they arrived.

That's what we should be doing in human resources management—or whatever it is called in the fifth phase. We should help people be better in the future than they were in the past. For those who work, better means more productive and more talented. And it seems plain that if we reach out to help people be better in the future, then we must know something about what the future will be like. That means we must be good at human resources management planning.

Robert E. Sibson

Vero Beach, Florida
June 1991

Strategic Planning for Human Resources Management

1

Planning and Personnel

Planning has always been regarded as part of management. In fact, management has often been defined as "planning, direction, and control." Personnel planning must then be part of human resources management, and planning work must be an integral part of the management of people. If the human resources management department is not doing planning, then it is probably not doing its work correctly.

In actual fact, the state of the art of planning in personnel generally is questionable in most companies and needs substantial improvement in many others. Inadequacies in planning represent a basic defect of work in the field of human resources management.

The focus of this book is strategic human resources management and strategic personnel management. Obviously, I think the subject of strategic personnel planning is of great importance, or I wouldn't take the considerable amount of time required to prepare the material for your consideration. But I am aware that there are many people who don't share my sense of urgency about strategic personnel management or my view that strategic personnel planning work is important.

The Value of Strategic Planning

The reason I think that strategic planning is important is very simple. I have worked directly or through associates for more than five hundred companies in the thirty-two years that I have been a personnel consultant. Approximately two hundred of these companies were my direct accounts, so I knew them very well. Every one of these companies that engaged in *real* strategic thinking and strategic planning as a core part of the style of managing has been successful by every measure of enterprise performance for as long as they managed in that manner. Every company I have known for more than ten years that has shunned strategic activities in their management processes has *failed* and is no longer in business. That's pretty compelling evidence for me.

I have seen essentially the same results in human resources management work. Almost all of my practice has been in the personnel field, so I know many personnel operations and personnel people very well. All of the human resources management professionals that I have known who were extremely effective and very successful in their careers have consciously and regularly engaged in some practical strategic thinking and planning. Those who engaged in no strategic thinking and planning activities or who rarely did such work were not very effective and were always hard to work with, even though some of them reached very high positions.

Of course, it's not that planning work means success. Rather, planning, done well, contributes very much to success in business overall and in human resources departments.

In my personnel audit work, there are a number of areas that I probe diagnostically, and one of them is always the degree to which those in the field are aware of both current trends and basic strategic matters. I think this is an important symptom of effectiveness because if there is not much knowledge about issues, how can there be effective human resources management work?

Thus the reason I think that strategic thinking and planning are important in human resources management is because they are important to success. Human resources management planning is important to the success of each business, each human resources management department, and each human resources management professional.

Some people do not agree with these observations, but whenever I have had an opportunity to discuss the matter with them, it turned out that they were judging strategic human resources management planning by the products of that planning and by those who claimed to be the planners. Planning work is often done poorly, and not everyone who does this work is equally good.

Make up your own mind about planning, but at least read this chapter. Let me start by discussing a few basic things about planning because they are essential to effective work, to an understanding of planning, and to the importance of planning in personnel work.

The specific advantages of human resources management strategic planning are identifiable, and I urge you to consider them. In outline form, the advantages of human resources management planning are:

- Strategic planning avoids costly and disruptive surprises that can prevent achieving goals and also avoids costly emergencies.

- If you do planning well, you are more likely to deal with key issues in a timely manner and avoid major crises. Crisis management is costly management and is subject to gross errors.
- The know-how gained from strategic human resources management planning should result in better work in human resources management, and ultimately this should translate to higher employee productivity and greater enterprise success.
- Strategic planning provides a sense of direction and sets priorities that affect what is done and the focus of work.
- Planning information also provides a screen against which new proposals can be evaluated, and this often eliminates needless projects.
- Generally, planning tends to bring relatively more order to work, although there will always be disruptions and unexpected events.
- Even when there are unexpected events that require immediate attention, planning helps the organization get back on the track quickly and without wasted motion or unneeded diversions.
- Human resources management planning work is an essential input to strategic planning for the business overall, particularly in high-tech and people-sensitive businesses.
- There is an educational value to strategic planning work, and the information can be used in the development of the human resources management staff.
- Strategic thinking and planning provide excitement in work and can be a leadership tool.

Strategic human resources management planning has a lot of advantages. These advantages meet real needs and in combination represent substantial values. The cost of effective strategic human resources management planning, as will be seen, is modest when compared to the real and clear advantages.

I concluded some time ago that *current* human resources management planning was essential work—that you can't do your job without that information. Strategic human resources management planning isn't essential, but it is of very high value and can provide an important competitive advantage.

Planning and the Management of Change

One very special advantage of planning during the next strategic planning period involves change. Strategic human resources management planning will assist in the management of change.

Planning has a great deal to do with change. If the environment surrounding business were unchanging, then there would be little need for planning. It is ongoing change and an increasing rate of change, due mostly to greater technology, that makes human resources management planning much more important today than even a few years ago. Because planning is so intimately related to change, it is a key element in the appropriate management of change.

In business, we talk about managing change, but we really don't do that. Rarely can even the largest company create basic changes or manage them. More accurately, what we do is manage in an environment of change.

How can a company manage in an environment of change unless it has reliable knowledge about what those changes are? Perhaps the most essential objective of human resources management planning is to assure effective management in an environment of change by providing information about that change.

Part of managing in an environment of change involves knowing when not to change. Every company has a tolerance for change, a limit to how much change the organization can deal with in a given period of time. Planning information supports sound decisions about how to change and when not to change.

Clearly, management consciously directs internally driven changes, such as new products. Similarly, there are internally driven human resources management planning changes. Companies generally know about internally driven changes. These are conscious actions based upon experience.

Increasingly, change in business is externally driven. A company must scan events in a thorough manner and be informed about the externally driven changes. This information is difficult to get and involves a significant amount of time. If you don't know about externally driven changes in a timely manner, they can be costly and difficult to handle.

Some changes are self-driven. The personal choices or special interests of very senior people are often causes for change that is self-driven.

Thus change is company-driven, world-driven, and self-driven. Information about all of these must be factored into your planning work. Planning is particularly essential for the effective management of change that is externally driven.

Basic Observations About Planning

We do planning all the time in the sense that we predetermine work methods. Planning has a more special meaning than that in business. Business planning means organized work to identify issues of importance and the evolution of specific methods and schedules for changing the business or business practices to achieve goals.

Organized work often means people in a separate department. In human resources management planning work, however, "organized work" usually means a number of project groups and assignments to individuals. Planning won't happen, however, without organization, so the work must be organized in some way.

The purpose of planning work is only to identify issues and events that will affect the business. It is not always necessary to explain events, and it is certainly not necessary to agree with the events. Actions may or may not be considered for dealing with each identified issue or event.

Planning must be done for an organization overall, and it must be done for each business area and each business function. You can't plan the whole without consideration of the parts. This is one reason why human resources management planning must be conducted. Personnel planning must be done as part of the overall organizational planning because it is part of the organization.

When you view planning as an integral part of the operation of the business, then planning work is essential work that must be done with excellence. Planning has often been done poorly or it was badly neglected because it was thought of as an activity apart from operations.

Some who think that planning is done well enough think of planning only as scheduling and occasionally looking ahead. I think that business planning in all areas, including human resources management, must be a much more comprehensive activity than that. Strategic planning is a part of management, and it must be an integral and ongoing part of management.

Most human resources management professionals agree that personnel planning in general needs to become an integral part of human resources management. Yet in a vast majority of companies, there is no organized human resources management planning activity at all. In other companies, human resources management planning is only done sometimes; when some special circumstance occurs or when there is a request by executive management that requires some element of personnel planning.

Planning of all types, including personnel planning, can be postponed, and that has been a special problem. If it is correct that planning is an integral part of operations, then work is postponed when planning is put off.

If you want a quick look at the state of personnel planning, ask companies for their personnel plans. Most companies don't have any human resources management planning material at all. Then ask to be shown how human resources management considerations are factored into the overall business plan of the company. More often than not, human resources management information is confined to forecasts of items such as payroll and employment.

Principles and Guidelines for Doing Planning Work

Those who do planning work must know the basic concepts and principles of planning. These principles apply to all companies that do any type of planning and must also be applied to human resources management planning work. The most important basic principle is that planning should be fact-based to the extent possible.

Whatever specific systems and styles are used, the foundation for planning in human resources management must be data and observable trends. Human resources management is not a scientific field and it is not always factual. But human resources management planning must nevertheless be based on whatever data are available and on observed activities.

Never allow any item or subject of planning to be based on someone's raw opinion or their vision of what the conditions of work should be. Be rigorous in checking sources and demand to know the observed facts or events that are the basis for each planning item.

A second principle of planning work is that it must be organized. You must have the correct structure, the proper process, and the right people.

Planning work in human resources management must be organized in the sense that it is done consciously and on a consistent basis, not just when it is convenient or interesting. Human resources management planning work must be organized in the sense that work is assigned and evaluated, and that there is accountability for results. Planning work is not an escape from the chores of the job but is itself work.

Don't even consider the notion that planning in this field will be done in a human resources management planning department. No one person or one group can do planning. Many or all professionals should be inputting to the process of planning. That's theoretically true for planning in general, but it's absolutely essential, in my opinion, in human resources management planning.

One person must be accountable for the planning work, however that work is organized. For the company overall, general business planning is the responsibility of the chief executive officer. It seems reasonable to conclude that the accountability for human resources management planning must be with the vice president of human resources.

Consider having a planning coordinator who works for the top human resources management executive. This person is the general contractor of human resources management planning work. The planning coordinator makes sure that work is assigned, monitors progress, and pushes to get things done if that's necessary. The co-ordinator then assembles the information and presents it for planning decisions and conclusions.

I urge companies to involve all human resources management professionals in planning. Give each one an information assignment that is related directly to needed human resources management planning work. Encourage inputs and ideas about trends and developments from every personnel person at every level of the organization, including lower-level personnel people. Lower-level personnel people may not have as much know-how as high-level people, but they are better able to observe trends and activities that are occurring in the operations.

A basic question is that of planning periods. For most companies, there are two planning periods: a short-term period, which is almost always one year, and a long-term period, which is most often five years. I urge companies to think about this matter, because it is at the heart of many of the problems in human resources management planning.

For most companies, short-term or operational planning in the human resources management area should be done at least once every six months, although for practical reasons you might make reports once every fiscal year. In my opinion, there are three long-term strategic human resources management planning periods. All of them are described in detail in Chapter 4, but it is important to note the matter here because it is a basic consideration in human resources management planning work.

Identify from the beginning the products of planning—what you expect to accomplish from your planning work. Unless there is a clear vision of what the result should be, why undertake human resources management planning at all?

The end product of planning must be identified planning items with commentary and action plans where appropriate. That information must be communicated to those who need it to do their jobs.

In most planning work, there is usually a planning report. You may conclude that a written report of some sort has communicative, administrative, and historic values, but a report alone is not a satisfactory product of human resources management planning.

A final basic matter of planning is the evaluation of results. Set up a system for evaluating the results of human resources management planning work from the very beginning. I think that every human resources management activity that takes a substantial amount of time should have a basis for assessing the value of the work. With respect to human resources management planning work, have specific measures: measures of accomplishments, not just that the process was completed and a report was written.

Identify things that are done better because of planning or that would not likely have been done without planning. Have proof that human resources management issues or opportunities were dealt with in a more orderly, more effective, or less costly manner because of planning. List mistakes that were probably avoided because of human resources management planning.

Don't make a project out of this review. You should be able to think of specific values by reviewing the product of planning. In addition, once in a while at a regular meeting of the key human resources management people in your company, ask for examples of how human resources management planning contributed to more effective results. If no one can remember anything, then the human resources management planning work may not be doing much good and it may not be worth the time required to continue it.

I also recommend setting a sunset date for every ongoing human resources management activity that involves a significant amount of time or cost. That's when the value of the activity must be proven again or be discontinued. The sunset period for human resources management planning is probably every three years.

Types of Planning

There are different types of planning activities, and this can cause confusion. Those who do planning should be familiar with these different types of planning activities. Here are six different variations or categories of planning, each of which is somewhat distinct:

- Conceptual—pragmatic
- Externally driven—internally driven
- Problem-oriented—opportunity-oriented
- Input—output
- Long-term—near-term
- Operational—strategic

The conceptual view of any planning starts with such questions as: What business are we in? Who are we? Where are we? The conceptual view of planning is very value-laden, with a heavy flavor of philosophy and concept.

Pragmatists (and I am essentially one of them) treat all conceptual issues quickly and with obvious answers. If we were doing planning work for Lenoir-Rhyne College, for instance, the pragmatist would answer the question of what business are we in by saying: We are in the business of education. With respect to the question of what are we, the pragmatist would answer: We are a quality liberal arts college with seventeen hundred students. And with respect to the question of where are we, the pragmatist would respond: We are in Hickory, North Carolina. Then the pragmatist would go to work.

In planning, you can actually do both conceptual thinking and pragmatic work, and that is what should be done. The emphasis in a business operation should be pragmatic, because business planning is a very practical business activity.

Planning of all types, including that done by human resources management, must consider external factors that affect business generally and internal situations that affect only that company. Identifying external forces impacting a business is a major job and requires commitments of significant amounts of time and support from outside sources. Internal factors are easy to determine, because these are issues you experience.

Internally driven and externally driven forces affecting the business are not unrelated. Every externally driven force that would impact your business will eventually be an internal factor.

Organizations experience problems, and thus a large part of planning involves the identification of vulnerabilities or problems. Vulnerabilities can be observed and recorded. Therefore, the identification of vulnerabilities is fact-based. Records of employee grievances or reasons for quitting might identify vulnerabilities. In addition, managers experience problems and can report them, which provides direct information about human resources management problems.

Opportunities are not always clear and apparent. In fact, one goal of planning is to make more certain that a company will recognize real opportunities as soon as possible so they can be exploited at the appropriate time.

There is planning input work and planning output work. In human resources management work, for example, we do planning to identify personnel matters that should be in the business plan or to identify subjects that should be on the agenda for action by the human resources management department. This is all input work.

When business plans are formulated, they must be reviewed to determine what human resources management actions need to be taken to help make the plans a reality. Then specific assignments must be made, schedules developed, and so forth. All of this is planning output work.

There are near-term planning periods that are generally operational in nature. For most companies, these are geared to the fiscal year of the business. There are also long-term planning cycles (three to five years) that are mostly strategic in nature.

Some like to say that planning is operational or strategic, and they usually equate operational with near term and strategic with long term. Never think that every near-term planning item is always operational or that every long-term planning item is strategic. That is simply not correct.

These are all terms and tools of planning work. They need to be understood by human resources management professionals who do human resources management planning.

Company Experiences With Human Resources Management Planning

In the fall of 1989, I was hired to direct a study on company practices with respect to human resources management planning. That work covered a period of about a year. The results were of value to those who commissioned the work and were very useful in providing some material for this book. Here are some of the highlights of that study in which one hundred and fifty-four companies participated.

Most participants could not correctly identify current human resources management trends and developments. At the same time, almost all participants agreed with all of the following statements:

> "We can no longer be surprised by trends in human resources management because they were not identified in a timely manner."
>
> "Human resources management planning is an integral part of the job of the human resources management department."
>
> "If we don't identify current items in human resources management, then we cannot be managing human resources."

Only one in ten of the participating companies had someone in the human resources management department who was responsible for coordinating human resources management planning. At the other extreme, one in twenty companies had a planning section in its human resources management department: people who spent all their time on human resources management planning work. Most of the people who discussed this issue with me thought that the organization of human resources management planning work was a problem.

In only 15 percent of the companies included in this study was human resources management planning information of substance included in the company's business plan. This was even true in companies that were very people-intensive.

None of the companies had budgets or expense information relating to human resources management planning work. Most of the companies could not estimate the cost of the human resources management planning work that they did.

Almost all participants agreed that human resources management planning was an essential activity. Six compelling reasons for doing human resources management planning work were identified for participants in the study. Every participant was in agreement on five of the six reasons for planning, and nine of ten agreed with all six. Yet four of five companies also said that they were not doing human resources management planning or that their organizations were not doing human resources management planning nearly well enough.

Most of the time involved in the study was spent talking with human resources management professionals and getting specific information about their company's practices and experiences in human resources management planning. A fair summary of the views of those who participated would be the following:

• There is a widespread view that human resources management planning work cannot be done well. Top management lacks confidence in the ability to do this work, and most top human resources management executives have some doubts about their company's ability to do human resources management planning work well enough.

• Until the last few years, there was little perceived need by management for human resources management planning, but that has now changed. It has changed mostly because predictable events in personnel management have surprised top management and involved a substantial cost. ·

• Most of the companies I talked to were in the start-up mode in human resources management planning (the spring of 1990), and they were having difficulty in organizing the work. Many of those start-up efforts have since fallen victim to the recession.

• Effective planning requires a reasonably consistent effort, and that's proven to be a special problem.

• More than half of these companies concluded that at least some of the human resources management planning work should be done by outside firms, but in every case the consultants used for this work proved to be unsatisfactory.

• In the minds of most human resources management executives who were interviewed, human resources management planning activities will be a routine part of the work of human resources management departments by the end of the decade. Most thought that planning work will be as much a part of the personnel job in the twenty-first century as salary surveying work has been during the twentieth century.

• It was clear that the companies included in the study were struggling with problems of process. Few were satisfied that they had the proper methods of human resources management planning work.

Doing Work in Human Resources Management Planning

Current human resources management planning work must be done. That is an essential point that is worth repeating, because if you don't have information about what is happening now that affects your work, it seems clear that you can't do your job very well.

Furthermore, each company should do current human resources management planning work for itself. It is practical to do current human resources management planning in-house, and you should do it yourself because you can't afford not to know about these current trends and issues in your field of work.

Inputs from outside sources on current human resources management planning can be helpful, but they should supplement your own work. In my opinion, even the most sophisticated current human resources management planning work done by consultants should cost less than $25,000 a year if it's done just for your company and about $2,500 a year if it's done for a group of companies.

Strategic human resources management planning is not essential work, but the list of advantages outlined earlier is very impressive to me. Furthermore, I have seen many cases where that strategic human resources management planning information was of tremendous value. Unfortunately, I have also seen cases where companies have wasted time and resources pursuing a prediction in someone's crystal ball that was simply incorrect.

Doing strategic human resources management planning takes a lot of time—and a lot of top-level time. That is one reason why many companies buy strategic human resources management consulting services from outsiders, usually consultants or universities. If you consider outside sources for strategic human resources management planning information, make certain that the suppliers are qualified to do the work.

In any event, you cannot avoid the responsibility for strategic thinking and planning by purchasing some service from an outsider. You buy these services to help you do the job, but the job is still the responsibility of the company's own human resources management professionals.

Those who do human resources management planning work will almost always be human resources management professionals. But those who do this work will also have to develop expertise in planning. The key things that should be known by those who do human resources management planning are outlined in this chapter.

Most important of all, make certain that top management supports the work done in human resources management planning. To ensure this, I recommend four things:

1. Above all else, make sure that you do this work well.

2. Make very clear the value of planning. Provide specific examples to illustrate how planning would have benefited the business in the past. Then structure your work from the beginning to provide information about success cases in the future.

3. Bury the cost of human resources management planning work. The cost of human resources management planning work is mostly a time cost, and it is moderate. However, activities like planning are the first to be the victim of cutbacks, cost savings, and budgetary reviews. You can easily bury the cost by not having a separate department and having all expenses charged to some other accounting item.

4. Build the planning process into the management system of the human resources management department. For example, get all levels of people in human resources management planning involved in the work. This results in better planning and also helps to assure ongoing support. In addition, by getting many people involved, the amount of time spent on planning by any one person is so small that it's not likely to be an issue.

Companies generally have great confidence in their ability to do planning for the business overall. Very often, that confidence has been found to be misplaced. There is usually much less confidence in their ability to do human resources management planning—perhaps because human resources management work has been done so seldom in the past. Yet human resources management planning work has been done with a high degree of excellence in many companies.

The most critical work in human resources management planning is identifying the issues. Twenty-four strategic human resources management issues are examined in this book. These are presented somewhat in the order of importance, from the most important to the very important. Sixteen of them—the most critical—are discussed separately in Chapters 5 through 20. The others are considered briefly in Chapter 21. All of human resources management issues will affect many companies and many people.

The twenty-four items identified are the strategic human resources management planning items that I have identified at this time in my strategic human resources management planning work. Obviously, in time, today's strategic planning items will be resolved or become unimportant. Others that cannot be identified now may emerge before very long.

There are many reasons for disagreement in strategic human resources management planning work. But there should be little disagreement about what the strategic items are that affect many companies and many people. Remember, if you follow the process recommended here, the identification of planning items is fact-based and should be free from bias.

We must never let our sense of right and wrong or our view of what should be done get in the way of doing strategic thinking and planning work. We must at least start a fact-based planning process with what exists, whether that's good or bad and regardless of our views.

Descriptions of the strategic items that have been identified should also be free from bias, but that is not so easy to accomplish. At least make certain that the descriptions are illustrative and not pure fiction.

Descriptions of human resources management planning items are to make sure that there is a common understanding of the items. The fact that we can identify the issues is important, and what we do about the strategic issues is important, but there can be errors in how the issues are described. We need to describe the issues well enough to communicate them.

Many recommendations are presented in this book, and all of them are mine. I make recommendations not because I am fond of my own opinions but because I think that's the right thing to do and because I am a consultant.

Because of their role, their training, and their experience, consultants give answers. That's what they are paid to do. Good consultants give better answers and are inclined to give their own answers, which are not influenced by the wishes or inclinations of their audience.

Most of all, however, I think a commonsense-*answer* approach has value because it presents a clear direction and provides a tangible alternative. There is more likely to be action to get solutions by focusing on possible answers than by just talking about the problems and issues.

Having considered the answers presented here, I ask that you think of better answers. If you work for a better answer, you may find a better answer, and then we will all be the winners. Perhaps others will not accept your better answer and they will seek to find still better answers.

This commonsense-answer approach is constructive and results-oriented. It is also, in my opinion, the correct problem-solving approach to complex matters like strategic human resources management planning.

2

A Process for Doing Current Human Resources Management Planning Work

There are a number of processes for doing human resources management planning. The process I use first involves the identification of current human resources management trends and developments. This is described in this chapter. The results of that planning work for one current planning period are reported in the next chapter. The current trends must then be projected in order to do strategic human resources management planning (Chapter 4). In briefest outline form, this is the human resources management planning system that I use.

Do Your Own Current Human Resources Management Planning

There are outside firms that do human resources management planning work for a fee. I did this work for a group of companies for a number of years. One of the most important results of the work I did for that group was to develop a process of planning *current* human resources management items that each company could use for itself, and that is described here.

The recommended process presented here relates only to *current* human resources management planning. Companies are less able to do long-range or strategic human resources management planning on their own. Strategic planning requires a lot of the time of high-level human resources management people.

Start your *current* in-house human resources management planning process by accessing general business planning information that is readily available. Very likely, your company already obtains some general business planning information from research firms, financial institutions, or others. The reports by such organizations cover many areas of the business and some will likely have some planning information that relates to personnel. Use this information as a starting point.

Next, use information that is already available in your own company. For example, your company has sales forecasts that relate to employment projections and perhaps changes in the workforce. Market research produces data that may be useful, such as a trend toward high-tech products. Production and engineering departments will have information about future technical changes affecting operations workers and facility requirements. Scour your company for information it now produces that relates to current human resources management planning issues and items.

For other needed information, organize your own human resources management staff. You can buy information from an outside service to supplement your own work, but I think there are compelling reasons for your company to do its own current human resources management planning work.

You can do current human resources management planning work in-house. Maybe an outside firm can do it better and maybe they can't. However, you can depend on yourself to get the planning information more than you can depend on others, and *current* human resources management planning information is *essential*.

You *must* know what is happening that is impacting your business and employee relations now or you can't do your job. That is the primary reason for doing the current human resources management planning work yourself, but there are other reasons as well.

If you looked at the work of consultants and others who report human resources management planning information as I have, you would see that they often came to different conclusions, even though they all looked at the same information. This necessarily means that some of them are wrong, partly because their planning process is flawed. You can't take the chance of relying on information that is essential to your work that might be wrong, incomplete, or biased.

If you knew the people who do much of the current human resources management planning for consulting and other types of firms, you would have another reason for doing the work yourself. Many of these firms use bright and able people, but very few of the people they use have much experience in business, and few of them know much about human resources management.

Information from outside sources may change because the company supplying the information may have changed in some way. For example, different people may do the work from time to time. The views of these different people may change the reported results, but you would not know this. You would reasonably assume that changes reported by outside services would be changes in the world of work, whereas they might only reflect changes in the suppliers' workplace.

Services like planning information purchased from outside firms are very vulnerable to budget cuts. If the organization of human resources management work by company people is done as outlined here, the human resources management in-house planning work will very likely survive budget cuts.

Also consider the personal value of doing human resources management planning work internally. I think (but cannot prove) that those who work in human resources management are more effective in their work if they are an integral part of activities like current human resources management planning. Ours is knowledge work, and the knowledge of company professionals is enriched if they work on and think about planning issues.

Finally, there is the matter of satisfaction. Not everything we do in human resources management work is of equal joy, interest, or excitement. Needed planning work is more interesting and motivational than many of the other things human resources management people do in their jobs.

The process for current human resources management planning work that is recommended here can be done in any company with ten or more human resources management professionals. This process isn't perfect, but it is good enough, and as people in your organization get experience in human resources management planning, the results from the planning process recommended here will be very good.

The Organization for Human Resources Management Planning

Human resources management planning work must be assigned. That doesn't mean that there needs to be a human resources management planning director or a planning department. It only means that planning work must be assigned or it probably won't get done.

First, recognize that the responsibility for human resources management planning necessarily rests only with the most senior human resources management executive. In all cases, however, there must be assignments of work to assist the vice president in

getting and evaluating information required to make planning conclusions and decisions. The top human resources management person spends only a small portion of his available time on planning,
just as the chief executive officer spends a small portion of his time
on general business planning.

It is often a good idea to delegate to one person the responsibility for coordinating support work for the current human resources
management planning activity. That planning coordinator is in the
mode of a general contractor and is the hub for communication. I
recommend that many people in the human resources management
organization have accountability for some part of human resources
management planning and that the human resources management
planning coordinator is the information center for this work.

The planning coordinator may be a person filling any one of the
key corporate personnel jobs. The planning coordinator's work takes
only a few hours a week. The person assigned that work must be
intelligent and should have had a significant amount of personnel
generalist experience. The personal qualifications and interests of
the planning coordinator are critical, and personal capability is more
important than current assignment.

I urge companies to rotate the assignment of planning coordinator about every three years. People can get stale in this type of
work, and new thinking and vitality are needed. Involvement in this
work likely means personal development, and a number of key
people in the human resources management department should
have an opportunity to do it.

Many human resources management professionals should have
specific information assignments in human resources management
planning work. For each of them, human resources management
planning work is a very small part of the overall work they do, and
to the extent possible, the work should be related to their current
assignments. The extra time spent on planning work specifically is
minimal and mostly involves time spent on networking activities.

Each person in the company's human resources management
planning network has accountability, mostly for providing information from prescribed sources and/or on specific subjects. Such information responsibilities are almost always in areas or subjects on
which the person is working anyway.

The planning coordinator mostly controls the flow of information and the organization of material. The planner is not the head of
the work in an organizational sense but is the center of a network.

The planning coordinator oversees the scanning of journals and
the administrative work of cataloguing, filing, and occasionally ana-

lyzing the material. The planning coordinator provides little actual information and does no more analytic work than most other people in the planning network.

For some people, the recommended organization of human resources management planning work seems to be untidy and unconventional. This way of organizing work is different from the traditions of the recent past, when an area of work to be done was translated into a department that appeared on organization charts with written job descriptions, manning tables, and expenses. More and more in business, there will be such unconventional organizational systems.

Sources of Information

Planning work is based on information. Therefore, once the organization for planning work has been decided, the next issue is to determine the sources of information and how they are to be accessed. Start by using what you already have in your company. As noted, start by using personnel data and general business information your company has now.

Also look for low-cost sources of information. This book is a low-cost source of human resources management planning information. Many articles and books are written each year that relate in one way or another to human resources management planning, and these should be reviewed.

The critical sources of information with respect to planning in any area relate to *events*—not someone's conclusions or opinions. So structure your information gathering for human resources management planning to collect information about events.

Recognize that there are existing organizations that observe and report events. This is the news media. Therefore, make sure that your planning system accesses the information reported by all branches of the media.

Scanning Journals

Have your human resources management staff people scan newspapers and magazines. Newspapers and magazines are in the business of reporting events. The media is very large and has many talented people. They will serve your purpose in human resources management planning admirably.

You will want to scan some nationally recognized daily newspapers, such as the *New York Times*. I have found that scanning three of these types of journals gets all of the national and international news events that I need for human resources management planning purposes.

Also scan a couple of general news magazines, such as *U.S. News & World Report*. Any two in this category will be sufficient.

You must also scan general business journals. I found that scanning *Business Week* and the *Wall Street Journal* did the job.

There is also a broad range of special journals you might consider. These are newsletters, such as the *Kipplinger Letter*, and special-purpose publications, such as the *AFL/CIO News*. I used only a few of these and got very little of value from them for my human resources management planning work.

Avoid regional publications and specific industry publications. They contain very little of value in the area of human resources management planning that is not available from the journals already identified.

A most important source of published information is the local newspaper. I scanned local newspapers from Vero Beach, Florida, because I live there and from Hickory, North Carolina, because I serve on the Board of Visitors of Lenoir-Rhyne College. Thus I could read about local events in these areas with some understanding because I had some knowledge of each of the communities.

I recommend to companies that they scan local newspapers in every community where they have operations of a significant size. Have local human resources management people do that scanning.

It is critical to the human resources management planning process to have your human resources management people involved in the journal scanning for three reasons. First of all, for the purpose of human resources management planning, they will be scanning material they read anyway. Therefore, the journals are scanned at zero net cost. Second, each of these human resources management professionals has his attention focused on issues, and the involvement is a learning experience for all of them. Third, this involvement helps everyone understand the process better, and they will use the resulting information about current human resources management trends and issues much more effectively.

Assign one or two journals for scanning to each person. Each of them may, of course, read or scan many other journals for different purposes. But don't burden anyone with accountability for scanning more than two journals for the purposes of human resources management planning work. Never have more than one person responsible for the scanning of any single journal, because then you clog up the system with too much paper.

Make sure that this work is done regularly. Never let the work be postponed. You have control because the scanners send the information to a central source. If any person in the network doesn't send in material as expected, or if they aren't doing a good job of scanning, then the central source will know this and the planning coordinator can take timely corrective action.

Your Network

In addition to scanning published information, you must scan people for what they hear, observe, and experience. You must set up a human networking system.

Start building your network with your own company's human resources management people. Include many if not all human resources management professionals in your company in your human resources management planning network.

Every person in the network should input the personal observations and conversations they have in the normal course of their work that contain information that they think may be relevant in planning. They should get such information from contacts inside and outside the company.

You need to structure this work. Scanning journals merely involves tearing pages out of a newspaper or a magazine and then sending the material to the office of the planning coordinator. The reporting of personally acquired information requires writing down that information or dictating it. That takes incremental time and work and involves a discipline that people must have or acquire.

When recording human resources management planning information becomes a habit or part of a routine, then the recording of the information won't take more than an hour or so every month. The information from personal contacts is really crucial, and much of it is not available from any other source.

Don't ask for long or fancy reports. Ask only for necessary identifying information, enough about the reporting to give the reader an understanding of the thrust of the report and the source of the information. The source of the information means mostly who submitted the information so interested people can contact that individual for more information if that proves to be necessary.

I always required such reporting in my own consulting companies. It was done on blue sheets—very simple forms that permitted only half a page of writing or typing. It was my judgment that this was the most important source of information we had in our professional work. It was also valuable in our human resources management planning work.

Also establish an external network system. Again, the first purpose is to get useful information and valuable contacts for an information exchange in order to do human resources management work with excellence. Some of the information acquired will also be useful in human resources management planning.

The quality of your outside network is important and worth some attention. For human resources management planning purposes, look for operations that have operating and economic characteristics that are similar to your own company. Look for organizations that have quality people in their human resources management department. Look for companies that are trying to access information from others so you can set up an exchange system. A dozen or so well-selected network firms will supply all the information you need for your human resources management work, including your human resources management planning work.

Consider using consultants as part of your outside network. They should be experts and by the nature of their work they should be constantly at the leading edge of knowledge. Network in particular with the experts you use and already pay. But if you know someone else who is particularly knowledgeable and thoughtful, you should try to budget a few thousand dollars each year to learn from that person.

I did something else during my consulting career that I will report because it can be useful to you in getting human resources management planning information. I noticed very early in my consulting career that there were down times when I was working with a client—times when there wasn't any real work to do, such as lunch periods. I always had x information and y information—and had a list of both for use during "down times."

The x information was extra—more information of value for the client than they had hired me for in areas where I knew they had an interest. Your clients are the operating managers, and you might do the same for them.

The y information involved "why questions" on my part. This was a structured and formal method of asking about people's experiences and thinking in areas where I felt there was a need for more information and insights. Some of the questions might properly relate to human resources management planning.

Information Handling and Analysis

The scanning of journals and the operation of the information networks results in an avalanche of paper. In my planning work, my associates and staff generate more than two thousand pieces of paper each year—and we learned over the years to screen information carefully and avoid a lot of duplication of material.

If your system doesn't screen items from scanning and networking, there can be twenty thousand items each year. In one year, for example, the issue of congressional pay increases alone generated over one thousand pieces of paper clipped from journals.

Because of the potential for so much paper, the information handling is important. You need a system for screening and review. The review should include feedback to the people who are doing the scanning so they do a more selective and intelligent job in the future.

From time to time, the planning coordinator should notify the scanners and those in the network about information that isn't relevant. But be careful not to shut off probing and inquiring attitudes.

Duplication is a problem because the number of pieces of paper on a subject is no real indicator of importance. Once you have enough to be satisfied that the issue is a planning item and you have enough information about it, start throwing away more papers containing the same material.

As you receive information, identify areas where you need more data or information. Someone must then probe and ask questions—probably within the network that has been established. You may even have to do some basic research; simple, basic research.

Reaching out for more information and research should be rather rare events in current human resources management planning, partly because they are expensive and partly because they aren't needed very often. Remember that the essence of the planning process involves an identification of observable items. That shouldn't require much of an additional outreach for more information, and it shouldn't require much research at all.

People who have not done this work often have concerns about whether they can do the information handling and analysis work well. I have no advice or suggestions for this. This is "soft science" work, and there are no analytic methods or proven scientific processes. But you are only out to discover what is observably happening and understand that well enough to prepare descriptions of the issue. Knowledgeable human resources management people who become immersed in the work and follow a reasonable process will succeed in identifying relevant items. The only requisites I can suggest are to keep at it with week-by-week consistency and don't let your preconceived notions cloud your vision.

Sorting and Cataloguing

As journals are scanned and networking memos completed, a considerable amount of material will be collected. Someone in the coordinator's group has to sort and file the information received from the network. This work takes a few hours each week.

Use any cataloguing system you wish. I keyed mine off the headlines in the newspapers, because editors do a form of cataloguing on their own.

In the course of a year, you can have hundreds of clippings and memos in one file, even though you have streamlined your information-handling system. You will also find from time to time that you will want to purge the system and get rid of duplicate information. You will want to review the system, and sometimes you will refile some of the items into a different system of cataloguing. This reviewing and resorting of information tends to be an ongoing operation.

Assign this work to "associate-level" people in the personnel department; people earning salaries of $20,000 to $40,000 a year in 1991 dollars. They can do this work as well as senior human resources management people. This practice will save money and will be an excellent experience for the reviewers and cataloguers.

This is the cataloguing method of doing planning work. You collect information about events and put it into some sorting system. With refinement, the categories become the planning items.

Obviously, cataloguing in the first year of planning work is the most difficult. In subsequent years, you start with last year's results and last year's folders. Trends and issues don't exist on an annual cycle, so there is always a considerable carry over of cataloguing from year to year.

With time, your people become more experienced, and those in the field send more relevant information. The planning coordinator and his assistants become more efficient themselves, which in this case means they do less rework.

Investigation and Analysis

In reviewing the information collected, there is a need for objectivity and care. Whoever does this work is looking at the material to determine if it is useful and whether additional investigation or information is needed.

This phase of the work requires a searching attitude and an investigatory inclination. Above all, this phase of the work requires objectivity. At this point, you are still determining information to report as a planning issue and not making any conclusions except about the relevance and the clarity of the information that has been obtained.

There will likely be some cases where there is a need for investigation and analysis. For example, when I first heard about upward mobility as an issue, my instincts told me to find out more. So we contacted a number of companies. Then we did some analyses to determine the source of the problem and the probable implications. Of course, we found that this was not a promotion problem but rather it was related to hiring unpromotable people in the first place. There are cases like this every year.

Very early in the planning work cycle, start the review, investigation, and analysis. Investigation work must be done regularly; it cannot be postponed. There must be time available to do a careful and thoughtful job. You can't rush this work.

I found that reviews every eight weeks worked best for me. You should develop whatever style or system that works best for the people involved in your company.

Each group needs to develop its own methods for doing this work. I use mostly memos and task groups. Define information assignments narrowly and specifically. Spread the assignments so that getting supplemental information is not a great burden on any one person.

Sometimes you will use the techniques of an investigative reporter. In getting more information, always try to get it in the course of regular work—or in the process of work contacts.

Also use library sources and your own company's personnel data. If you have a computer-aided personnel data system, it can be very helpful in getting quick, fact-based supplements to information needed.

Eventually, you will be evaluating the reliability of information and exercising difficult judgments about what is relevant, what should be reported as a human resources management planning item, and how the material should be grouped and presented. This requires analytic work and imaginative thinking.

Your investigative and analysis work should avoid eight tendencies:

1. Don't do more investigation and analysis than is needed. This work can consume you. Remember that your main goal is only to identify and describe current planning items.

2. There is a tendency for planning work to become more and more centralized with time. The planning coordinator and the vice president of human resources management will increasingly tend to dominate input. Avoid centralization of observations and ideas.

3. After the first year's report, you will find that prior years increasingly influence future reporting. For example, if you put "con-

tract work" in this year's report, it will be clipped and reported with regularity the following year.

4. Circulate reports, restructure the planning organization, rotate assignments, and consider other actions to maintain vitality and an inquiring mentality by those who do scanning and those who are in your network.

5. It is critical to keep independence of reporting out in the field. Encourage inquiring and innovative reporting, even if it seems pretty wild at times. You can always disregard or further review information, but you will never know about some things if people are discouraged from submitting unusual items or items that may be unpopular or controversial.

6. Avoid the tendency to hold meetings and form committees. In the evaluative process of the work, some meetings to exchange ideas and for brainstorming might be useful. My strong feeling is to have no standing committees at all.

7. Avoid a formal structure or separate organizational identity for the planning work. That gets the empire-building syndrome into operation and sets up the entire work process for budget cuts.

8. Finally, be very sure you don't set up elaborate systems to justify preconceived notions. There are many cases where planning processes of different types have been prostituted to justify someone's vision of how the world should be. There are also cases where results were distorted to make good copy and please the ultimate audience.

An Annual Product

Current planning in all areas is an annual event. That isn't necessary or even logical, but that's what happens. If nothing else, your "customers" expect a reporting once a year—mostly for use in preparing their annual to-do list, for operational planning, and for budgeting.

You should obviously tie your cycle of work in human resources management planning to the company's operational planning and budgeting cycle. If your company is on a fiscal-year/calendar-year basis, this means that your customers need the results of your annual effort mostly in the six to eight weeks starting around the first of September. A September reporting date means that you must be preparing your reporting material in the summer months.

Each year, the end-product of current human resources management planning is some type of report—or a series of reports. It is necessary to record conclusions and communicate them to the ultimate users of the information.

In fact, too often the product of planning is prepared and filed, and then another report is prepared the next year and filed. Nothing happens when you prepare a report. Something only begins to happen when people read the report and have a reason for doing something.

The communication of the results of the work is crucial. I strongly advise that you don't even start out doing work in current human resources management planning unless you have a realistic and assured method of communicating the results.

Some good work has been done in human resources management planning activities. I was proud of the results of my planning project. But I have never seen a case—including my own—where the job of communicating the results was done well enough. When you set up your own in-house current human resources management planning activities, start with the communication issue.

3

Current Human Resources Management Planning Items

The result of scanning and cataloguing work is a list of planning items, and that completes the human resources management current planning process. These are events in the field that are now occurring and are observable, the human resources management items that confront the business *now*.

Many items are identified from the scanning and cataloguing work. As many as one hundred current human resources management items can be identified every year. Inevitably, some of these will be relevant to your company.

Just the list of planning items is worth a great deal. If that information is communicated properly, then the time and the cost of identifying and cataloguing the items of current human resources management planning are probably justified just by the information that was identified.

For the most recent current human resources management planning period, my work identified sixty-plus observable current issues and trends that would probably be important to many companies. I think that these items should be evaluated and weighted for effective communications, and so I weight them carefully and get a rank for each by importance. Of the sixty-two items reported, however, less than half are really important to any single company. The rest are important for other companies, and you should probably know about them and track them.

It is important to get information about the year-to-year changes in current planning items. This will give you a sense of the trends. It is also important to decide what you are going to do with the planning information. I think that current planning information should be communicated. Action steps will likely be necessary for some of the items. Finally, the current planning items represent the basic first step in strategic human resources management planning work.

Evaluation and Weighting

Not all planning events are of equal importance, and not all items are of equal importance to your company, either now or in the future. There is, therefore, a need to consider some system to evaluate and weight the planning items.

The evaluation and weighting of human resources management planning information improves the quality of the communication and understanding. By weighting the items, the reader's attention is concentrated on the more important items (not necessarily the most newsworthy), and that contributes to better communication.

The primary value of weighting is for company action. The weighting system is an objective approach to identifying items that require attention the most. No organization can deal with all current planning items. Weightings of planning items are helpful in setting priorities for action.

Simple groupings may be all you need for human resources management planning items. If you do this, use at least five categories to distinguish the planning items. The five groupings I would recommend are as follows:

1. Items clearly of great importance to your company, where you should be taking action now. There should be no doubt on the part of any professional or operating executive that planning items in this category need to be addressed.
2. Intermediate. (It is not necessary to define intermediate ratings.)
3. Items that will probably impact your company or have some impact on some parts of your company. These items should at least be monitored carefully, and you should be learning about the experiences of others in these areas. Top management should be kept informed about these items.
4. Intermediate.
5. Items of doubtful importance to your company. But human resources management professionals should at least know about the trend or issue, and the item should be tracked in the human resources management planning process.

Procedurally, it is a good idea to have a number of managers participate in the grouping. Have them straight-rank all the items first—from most important to least important. Collect those rankings for future reference. Later, have each of the same people categorize the planning items into five groups, such as those that have been described.

You may be surprised by the high degree of agreement that you will get among managers by using such a simple system. It's very likely that there will 80 percent agreement, and 90 percent of the disagreement will be one degree—one gradient in a five-gradient system.

There should be agreement among top executives about the top dozen human resources management planning items, because these are the items that will most likely impact your company. Don't be too concerned about disagreements about the last third of the planning items; they are items on which you are not likely to take action anyway.

If the straight-grouping method seems to be inadequate, then factors can be identified and degrees under each factor can be defined. Point weightings can be assigned to each degree of each factor. Then for each planning item, points can be totaled and relative importance determined in a very formal manner.

For companies that want factor-point systems, the weighting factors I use are:

- Likely consequence of impact
- Probability of occurrence
- Manageability of the item
- Reliability and validity of sources of information about the item

The degree definition under each criterion should be in three levels. Here is a summary of the criteria and standards that you can consider if you decide on such a formal system of determining the relative importance of planning items.

A. *Likely consequence.* The potential impact of the planning item on the operation of your business, the productivity of employees, and existing human resources management policies, programs, and practices.
   1. Substantial impact affecting reported results, employee productivity, manpower levels, and human resources management practices.
   2. Will have important consequences, although it may not be clear how great the impact will be or exactly how the planning item will affect the company and its employees.
   3. A valid item to report and track, but the consequence at this point is uncertain or probably not very great.
B. *Probability of impact.* The likelihood that the trend will have the consequences that have been identified.

1. The trend is already impacting the company.
2. For identifiable reasons, there is a very high probability that the trend will impact the company in some way this year or next.
3. The item is only impacting some businesses or some areas, and there is some doubt that it will impact the company at all.

C. *Manageability.* The degree to which an individual company can act to effectively manage the trend or issue.
   1. Highly manageable—as manageable as most important areas of human resources management.
   2. Manageable in part only—or at a considerable cost.
   3. Cannot be managed well by an organization; mostly individual companies react or adjust to the situation.

D. *Reliability and validity of sources.* All trends reported are observable, but some are assured, in the sense that we can count data and know of cases.
   1. Clear and provable evidence.
   2. Based on observations of others, interpretation, and judgment.
   3. Identified by observations subject to different interpretation.

The biggest advantage of a formal weighting system such as the one recommended is objectivity of view. Without a formal evaluation system that is consistently applied, there is danger that the work will be focused on conclusions that, in turn, were based too much on one person's view. In addition, a point weighting system gives you an idea about the relative importance of each strategic planning item.

If you go to a detailed system of weighting, then the identification of the criteria, the definition of degrees under each criterion, and the point weighting systems can become an issue—and sometimes a distraction. Consider having a small cross section of people, composed of line managers, executives, and some human resources management professionals, review whatever criteria and weighting system you want to use. Get their endorsement or get a different weighting system.

Current Planning Items

There is a list of items and issues for each current planning period. The items that resulted from my work during the latest planning period are listed in order of importance in Exhibit 3–1.* Each item is

---

*The work cycle in my current resources management planning project begins in July. In this way, my material is printed and distributed to subscribers before Labor Day so they have it for their fall operational planning and budgeting period.

Exhibit 3-1. Current human resources management planning items (from September 1991 to September 1992).

Rank	Item	Percent of Importance Rating	Years on List of Current Items*
	(Group I)		
1	Productivity Management	100%	5
2	Delegative Management— Empowerment	96	5
3	Fairness	93	5
4	Equal Treatment	92	3
5	Special Interest Groups	91	3
6	Unpaid Leaves	89	2
7	Pay for Performance	88	5
8	Unit Management	86	2
9	Functional Illiteracy	84	3
10	Executive Pay Excesses	83	4
	(Group II)		
11	Institutional Educational Deficiency	82	5
12	Privacy-Secrecy	80	3
13	Benefit Cost Containment	78	5
14	Job Security	76	2
15	Managing Differences	74	3
16	Retirement Plan Issues	73	2
17	Computerized Personnel Systems	72	3
18	Flatter Organizations	70	2
19	Paid Leaves	67	1
20	Reallocation of Talent	66	2
	(Group III)		
21	Reeducation	65	4
22	Second Careers	63	2
23	Drug Use by Workers	60	5
24	Protection at Work	58	2
25	Chronic Labor Scarcity	55	5

*These ratings have been used for five years.

Exhibit 3-1. *Continued*

Rank	Item	Percent of Importance Rating	Years on List of Current Items*
26	Revitalization of Recruiting and Testing	54%	2
27	The Problem Employee	53	1
28	Support for Working Mothers	51	2
29	Escalation of Recruiting Costs	50	3
30	Contract Workers	49	4
	(Group IV)		
31	Leadership	48	3
32	Impact of Technology on the Work Experience	47	3
33	Democracy at Work	46	2
34	Child Care	44	4
35	The Media	41	5
36	Restrictions on Location of Facilities	39	3
37	The Changed Role of the HRM Department	38	3
38	Less Company Loyalty	37	5
39	Employee Counseling	33	1
40	More Downsizing	32	1
	(Group V)		
41	The Working Poor	31	4
42	Personnel Management in a Recession	30	2
43	Technological Unemployment	29	2
44	Trust	25	2
45	Further Decline of Unions	24	5
46	Restrictions on Relocating Jobs	22	3
47	A Multilingual Workforce	21	1
48	Immigration	20	1
49	Flexplace Work	18	1
50	Stress at Work	17	1

Exhibit 3-1. *Continued*

Rank	Item	Percent of Importance Rating	Years on List of Current Items*
	(Other Items)		
51	Employee Stock Ownership	14%	3
52	Comparable Worth	13	5
53	Executive Accountability	12	2
54	Influence of Foreign HRM Practices	11	2
55	Workers vs. Nonworkers	10	3
56	Deregulation in the Workplace	9	2
57	Human Asset Redeployment	8	3
58	Changing Social Values	7	1
59	Changes in Workforce Demographics	6	5
60	Work Ethics	5	1
61	Community Regulation of Work	3	1
62	A Four-Day Work Week	1	1

given an index of importance. This was the numeric result of applying the factor-degree weighting system just described.

The nature of most of these *current* items seems to be apparent from their labels. They need to be sufficiently described in the planning work so that each item is clearly understood.

This book is about strategic human resources management planning. In my process of strategic planning, identifying current trends is the first essential step in identifying strategic issues in a fact-based manner.

Here are a few comments about the sixty-two *current* human resources management planning items for 1991–1992 that have some relevance to understanding the process. Some of the comments also have relevance to strategic human resources management planning.

All of the twenty-four strategic items identified and described in the remainder of the book are based upon one or more of the current planning items. You might take a few minutes now to scan the list of current planning items and check which items you think have strategic implications.

It is normal for an item that is on the current planning list for the first time to be in one of the lower ranked groups, even though it later becomes of major strategic importance. Only if a current planning item is caused by a change in the law or a catastrophic event would it likely be in the top group of current human resources management planning items the first year it appeared.

All I have done with the current items is identify them, because that is sufficient for the purpose of this work. Remember that all of these are observable trends and issues, so they don't require detailed descriptions and evaluations as strategic issues usually do.

In working with worknetworking clients, I have found that with a list of sixty items, about one-third or up to two dozen items are relevant to any one company. The others are of interest but are not directly relevant in that year. Of the twenty or so items that are of direct interest, a company usually needs to take specific action with respect to five or ten of these current items each year.

The list of current items will vary a great deal among companies. Very few issues will affect all companies or almost all companies.

My goal each year is to identify the top sixty items. I think that is a very comprehensive list of current human resources management planning items. In the process of reviewing my work each year, I will find another forty to sixty items that have been reported by some source. I would add them if I thought they had any relevance to even a few subscribers, but they don't. There are a lot of false prophets in planning work and some evangelists who report their wishes as trends.

I think that reporting about sixty current planning items each year is very comprehensive. You need a complete list—you cannot afford surprises. I tell subscribers that the sixty current items reported are 99.9 percent complete.

Changes in Planning Items

It is necessary to do the *current* planning cycle *annually,* partly because the planning items change. The change in current planning items from year to year is a measure of the rate of change at work today.

Based on my experience, a human resources management planning item remains a current item an average of about three years. Each year there are always at least a dozen new items, and, for one reason or another, there are at least a dozen items that are not on the list that were on the list in the previous year.

Items become relevant for a variety of reasons; and understanding the reasons helps insure good scanning. Computer-aided personnel became an item last year because new MIS technology became available. Human resources management in a recession became an item because a half-dozen major industries started to experience a recession. Drugs at work became a planning item because of a ground swell among workers against drugs and because of some instances of death or injury because others were using drugs. Retirement plan issues were on the list because there have been so many pension plan cancellations and pending reversion cases. Pay for performance was a management-initiated trend, related no doubt to payroll cost management.

Current human resources management planning items drop off the list mostly because items run their course, because affirmative action by employers resolves the issues, because of a loss of interest or more interest in other matters, or because the item becomes unimportant. For example, contract work was ranked high in 1986, but the growth in contract work has ended. Small employers now dominate markets, so the issue of small employers increasingly dominating labor markets wasn't relevant any longer.

You can get a sense of the rate of change in current human resources management planning items by scanning Exhibit 3-2. This lists the top twenty planning items in 1992 and shows where each ranked in 1987. The exhibit also shows whether the item will likely be a strategic human resources management planning issue, which is one indication of how long it is likely to remain on the list of current human resources management planning items in the future.

Communications of Current Human Resources Management Planning Information

I recommend that companies consider communicating the results of current human resources management planning work to *all employees*. A brief article-type report of about twenty-five-hundred words would be sufficient. The material would identify a few dozen planning items that were of greatest importance to the company. This would be enough to inform employees without getting into unnecessary detail.

This report should be informational, without commentary and without weighting the planning items. Such communications are about employees and work, and your employees will be interested.

A knowledge of the issues may diffuse problems because of more understanding that what your employees experience at work is part of very general trends affecting work and those who work in

Exhibit 3-2. Changes in current human resources management planning items (top twenty in 1992).

Rank in 1987*	Current Planning Item	Strategic Item
High	1. Productivity Management	Yes
Low	2. Delegative Management	Yes
Not Listed	3. Fairness	Yes
Low	4. Equal Treatment	Yes
Not Listed	5. Special Interest Groups	Yes
Not Listed	6. Unpaid Leaves	No
High	7. Pay for Performance	Yes
Not Listed	8. Unit Management	Yes
Not Listed	9. Functional Illiteracy	Yes
Medium	10. Executive Pay Excesses	No
Medium	11. Educational Deficiency	Yes
Not Listed	12. Privacy-Secrecy	Yes
High	13. Benefit Cost Containment	Yes
Medium	14. Job Security	Yes
Not Listed	15. Managing Differences	Yes
Not Listed	16. Retirement Plan Issues	Yes
Not Listed	17. Computerized Personnel Systems	No
Low	18. Flatter Organizations	Yes
Not Listed	19. Paid Leaves	No
Not Listed	20. Reallocation of Talent	Yes

*A different rating system was used, so the listing is in three gradients only—high (top third), medium, and low (bottom third).

many places. In any event, employees should know what's going on in the world of work. Just make sure that the information provided to employees simply reports events and that it is written in the employees' language—without cartoons.

All managers of personnel in a company should also have information about current human resources management planning items. If a person manages people, then he must know about current trends and the changes in conditions impacting people at work.

In fact, in my opinion, current human resources management planning information is a *must* for managers. In addition to the article about planning items distributed to all employees, consider a briefing to managers on the current issues judged to be of greatest significance to your company. Consider meetings with managers of people that would give them an opportunity to ask questions about the report they received on current human resources management planning.

It's hard to prove in a concrete way that better informed managers are better managers of people. It seems reasonable, however, that being better informed with correct information about current employee-employer relations issues would contribute significantly to the excellence of the management of personnel.

You should also report in some way the results of human resources management planning to the senior executives in your company. Each company has its own preferred way of communicating such information. If given a choice, I would prepare brief written reports for executives followed by a personal presentation. Then throughout the year, communicate to top management planning information as it relates to subjects under consideration.

Finally, information about the results of human resources management planning must be communicated to human resources management professionals. This reporting should be done in substantial detail. In practice, communicating the results of human resources management planning to human resources management professionals is best done as a series of events, in the normal course of communicating within the department.

Everyone in the personnel field needs current human resources management information in order to do their jobs well. Such information is also a form of training.

Action Steps

The result of planning is a list of planning items that should be described. The sixty-two items presented are the *current* human resources management items based on work performed in 1991. Planning work requires action. The first action requirement with respect to all the important human resources management planning items is that they should be communicated.

There are three additional action steps to consider:

1. Input current human resources management planning information to operational plans and budgets.
2. Identify separate actions that the personnel department itself must take during the current year in addition to actions identified for input into the operational plans and budgets.
3. Input the information into strategic planning.

Items will be identified in the human resources management planning work that will not be used in operating plans but which should be the basis for independent actions by the human resources management department. These types of actions often relate to doing the personnel job or to employee-employer relations matters that are not directly limited to any particular business plan or action.

Separate human resources management department actions would obviously vary a great deal from time to time and in different years, but here are a few illustrations:

- In response to career hiring needs, you might change the role of the personnel department's interviewing during the hiring process.
- To increase the effectiveness of the human resources management department, you might start the use of time sheets.
- Because of escalating employment costs, a new employment process and tests might be initiated at one location for one category of jobs, with the results being monitored.
- In connection with the fairness issue, to lower costs and have greater assurance of competitiveness in pay, a system of pricing by employment experience might be initiated.
- Because of functional illiteracy, you might start giving educational achievement tests.
- A computer-aided personnel system might be installed, replacing a number of fixed, hard, special-purpose computer programs that are now in existence.
- You might start to post job openings to improve the excellence of staffing and as a matter of fairness.

Consider the next logical planning action: Do strategic human resources management planning work. If you do strategic human resources management planning work, then it must largely be based on current human resources management planning items. The work on current human resources management planning represents a substantial part of the work necessary to do strategic human resources management planning.

Mostly, however, current planning is an essential part of doing the human resources management job. You really can't do the work in human resources management unless you know the issues. Human resources management planning is an important part of knowing current items and issues.

4

Strategic Human Resources Management Planning

This is a book about strategic human resources management planning, but it is my view that you cannot do strategic planning without doing current planning first. I recommend that you start your strategic planning by reviewing the current planning items that have been identified and determining which current human resources management planning items have significance beyond the current time frame. Then do an extrapolation and the other tasks of strategic planning.

Strategic Management of Human Resources

Strategic human resources management planning is part of strategic human resources management work, which, in turn, is part of strategic management. This suggests that you start strategic personnel planning with your *current* human resources management planning information *and a deep understanding of strategic management.*

Here are nineteen basics about strategic management, briefly stated in a paragraph or two. I think that these points are important in understanding strategic management and strategic human resources management planning. These thoughts are also important in determining whether strategic human resources management planning is practical in your company.

If you consider a strategic human resources management activity, the very first thing to do is to assess the extent of strategic management that now exists in your company. Make sure there is enough strategic thinking and strategic management practices to support strategic planning in any field, including human resources management.

Strategic management involves plans, methods, and actions to improve the business. Strategic human resources management planning should, therefore, involve activities designed to improve the future capabilities of employees and increase productivity.

It isn't likely that a company will have strategic management skills without current operational management excellence. In human resources management, this would mean that if a company cannot (or does not) properly manage the current capabilities of its employees, that company would not likely improve the capability and productivity of its workforce in the future. Therefore, if a company lacks skill or interest in managing people, strategic personnel planning would probably be a waste of time.

Strategic is too often assumed to be just long term. In fact, while most strategic issues are long term, they have various time cycles. The dividing line between long term and short term cannot simply be more than one year or less than a year. Activities are continuous and do not change in nature at 365-day intervals.

The strategic management of human resources is not a few grand plans that can be put into a three-ring binder or shown on a video in the boardroom. Much of the real strategic achievement in personnel happens one-on-one and day-to-day over various periods of time. Real strategic achievement in the field of human resources management is the combination of many critical incidents that fashion the capability and productivity of the workforce.

For example, organizational enrichment is a strategic human resources management activity. That happens or doesn't happen one hire at a time. Furthermore, *every* hire does not have to be more effective than the person he replaced in order to have organizational enrichment. Organizational enrichment happens if 60 percent of the hires are more effective, if 30 percent are about as effective, and even if 10 percent are less effective than the people they replaced.

We also tend to think that strategic work is done at the top and that work done down in the organization does not involve strategic matters. That isn't always true and is absolutely not correct in human resources management. There must be policy guides, strategic directions, and leadership from the top. After that, much of the strategic management of human resources happens down in the organization through the managers of personnel, who are supported by human resources management generalists at various levels.

Strategic management often relates to actions that cover a whole class of cases. In effect, a strategic action deals not only with the case at hand but often impacts or sets precedents for many other cases of that type or category in the future.

Strategic relates to actions that impact the basic nature and character of the company or any part of the company. In human resources management, this means that such basics as the capability and work ethic of the workforce are strategic matters.

In matters of personnel relations, strategic actions must also relate in some way to work on social issues, including matters of compliance. Failure to comply with laws or the failure of a company to act in a manner that is consistent with the social culture of the times can cause major and long-term problems in human resources management.

We tend to think of strategic as important, but that doesn't mean that other work is unimportant. Selling a large order is important, but it is not a strategic action. Strategic actions are usually important because they affect many cases, the way the business operates, or because strategic matters affect a company for long periods of time.

There are strong links between operational work and strategic work in any area of activity. Thus it is not a matter of sound operational management or sound strategic management. For example, if people are managed well and work productively in the short term, many more strategic human resources alternatives are available for the long term. If employees are managed poorly in the short run, the company may have no future.

Policies are always strategic. In fact, one test for determining if a statement really involves a policy matter is whether it involves strategic issues. Thus policy management relates in some ways to strategic human resources management planning.

Programs are sometimes strategic because they require the same processes and guidelines in many cases. Therefore, as we move from programmatic to delegative management methods, a strategic tool that was central to the management process for many years becomes less determining. That is one reason why companies often experience difficulties in the transition from a programmatic style to a delegative style.

You can take strategic actions without any strategic planning, and that is often done. However, one major purpose of strategic planning is to provide information needed to make more intelligent strategic decisions and take long-term actions based on more information and better knowledge about alternatives.

Some business writers have created a fancy and stylized vision of strategic management practices that doesn't really resemble the real world of work. The stylized version describes the gathering of many facts and an orderly, deliberate, and intelligent charting of the company's future by those at the top. It rarely works like that. If you ever want to get a realistic sense of how strategic planning really works, talk to the people who do the work and read some planning reports that were prepared a few years ago.

Strategic successes often happen because executives recognize an opportunity and seize it. But, of course, if executives are better informed about the alternatives they have, as would be the case if there were sound strategic planning, then those at the top are more likely to recognize opportunities. This also applies to strategic human resources management issues.

There is also an idea that strategic management is always complex and many faceted. Very often, however, the companies that have been most successful had simple strategies they stuck to with the fervor of zealots. Companies are more likely to stick with a simple strategy commitment than with complex commitments; this is especially true in a rapidly changing work environment.

In most cases, you should be able to write out a business strategy in a few pages. At any point in time, all human resources management strategic plans should be shorter than this section of this chapter—they should be less than a thousand words.

Effective strategic management requires that executive management has a deep understanding of the businesses of the enterprise and a knowledge of external factors impacting each business area. You can't improve substantially what you don't understand well, except in the case of raw luck.

This means that strategic human resources management requires managers of people at every level who possess intelligence in human resources management discipline areas. This also requires human resources management professionals who know people in the organization well and understand the operations.

Specifically, the process of strategic management also requires two aspects of knowledge about the future:

1. How each area of the company might be changed and the possible consequences of the change.
2. How the environment impacting business is changing and how these external factors affect each business.

Knowing about the possibilities for change in the business requires a deep knowledge of the business, and that includes an understanding of basic operational matters. Knowledge of the environment affecting people at work means strategic human resources management planning information.

Strategic planning is an activity requiring high intelligence, deep understanding, and sound, commonsense thinking. These few general principles of strategic management are essential elements that are required to understand strategic human resources management planning work.

Strategic Human Resources Management Planning Work

There are some basic guidelines for doing effective strategic human resources management planning work. Most important of these is that strategic planning should essentially use deductive analysis. The key to the deductive process, in my view, is that all plans must be based on observable current human resources management planning items in the first instance. When you have that view, you start with what you know and then make forecasts.

Second, you must develop a sound method of forecasting and monitoring. The strategic human resources management planning process starts with fact-based observations of current trends. The validity of the strategic items that are identified then also depends upon logical methods of forecasting.

Forecasts are predictions that are never completely accurate, except by chance. It is crucial, however, to use some reasonable method of forecasting in an objective and consistent manner to get an appropriate description of what each strategic planning issue might be like in the future in order to have a proper understanding of the issue. Then persistent monitoring will make the predictions more reasonable each year.

In my opinion, there is too much concern about the accuracy of forecasts in strategic human resources management planning work. If strategic human resources management planning is geared in the first place to current observable trends, uses reasonable forecasting methods, and is monitored regularly, then descriptions of each item will be good enough to communicate the issue to all concerned persons.

A third guideline of strategic human resources management planning is to learn from your experiences. I like to ask planners in our field, "Whatever happened to the guaranteed wage, the four-day work week, and the cottage workforce?" At one time, each of these was heralded as a key strategic human resources management megatrend. We know why each of these forecasts was incorrect at the time and should have learned from these lessons.

A fourth guideline involves manning the work. Strategic human resources management planning work must be done mostly by senior human resources management professionals. There is little low-level work, like scanning and cataloguing, when it comes to *strategic* personnel planning.

A fifth guideline of strategic personnel planning is that there must be constancy of effort. In good times, executive management too often says of activities like planning, "We don't need it" and in bad times the same executives will say, "We can't afford it." If you get even a few months behind in strategic planning, you may never catch up, or worse yet, you might miss something.

Because of the requirements for constancy of attention and the time required of top-level people, some argue that companies should use consultants for at least part of the required strategic personnel planning. Another reason for using consultants is that the same external factors that impact your company impact many companies, and therefore consultants should be able to do strategic human resources management planning work more effectively and for a lower cost than each company can do individually. I think that as a sixth basic guideline, you should consider using consultants in some ways in strategic human resources management planning if you can get really good ones for a reasonable fee. Specifically, consider buying an independent identification of strategic human resources management planning items and network those consultants from time to time.

Not all strategic planning items are of equal relevance; nor should they command equal attention. You must, therefore, weight the strategic factors in some manner, and that is my seventh guideline for strategic human resources management planning work. Start with their overall importance now—as a current planning item. Then consider the probability of the future impact and the time of impact.

Finally, my eighth guideline for strategic planning relates to actions. Planning can be valuable in gaining knowledge, but mostly you do strategic human resources management planning so you can *do something*—and do it better in some ways than you would have if you had not done strategic human resources management planning. Thus planning should result in actions taken, or actions to be undertaken, or actions to be avoided because of strategic planning information.

The Strategic Personnel Planning Process

There is a current planning process that I use because I think it's the best process. This process is described in Chapter 2. The process uses the scanning of journals, networking people inside and outside the company, and cataloguing. Then each category is evaluated and weighted, and the result is a list of current planning items.

There is also a strategic planning process. The strategic human resources management planning method I recommend starts with the current planning items. There are thus a half-dozen steps in my method for strategic human resources management planning.

Here, in outline form, is the combined human resources management planning process that I have evolved over the years.

A. Current Human Resources Management Planning
1. The base of the planning process is scanning journals and inputs from network contacts inside and outside the company.
2. The current planning actions that are identified are catalogued.
3. The result is an identification and description of *current* human resources management planning trends and issues.
4. These current planning items are weighted to assess relative importance.

B. Strategic Human Resources Management Planning
5. The current trends are examined to determine which might have strategic relevance.
6. The most likely time span of each strategic human resources management planning item is judged.
7. Then there is a forecasting of each strategic human resources management planning item through the time period determined for each.
8. At predetermined periods, forecasts are monitored and adjustments are made when necessary.
9. The result is an identification of strategic human resources management planning items.
10. These results should also be weighted to determine relative importance.

For some current planning items in any planning work year, there will be no likely relevance much beyond that planning period. Those items are current trends and will not be strategic planning items. In my system, *all* strategic planning items are also current planning items.

About a third of the current items in any planning period will usually also have some longer term relevance and, therefore, they will be strategic planning human resources management planning items. Almost always, the nature and relevance of the item is different in the future than the identified current trend, but it is in the same category.

Strategic Planning Period

For items determined to have strategic possibilities, it is first important to make judgments about the approximate planning period. Specifically, as part of the second step in strategic human resources management planning, you must make a specific judgment about how long it will take that item to achieve maturity or be of maximum importance and have an impact on business.

There are three long-term planning periods, and I think it is only necessary to judge which is the most likely time period for each strategic item. One is up to three years. The intermediate period is anywhere from three to ten years. The long-term planning period is more than ten years and may be as long as thirty years.

Each of the strategic planning periods has relevance in terms of resource application. These are the considerations in categorizing each strategic planning item to one of the time periods.

The two- to three-year cycle is the time needed to change the workforce, to change basic human resources management programs, and to take actions that will impact productivity.

As an example, the average strategic time of two to three years is the period in which a company could develop and implement new performance appraisal systems or a new management bonus system—and have them in effect long enough to evaluate results. This is the period of time in which you could change the quality of the workforce by organizational enrichment, by improved recruiting, or by developing basically new reward-for-performance systems.

The next longest strategic time period is from four to ten years, which I label the seven-year period. The seven-year business period relates mostly to changes in basic styles of managing personnel, a change in the excellence of managing people, and in enhanced employee-employer relationships. Examples would be the implementation of a delegative management style of managing people or the processes of productivity bargaining or union decertification.

A period of more than ten years relates to new technologies that impact work and that could result in fundamental changes in politics, values, and social relationships. Examples would be EEO initiatives and the decline in company loyalty.

Determining the likely time of impact of a strategic human resources management planning item is mostly judgmental. Relating time periods to the type of activity that must be deployed and used for dealing with them makes these judgments practical.

Having identified the time period, it is necessary to do forecasting and monitoring and determine action steps. That is the overall planning process in human resources management. Forecasting and monitoring activities require careful consideration.

Forecasting

The technical work in strategic human resources management planning mostly involves forecasting and monitoring. Forecasting involves some method for determining future items, and monitoring involves a periodic review of the forecast.

There are basically six methods of forecasting that can be used to identify information items about the future:

1. Extrapolating past trend data into the future
2. Category planning—where the frequency with which trend items are reported is the basis for conclusions regarding future items
3. Intuitive forecasting—where a desired future state or condition is the starting point, even though the sum of the supporting evidence cannot reasonably justify the prediction
4. Feasibility-based forecasting—the identification of a capability and the assumption that the capability will be utilized in certain ways
5. Value-based planning—where people express their desires about how things should be and then seek to affect actual future events
6. Forecasting observed current trends

Business planning often uses all of these methods. Sometimes business planning people have used all six methods in a somewhat random manner.

All six methods of forecasting have some value in the strategic planning process under certain circumstances. However, planning based on observed trends should be the *basic* method of human resources management strategic planning.

Statistical extrapolation is often used in planning. Extrapolation is the core of financial planning and market research forecasting. Extrapolation is mathematic and, therefore, appears to be factual. It seems so reasonable to extrapolate past facts and trend lines into the future. And statistical extrapolation is simple, requiring only basic mathematics that, in turn, can be computerized.

Use statistical extrapolations whenever possible. Extrapolation is the most reasonable and objective method of forecasting. We know that the future is always different than the past and that extrapolating the past into the future statistically will always be wrong. But each year you are able to monitor those extrapolations, and they become more accurate with each monitoring.

Category planning is used as a basic method of forecasting by some well-known futurists. When this method is used, the volume of the material accumulated for each subject is the basis for determining the importance of the items. Obviously, this method of forecasting assumes that the most newsworthy current trends are those that will have the greatest strategic significance in the future.

Intuitive planning identifies desired facts or practices and, based on logic, builds proof that these may be trends of the future. This type of intuitive planning is a cousin of value-based planning, except in inductive or intuitive planning the observations are real, however infrequent or special, and the process can be extremely logical. For example, planners saw productivity management practices that were called quality circles used in Japan, and with great reason and some logic, predicted that they could be used in this country. After costly experiments, the prediction proved to be incorrect, because the inductive process never factored in cultural differences between Japan and the United States.

Feasibility-based forecasts are factual in the sense that half the equation is observable. This basis of forecasting assumes, for example, a reaction to technological capability, which is anything but certain.

One specific example of the application of feasibility-based forecasting is the forecast of the cottage workforce. MIS experts were, in effect, predicting that what computer technology could do would happen, without considering the requirements of the law or management. Just because something can happen doesn't mean that it will happen. But anything made feasible by technology is a possibility to observe, to consider, and to monitor in planning work.

Value-based planning mostly reflects wishes. Obviously, management can't base decisions on pure desire, regardless of the nobleness and virtues of the wishes. But there is a legitimate place in planning for the consideration of values as inputs to planning. There is always a range of likely reality in the future, and values held by the leaders can influence actual future results within the range of possibilities.

There are more value-based planning methods in strategic business planning than many may assume. A bright person can start with a vision of how the world should be or how he would like it to be and then develop data, logic, and reason to support that predetermined view. If the planner then has the ability to get media attention, his biased views will get so much publicity that his fantasies will take on the appearances of fact.

Planning based on observed current trends is the last method. It is the method I recommend as the core of forecasting.

The methods of forecasting used in extrapolating the current conditions to a future prediction are also important. Mathematical extrapolation is best but, as noted, is seldom used in personnel planning. The extrapolation method I use is a form of linear logic, often supported by extrapolated data related to the trend.

For example, data on capital substitution and the effect of the new information capital on productivity can be extrapolated forward. This can be directly related to possible productivity levels, but there must then be judgments about what that means in terms of productivity management actions.

You can extrapolate public school data: grade point averages, SATs, dropout rates, etc. But logic tells me that employers and parents will not accept the consequences and that they will start a parade of actions for improving public education. Then the politicians will get at the head of the parade.

You can count the great number of special interest groups that exist today. There is no reason to think that there will be fewer of them in the future. For this planning item it is sufficient to conclude that there will be many special interest groups in the strategic future.

Each strategic planning item needs to be approached and considered differently. But in each case, some combination of data/information is extrapolated by some system of linear logic. Allocate most of your time and effort to the two-to-three-year items, and review them carefully each year against actual events by monitoring methods.

Monitoring

Monitoring is an art, and it's impossible to describe specific techniques that should be used by everyone. Here are a few suggestions from my own experience.

Tailor the monitoring method to the item. That sounds very complicated, but there aren't that many items.

Emphasize the top dozen or so items in your own monitoring. They should get 80 percent of the monitoring time. The top six items should get 50 percent of the monitoring attention.

Also consider the planning time interval. In my planning work, I monitor the two-to-three-year items every six months, the three-to-ten-year items every year; and the more-than-ten-year items every three years.

There isn't a method for doing monitoring work, but there is a process. One is by periodically reviewing current trends. Look for dramatic changes and headline events. These signal shifts—and shifts change forecasts.

For example, upward mobility signaled a shift in equal opportunity to equal treatment. This rather subtle shift was more powerful and more permanent than all the demonstrations, speeches, and articles that had been reported in the media.

Some planning items can be monitored by data, and planners should use data whenever possible. Some retirement issues, for example, were forecasted and monitored by data based on plan cancellations and reversion cases. Others items, like delegative management, can be monitored only by tracking developments in many companies.

The best monitoring is always factual and statistical. When reports of productivity increases showed only a 2 percent increase a year instead of the 4 to 6 percent that was possible, there had to be a change in forecasts relating to the number one strategic issue.

I also ask a lot of questions, usually as a by-product of a contact for some other purpose. At any point in time, you will find that there are three or four strategic planning issues where you have particular difficulty in monitoring the results. At the time this book was being drafted, these were: equal treatment (Chapter 8), demands of special interest groups (Chapter 11), multicultural differences (Chapter 10), and the impact of technology on employee work experiences (Chapter 17). I average a dozen questions a week on these issues and will continue this for any item until I feel I have enough information to intelligently monitor the trend.

I have no other suggestions to offer. Monitoring is a central part of strategic personnel planning work, but it is a matter of judgment and personal style.

Strategic Human Resources Management Planning Recommendations

Don't ask whether your company should do human resources management planning. Current planning is essential work. You must know what is happening now that is significant in human resources management. In fact, I argue that companies should do current planning in such a manner that they are 99.99 percent certain they know what is happening so there will be no surprises.

Strategic planning of all types is discretionary—or at least it can be postponed. Nevertheless, I recommend that every company that has a human resources management professional should do human resources management strategic planning in some way. Any company with five or more professionals can do strategic planning work in the manner just described.

I think that failure to do strategic planning and to do it well has been one of the foremost critical defects in the human resources management field.* Without strategic information, those who work in the field necessarily take a "this year" view and are constantly embroiled in fire drills and crises. This deficiency will become greater as the work environment becomes even more technological and the rate of change increases even more.

Strategic thinking and planning in any field are difficult, and human resources management is no exception. But sound human resources management strategic planning can be done, and it doesn't cost very much.

For example, from my own personal experience in doing strategic human resources management planning work, I would say that to do a good job of strategic human resources management planning, top-level human resources management professionals should spend about two hundred hours each year, and about an equal amount of time should be spent by support persons. This does not include the time spent by people in the company and by outside people who have to gather current planning information, and it does not include communication of the material. The time estimates only include the time spent on strategic personnel planning work.

Doing strategic human resources management planning work is not so much a matter of time but the management of time. The top human resources management person, for example, may personally spend fifty hours a year on strategic personnel planning. But the time must be applied with reasonable consistency—at least some time must be spent every month. Furthermore, the time must be confined to matters that can only be handled by the top human resources management person, and then he must stay out of other planning activities.

The product of strategic human resources management planning is first a list of items. The top sixteen strategic items resulting from my independent work are show in Exhibit 4–1. These are covered in the next sixteen chapters in this book (eight additional planning items are treated very briefly in Chapter 21).

In evaluating strategic planning items, it is necessary to consider the importance of the item as a current human resources man-

*If you are interested in my opinion of all four major defects in human resources management, they are: lack of strategic thinking; failure to take affirmative action on matters of critical importance, like productivity management and downsizing; lack of knowledge of operations and operating workers; and failure to stand up and represent employees' views and interests in important business decisions.

Exhibit 4-1. Strategic human resources management items.

Strategic Planning Item	Index of Importance	Time Period* (Years)
1. Productivity Management	100%	2–3
2. Educational Deficiency	98	4–10
3. Delegative Management	92	2–3
4. Equal Treatment	83	2–3
5. Managing Differences	67	4–10
6. Demands of Special Interest Groups	62	2–3
7. Fair Pay	48	2–3
8. Benefit Cost Containment	47	2–3
9. Retirement Issues	44	4–10
10. Labor Scarcity	39	4–10
11. Impact of Technology on the Work Experience	37	4–10
12. Employee Owners	31	4–10
13. Restructuring the Organization	23	4–10
14. Job Security	20	4–10
15. The Working Poor	17	2–3
16. The New Work Democracy	13	4–10

*This is the period in years when the item is most likely to have the greatest impact and affect the most companies.

agement planning issue, plus the likely time impact before the item will become a current trend item, plus the manageability of the item. You must also make judgments about the probability that the item will, in fact, impact *your* company and how.

In a book like this, I can only outline the top strategic human resources management planning items affecting many companies. I can describe them and suggest actions in general. It is still the job of the human resources management people within a company to determine exactly how each strategic item will impact their company and evaluate different action recommendations to develop specific actions plans for their own company.

As you consider each of the strategic personnel planning items presented, concentrate on the relevance of each item to your company and how that item might affect your company. Then think about possible actions.

The descriptions and commentaries on each of these items are mostly presented to make sure that the item is communicated. If you have other opinions about the item or choose to describe it differently, that would be fine, and I hope that my commentary helps to sharpen your own view. The critical thing is to identify each strategic human resources management planning item. We should not let commentary and opinion deflect us from consideration of the item itself.

The process for strategic human resources management planning described here is fact-based. It is also an objective system and process. Reasonable people who are at least somewhat familiar with the subjects would come to the same conclusions if they followed this process.

To test the reasonableness of this view, I have had different people in companies and in consulting firms who had an interest in the subject of strategic planning follow the process that has been described. In each case, *they arrived at the same conclusions*. The rank of importance varied, but the items are essentially the same.

Specifically, twenty-three different people identified, on average, twenty of the twenty-four items listed at that time. Every one of these people identified the top dozen items as being very important strategic human resources management planning items.

You may not *like* the results of strategic human resources management planning. I don't like a lot of the items I have reported in this book. Strategic items are usually distasteful to someone, which is one of the reasons why they are so difficult to resolve. Our likes and dislikes should not affect our strategic planning work.

You may not agree with my recommendations for actions. I hope you will find that some of them are useful and that the others will at least help to illustrate the planning items and perhaps stimulate your thinking about other actions.

5

Productivity Improvement

The number one challenge of the future planning period is productivity improvement. We are now in the productivity era, and it will likely continue through the 1990s and well into the twenty-first century. Productivity management is the number one strategic human resources management issue. I think that productivity is the number one business issue in this country. In addition, productivity is certainly a major national issue.

The Productivity Opportunity

There is an incredible opportunity to increase productivity for the next twenty years. Productivity can increase at the rate of 4 to 6 percent a year in that period. This would mean that by the year 2010 productivity would be more than triple what it is today.

Looking back, we have experienced a miracle in productivity, and it propelled this country to a position of economic leadership in the world. However, past increases in productivity were modest compared to the potential for productivity improvement in the future strategic planning periods.

Productivity in the past hundred years in this country increased at the rate of somewhat less than 2 percent a year compounded. In the future, the rate of productivity increase can be at least twice as high, and many believe that productivity can increase three times as much in the future as it did in the past.

These forecasts are not guesses. We know that productivity improvement of 4 to 6 percent a year can happen because of the investment in machinery, including computers and communications equipment, and from the demonstrated impact of such technology on productivity levels.

Productivity improvement in the future strategic period will occur by the traditional method: substituting machine power for human effort. But more and more in the future, machine power will replace capability of the mind as well as physical effort. When machines extend the brain as well as muscles, the potential for improving productivity is very great.

Computers cannot think yet, but they can do many thinking tasks—like calculate and memorize. The computer can do such tasks many times more productively than the human mind.

Computers represent much of the capital that will make enormous increases in productivity possible, but they are not the only new capital that will contribute to greater productivity. Communication equipment will also make productivity improvement possible and is often closely interrelated to computers. Robotics, materials, and new energy sources will also facilitate productivity increases in the forthcoming strategic human resources management planning period.

The effect of a productivity impact of up to 6 percent a year on standards of living is mind-boggling. By the year 2010, it is quite possible that living standards would more than double. The family income of the lowest-paid full-time workers would be equal to the average of all workers today, net of inflation. By the year 2010, the *average* family income in the United States could be $40,000 (in 1990 dollars). There would be no poverty in this country.

To get an appreciation of the impact of greater productivity, think of the life-styles that existed a hundred years ago. Think about how much better our material condition is today than it was then. Then extrapolate that into the future at two or three times the rate of improvement of the past. Then by the year 2010, standards of living can be as much greater, compared to today, as the living standards of today are compared to the living standards in the early 1890s.

This economic miracle of future productivity improvement and its incredible effect on our economy and our living standards won't happen automatically. Potential productivity improvement results only from the effective management of workers and from a workforce committed to excellence; all facilitated by reasonable government policies.

Buying the equipment won't bring about the new productivity miracle. The proper *use* of equipment is just as critical in order to achieve potential productivity improvement.

There are big differences between the capital substitution of the past and much of the current and future capital substitution. In the past, the capital controlled the work. In more and more cases today, workers, not machines, control the output.

In the past, machinery substituted for labor was expensive compared to the pay of workers who used the capital, and the equipment was usually for a single purpose. Today, capital is cheap compared to pay, and the equipment that substitutes for labor is usually multiple purpose.

In the past, savings from substituting capital for labor were calculable and definite, but now that is much less true. We know there can be savings, but the amount of savings, if any, depends on how the equipment is used.

The differences in capital substitution that have been described generally mean that the productivity potential is greater but that productivity increases from capital substitution are not assured. Differences in the nature of capital substitution also mean that the methods of productivity management must be effective if there is to be productivity improvement at the rate of 4 to 6 percent a year in the next strategic human resources management planning period.

Partly because productivity is worker controlled in the new capital substitution, the management of people is critical to productivity management. This means that productivity management must be of highest importance to professionals in human resources management.

Failures of Productivity Management

So far we have failed to achieve the potential productivity improvement. Productivity has been increasing at about 2 percent or less since the productivity age started in the early 1980s. That failure, in large part, has necessarily been the failure of executive management to understand the opportunities and respond appropriately. That, in turn, may be largely a failure of those in the field of human resources management.

Essentially, we may all be too inclined to go on in the same old way with programmatic and bureaucratic management systems. The knee-jerk reaction to productivity problems and opportunities was usually to establish a productivity *program* like quality circles or quality management. That often meant that the answer to too many programs was another program.

The productivity age is also off to a bad start because of failures of leadership in the government. For instance, Congress keeps ignoring the issues of productivity and, in fact, passes law after law, each of which may have good goals but many of which seriously retard productivity improvement.

Congress must find a way to promote productivity before it spends the productivity dividend. What we can't afford is legislation that reduces productivity, and a great deal of human relations legislation has done exactly that in recent years.

The productivity failure of the 1980s was also due to a failure to properly reward those who increased productivity. Rewards for greater effectiveness are essential for sustained productivity improvement.

Productivity improvement is also increasingly dependent on the excellence of education. Educational deficiency has hindered productivity improvement, and there have been few reasons to be encouraged about education.

Unions and special interest groups have had their own agendas. This very often caused reductions in productivity or retarded improvement in productivity. Unions and special interest groups often seem to be uninterested in productivity, although they must realize that productivity improvement is really the only thing that will finance their wish lis⁺s.

Many special interest groups think that an exception should be made in their case. But, of course, every special interest group thinks this way.

There are plenty of people and circumstances to blame for the failures of productivity management in the 1980s. All of these factors are at least partially manageable, so the failure in productivity is basically a failure of executive management.

Overall, there seems to be little reason for optimism about productivity improvement. But I think that leadership for greater productivity will come from the working people. I think that working people will cause a great change in political attitudes and legislative priorities, resulting in much more support of productivity improvement.

Executive managers may also let workers be more effective through delegative management and empowerment and facilitate effectiveness in other ways when it becomes important enough to do so. We must all hope that executives will provide leadership in productivity management work.

Another reason for optimism about future productivity is that the economy will increasingly be dominated by smaller enterprises. These companies are almost always productivity conscious and generally have delegative styles and the ability for quick reaction.

Expect productivity to drag on at about 2 percent for another few years. Then workers, some executive leaders, many small entrepreneurs, and international competition will likely force the leaders in Congress and other business executives to change their attitudes and their actions. Then I predict that starting about 1995, productivity will begin to increase at about 4 percent a year. By the year 2000, productivity improvement might reach 6 percent a year.

Essentials of Productivity Improvement Work in the 1990s

Failure to achieve anything like the productivity opportunity that exists suggests the need for rethinking productivity improvement work. Here are a few essentials for work on productivity improvement in the next strategic planning period.

Above all, in my opinion, we should have learned from past experiences that productivity improvement doesn't result from one grand program administered by the corporate office. The big-bang approach to productivity improvement was perhaps one of the last products of the programmatic management era.

You can be sure that there will be organizations that knock on your door with some panacea productivity program. They will have polished presentations and claim that *they* have the answers to productivity for you—and for everyone else. My advice is not to waste your time listening to their presentations.

Another lesson that should have been learned is that productivity improvement work must be geared to each company's operations and culture. This means that you should learn from the experiences of others, but be careful about copying what seems to have worked for them.

Not only is every company different, but each company has different issues relating to productivity, and each has its own unique successes and roadblocks with respect to productivity improvement. In productivity work, the questions and issues are different in every company and, therefore, specific productivity management practices must also be different.

In fact, within organizations, there are business areas and divisions with unique operating and economic characteristics. Therefore, there often should not be a program for a company overall, let alone all companies.

When it comes to productivity management in the future, think big. Remember that productivity can be increased in the next decade at two to three times the rate of productivity improvement in the past. Get information about this incredible opportunity in front of your top management so they will know about the potential opportunity for your company.

The potential for productivity improvement will not be limited by machine capability in the foreseeable future as it was in the past. For example, the rate of new computer equipment being introduced in the technology era has been so rapid that the users have not come even close to taking advantage of the capability of the equipment before new generations of more productive machines were forthcoming. Based on known technology, that cycle will continue well into the twenty-first century.

Also remember that the machines now being substituted for manpower extend the mind as well as substituting for muscles. Translate that into your business.

Your company is not in the productivity business. Whatever the success factors have been in your business, those factors will remain the same in the future. If, for example, yours is basically a marketing-oriented business, it still would be. Productivity management will improve the business but not necessarily change that business focus.

Productivity makes it possible for your business to do things better—much better. Productivity makes it possible for your business to do things quicker—much quicker. Very often, productivity makes it possible for your business to operate at a lower cost—a much lower cost. Doing things better, quicker, and at a lower cost is the productivity dividend.

Productivity work will be much different in the future than it was in the past. For example, large companies have accomplished productivity management in the past largely by committing great financial resources. With large amounts of money, big companies could buy capital for mechanization, and the machines then controlled the work. Thus in the past, big companies largely managed productivity because they *bought* productivity improvement. Productivity improvement was mostly a *purchasing* function. There will be less of an ability to buy productivity in the future, mostly because workers have more control of the output. More and more in the future, productivity must be managed, not just purchased.

In the future, buying the machines and spending money on research and development will be only part of the job. For example, because the machines are often worker controlled, managing the use of the machines is now a critical part of productivity management. Thus the effective management of people is a critical element of productivity management now and will continue to be in the future.

Productivity and enterprise success are always linked, although not necessarily in a single year. Higher productivity will always mean greater profitability in a commercial firm in the long run. To get high productivity, there must be effective productivity management by all the operating managers in the company.

Productivity improvement must be managed, which is a good reason to call this work productivity management. Productivity management must have policy direction and leadership from the top. Productivity management needs a human resources management department with a deep knowledge of the subject that will be helpful to managers when they work on productivity issues. Above all else, every manager of personnel must be a productivity manager, and productivity improvement mostly occurs because of thousands of incidents and actions every year in every company.

Finally, achieving higher productivity requires an organized effort. Then sustaining high levels of productivity depends on making productivity management an integral part of the management style of the company. Most companies today have a great opportunity to improve productivity, and they need to determine methods of productivity management that will work the best for them.

Productivity Management Methods

Effective productivity management methods evolved over many years. I have personally been working on productivity management since the early 1970s.*

The basic method that I think is the most effective is presented here in summary form. Each company must customize this method of productivity management, but the twelve steps outlined below are, I think, applicable to every company, usually in the order listed here.

Step 1: Get Executives Involved

The first step in improving employee productivity is to make sure that executives are really committed to productivity management and personally involved. This means four things:

1. Executives must be well informed on productivity management.
2. They must be convinced that an improvement in productivity is possible and necessary.
3. The executives themselves must be productive.
4. Proper policies and direction must come from the top.

Here are a few comments about each of these elements of executive involvement in productivity.

Make sure that your top executives are well informed and intelligent about the potential for productivity improvement. That knowledge should be about productivity management generally and about specific opportunities in your company.

*Robert E. Sibson, *Increasing Employee Productivity*, AMACOM, New York, 1976.

Information about productivity management must be transmitted in the normal way that things are communicated to top executives in your company. Avoid making one big formal presentation, but rather have a series of specific items that are presented in the normal course of communicating to executives. Most importantly, take advantage of cases to demonstrate productivity management matters.

Obviously, executives must have a commitment to productivity improvement. I have never met an executive who didn't want higher productivity, but I have met some who thought that levels of productivity didn't make much of a difference in their company's business results and many who doubted that people in personnel could impact productivity through human resources management efforts.

Management at each level of the organization should set a good example with respect to productivity. That should start at the very top of the organization. If employees throughout the organization are to work effectively, executives must be productive and set a good example. If executives don't do their best, it is unlikely that others will work to optimum effectiveness.

One way to get executives to set a good example is to include them in efforts to improve productivity. Make sure that their direct involvement is visible throughout the organization. It isn't necessary that executives spend much time on productivity activities, just enough involvement to demonstrate a commitment to productivity improvement.

Executives are most directly involved in their own productivity and that of their immediate subordinates. How executives manage the productivity of direct reports can be critical in productivity management. How each level of management handles productivity sets the tone of conduct for the next lower level. This is the trickle-down theory of work in productivity management.

When you think of productivity improvement activities, don't forget to include the executives themselves. If executives think that they have increased their productivity, they will be committed to productivity improvement for everyone.

Obviously, executives must also set the policies and basic strategies for productivity improvement and exercise ongoing executive control. A few basic policies rigorously enforced are what is needed.

Step 2: Develop a Productivity Consciousness

The second step is to develop a productivity consciousness throughout the company. Every manager must think about productivity every day and with respect to every incident.

Developing a productivity consciousness is a matter of persistence. Whatever the question or issue, just ask whether practices support or detract from the effectiveness of work. This should be done in all areas of a company's operation, including the personnel department. Then whenever there is a success case in productivity management, broadcast it widely.

You will enhance productivity consciousness throughout the company as you build know-how and skill in productivity management on the part of those in the personnel organization. As the professionals gain effectiveness in productivity management, they will think productivity and communicate productivity. As human resources management professionals help managers increase productivity, then the managers will see the results of productivity and become more productivity conscious. Mostly I have found that you make believers by actual success experiences.

Some people think it's useful to have a lot of communications, ceremonies, celebrations, and hoopla associated with productivity management. Such publicity often seems juvenile, but it will keep productivity in front of everyone. Because some think that public relations for productivity is so important, I include it in this step.

In fact, you will find that what really develops a productivity consciousness is accountability, success, and reward for success. Those things will come with time, but you also need a productivity consciousness in the early stages of productivity management, and the communication actions can be helpful in those early stages.

Whatever specific techniques you use, there must be persistence in your efforts and a constant focus on the effectiveness of work. What you are doing is building a productivity culture.

A productivity culture values performance. Personnel actions of all types consider only performance when there is a productivity culture and have little tolerance for any other considerations in personnel actions.

Step 3: Establish an Organization for Productivity Management

Never set up a separate productivity department. But there must be an identification of accountability assignments and, at times, project groups to accomplish specific tasks. What is recommended is a *system,* not a bureaucracy.

The vice president of human resources management must be the head of the organization. Avoid having a coordinator or team leader. Actually, each human resources management professional is a productivity coordinator.

Consider having one person in the office of the chief executive officer oversee the work on productivity throughout the company. This assures executive involvement. This officer should monitor the work initiated in operating divisions and units. When necessary, this executive can obtain needed support or required corrective action.

Step 4: Remove Unproductive Practices

Early in your organized efforts on productivity work, you should launch a vendetta against unproductive practices of all types anywhere in the company and at every level. The senior executive in the office of the chief executive officer might make this a matter of personal interest.

When there are unionized employees, removing unproductive practices means productivity bargaining. Productivity bargaining has often resulted in productivity being doubled in a few years.

Don't think that unproductive practices only exist in union situations. There are many cases of unproductive practices at every level of a company's non-union operation.

Today and throughout this strategic human resources management planning period, there will be many special interest groups who seek changes in the workplace that they think will improve conditions for their constituency. These proposals very often result in new unproductive practices that cause a decline in productivity. The combined effect of all special interest groups has caused the introduction of many unproductive practices.

If you have never tried to remove unproductive practices, the chances are that productivity can be improved through this step by 10 percent. New unproductive practices in the future will deter productivity increases by 1 or 2 percent a year, so there is a need for an assault on unproductive practices every three to five years.

It is at this point in my productivity management method that the work will encounter very serious opposition. Many unproductive practices were thought to be useful or necessary by someone at some time for some reason, and that will inevitably cause reactions, objections, and opposition.

Be prepared for a lot of opposition to the removal of unproductive practices, sometimes from very high places. Attack the unproductive practices like a desert storm, but try to leave all the participants unwounded.

Step 5: Make Productivity Part of Every Manager's Job

Assign the job of productivity to every manager. Give managers time to do the job and provide the support they need to do this work. Measure managers' performance partly by how well they manage people and how well they manage productivity. Reward those who increase productivity. Replace those managers who don't manage productivity well.

When all managers are accountable for productivity management, then many people are working to improve productivity. Those doing productivity management work are experts in the work being done, and each can apply methods that work best in his own area of work. Thus there are many productivity experts. Productivity gains may be small steps forward, but there will be many steps every year, and for that matter, every day.

Making productivity a part of every manager's job is, in my opinion, the key activity in any method or process of productivity management, including my own.

The key to making productivity a part of every manager's job is delegative management (Chapter 7). Delegative management is thus an important part of productivity management.

Step 6: Establish an Ongoing Management System for Manpower Management

A chronic problem of productivity management is excessive manpower. Your company can have high productivity by increasing the numerator of the productivity formula (measures of output) *or* by reducing the denominator (man-hours of work). Manpower management has to do with man-hours of work.

Manpower management in many operations was pretty mathematic. The complement count could often to tied directly to sales or other volume measures. With more complex work and with more knowledge workers, manpower management is much less mathematic and must mostly be determined by operating managers down in the organization.

There has been a substantial amount of downsizing during the past five years; support staffs at the corporate and division levels have been reduced regardless of operating volume. Expect much more downsizing at corporate and division levels. Also expect that a form of downsizing or rightsizing will occur in operations jobs in many companies.

If you will, reflect on the many stories about downsizing that have been in the press. In large companies, many thousands of people have been let go. If a company can be operated without this vast number of people, what did these people do when they were on the payroll and how is it possible that they were ever hired in the first place? These are critical clues to productivity management in the future.

In essence, only the managers of personnel can determine correct manpower levels. Various administrative practices can monitor manpower, and competent human resources management professionals can help the managers of personnel in their manpower planning. But manpower management is a job that must essentially be done by managers who know the work and the people who do the work.

Manpower management presents a major opportunity for productivity improvement. This must increasingly be done as the ongoing management of work rather than a periodic body count.

Step 7: Increase the Capability of the Workforce

Performance management is a critical part of productivity management. This is particularly true because workers now often control the machines that make higher productivity possible. Capability assessments and actions to improve performance must also be the responsibility of the direct manager of personnel.

Performance management means increasing capability and work excellence. It focuses on optimizing the effectiveness of each individual.

Performance management relates to work done and the talent of those doing the work. These variables are known only by the operating managers, and it is absurd to claim that any one program will improve capability and the performance of many people with different capabilities.

Performance management starts with effective recruiting and selection. For a hundred years, personnel professionals have been saying, "Put your personnel dollars up-front," and that is certainly true of performance management.

Performance management requires effective performance appraisal. In addition, in the process of performance appraisal, the manager can identify ways in which each person might improve. Then when practical, the manager, who might be assisted by human resources management professionals and training specialists, plans and executes actions to improve performance.

Training can obviously affect capability and performance. However, many companies need to go back to the basics of training. This mostly means that companies must have training that is focused on meeting needs and improving work capability. There must also be recognition that most real training is related to work incidents and occurs in the operations. In capability training, the managers of people must essentially be the trainers, and professional human resources management professionals should mostly be training the trainers.

Performance management must also include organizational strengthening. This means reassigning people to optimize their talent. It means replacing people with more effective people.

Step 8: Empower Every Employee to Increase Productivity

The delegation of responsibility for productivity improvement should go through management levels to every worker in the company. Productivity improvement is the job of every employee.

Delegative management makes productivity part of every manager's job. Empowerment makes productivity management part of every employee's job. Empowerment must be delegated by each manager of personnel. Empowerment without delegative management is, in my opinion, a formula for disaster.

Participation is not enough. Voluntary individual participation is insulting to many employees, and a form of compulsory participation won't work. Group participation is an unproductive suggestion box.

Employees know things about their work that no one else knows, and employees who know the work the best are likely to have many ideas for productivity management. They should be able to *act*, not just suggest ways they can do their work better.

Employees will also have ideas about how others might be able to do their work better, and that should be encouraged but not imposed. It must be the worker himself who is empowered to accept or not accept the ideas of others.

The relevant word is *empowerment*, not participation. Empowerment means the same as delegation. Delegate to every worker the job of being as effective as possible. Make every worker responsible for working as effectively as possible. Reward high productivity.

Step 9: Make Sure There Is Reward for Greater Effectiveness of Work

Pay for performance is key to effective productivity management. It is fair to reward for greater effectiveness of work. Such rewards incent people to increase the effectiveness of their work.

Pay for performance is a complex matter. It has been the focus of attention in human resources management for many years. Plainly, however, pay for performance is an integral part of productivity management.

In the forthcoming strategic human resources management planning period, it will be absolutely essential to have effective pay for performance. The great potential for productivity improvement will not likely be achieved unless there is effective pay for performance.

Step 10: Measure Productivity

It isn't possible to manage productivity as an ongoing part of the management process unless productivity is measured. Therefore, establishing and administering proper methods of measuring productivity are an integral part of productivity management.

Establish productivity measures for every unit in the company, without exception. Such data then represents a measure of results for each unit and the effectiveness of management of the unit.

Productivity measures have another value. A company will never know whether an action designed to improve productivity is really effective unless productivity is measured.

You may hear from some managers that it is not possible to measure productivity in their operations. I heard that statement many times and had a standard way to deal with the problem, which you may want to use. I would personally take on the job of developing productivity measures for a unit that claimed it couldn't be done. It is always possible. After I had developed measures of productivity for a unit, the manager of that unit would often develop a much better measure of productivity.

Step 11: Work to Develop Effective Teams Throughout Your Company

A company's productivity is improved by increases in the productivity of individuals and by the increased productivity of groups or teams. Developing productive work groups and effective teams is an important part of productivity management.

There has been a lot of talk about teams in business over the past thirty years, but most of them resembled teams I never played on. All the teams from T groups and OD through today's variations of participative management stress getting along and going along. The teams I know play to win.

Winning teams have qualified players. Each player has a position and concentrates mostly on that job to the best of his ability.

Effective teams don't talk their opponents to death. And they don't require or expect concurrence. Members of winning teams don't expect to be pampered or involved, other than as a player on a team.

The coach designs the systems and often calls the plays. The coach's assistants teach each player, but each player is also empowered to do what he can (within the rules and following the coach's instructions) and to do his best.

This is the type of team that we must build in business. We need to focus on *winning* teams, not happy teams or tranquil teams.

Structure your team's attitude on the real world of business, not the laboratory world of academia. Design your team's systems to play the American way. Incent each player and each team to excel, and reward the winners.

Step 12: Build a Productivity Culture

Productivity management should be an ongoing activity, not a once-in-a-while effort. What is created during a productivity management effort must be sustained. Productivity must become part of the company's management style, part of the company's culture.

One of the advantages of the productivity management process that has been described is that each step is a building block for an ongoing productivity culture. Each step relates naturally to operations and, therefore, readily becomes part of management: a management process and the management culture.

Remember that there are many reasons for a decline in productivity; many deserving issues and worthy cases that result in actions that erode productivity or retard productivity improvement. A company with a productivity culture won't permit the erosion of productivity for any reason.

Conditions change, and new steps will be required to sustain high levels of productivity and achieve even higher levels of productivity—productivity levels that are unthinkable today. As a result, part of the productivity culture must be an alertness to change and an inclination for quick and affirmative reactions to opportunities to improve productivity even further.

To preserve a productivity culture, there are, I think, two essentials:

1. A continued measurement and reporting of productivity
2. A vice president of human resources management who is a productivity evangelist and who exercises strong leadership in productivity management

There are also a few other key areas to monitor. The areas I reviewed during an audit included such things as:

- The degree to which productivity management was part of the manager's job
- Whether employees were empowered to work more effectively
- The excellence of pay for performance
- Unproductive factors, particularly committees and meetings

Productivity Programs

Note that this twelve-step method of productivity management contains no mention of programs. In my opinion, productivity programs should only be considered as a method of dealing with a specific problem or issue of productivity management.

Never doubt that productivity programs will be offered as panaceas in the future as they were in the past. Productivity programs have made some suppliers rich, and some people will try to do the same thing in the future. There are also, of course, people who think that a productivity program will contribute significantly to greater productivity in spite of the lessons of the past.

High levels of productivity result from attention and action by operating managers. If they help at all, productivity programs are most likely to contribute to more effective productivity management because the programs focus attention on productivity and provide examples and cases.

If you follow the method recommended for productivity management, you will rarely if ever use a productivity program. However, a program may be a way to deal with a special problem or situation, so human resources management professionals should know something about productivity programs.

There are three basically different types or categories of productivity programs to consider. These are:

1. Business strategies
2. Company cases
3. Practices, activities, and gimmicks

Business Strategies

The most elaborate and comprehensive productivity programs involve the development and implementation of strategies to improve the business. Like any general business strategy, this one aims at improving the business, in this case by increasing workers' productivity.

Business strategies for increasing productivity generally involve some restructuring of personnel practices and methods of work. A business strategy of improvement by productivity management also usually involves a number of phases or steps. There may be a half-dozen separate steps or phases in this work, and it usually takes at least three years to complete the implementation of all the steps.

The best example of basic strategies are the quality management programs. These involve many steps and many phases of work, all of which are designed to get work done correctly the first time and reduce rework. Really successful quality management activities have involved many of the steps outlined earlier.

Another example of a business strategy to improve productivity would be performance management programs. These involve focusing on the seventh step in my process. Then performance management systems almost always involve staffing, appraisal and training programs, plus some form of incentive pay.

Company Cases

A second basic type of productivity program is to identify one organizational unit or location that will be used as a case. With one success case, the managers of other units will be encouraged to improve productivity and will have the experience of that case to guide them in their productivity improvement efforts. Each success case provides more background and encouragement for others.

Select each case by asking for volunteers. Some managers will want to do this to make a name for themselves. Then let that volunteer manager pick the method for improving productivity in his unit. The human resources management department can assist in the determination of methods used and in the implementation phases.

The best first case is the human resources management department itself. Those who work in the personnel profession should know more than anyone else about how to increase employee effectiveness of work. Success by the personnel people would then enhance their credibility throughout the organization when they go out and give advice on productivity improvement to other departments.

Productivity Practices

When I was first involved in productivity consulting projects, it was tempting to develop a canned program because that is what usually sold and I had a business to run. But even in the early years of productivity work in the early 1970s, there was plenty of evidence that canned programs didn't work.

Canned programs did sell. The first and most widely used was organizational development. Quality circles was a close second. There have been many others.

These canned productivity programs have cost businesses in the United States billions of dollars. On balance, it is most people's opinion that they have done more harm than good.

From that experience, it is likely that canned programs will not be used much in the 1990s. No doubt, new programs will be developed and some companies will buy them. But that will be an unusual experience in the future strategic planning period.

The reason for the failure of canned productivity programs is mostly because each company is unique and the problems and opportunities for productivity management vary enormously from company to company.

Of course, some basic issues of productivity are common to many companies. These essentially relate to the twelve steps in the productivity method that has been presented.

If you do decide to base productivity management in part on canned programs, I recommend that you do so by identifying a number of alternate programs that have been used somewhere. Then let each manager pick whatever program best meets the needs of that manager's organization.

This laundry-list approach to productivity improvement makes the job of those in human resources more difficult. Under this approach, the human resources management professionals must be expert in a number of different systems, and they must be able to indicate the features of each of these practices in advance. Only in this way can the managers intelligently choose the practices that will most likely facilitate productivity improvement in a particular operation.

You should keep the list of alternative methods to a *maximum* of a dozen proven methods. With a dozen choices, each manager should be able to find some method of productivity improvement that is applicable in his unit.

Productivity Management in the 1990s

Everyone who reads this book must have wondered why business has not improved productivity. If it is correct that there is a great productivity opportunity, then business results could be improved enormously. For example, a business that is now earning $1 a share could be earning $1.50 a share in real 1990 dollars by the year 2000 through productivity management alone.

One explanation for this apparent contradiction is that the assumption is not correct. Fortunately, a productivity improvement opportunity at a 4 to 6 percent rate is provable, partly because it has been done, but by analytic methods as well. A productivity rate of 4 to 6 percent for at least the next ten years can be proven for your company—at least it has been proven in every case so far that I know.

I don't know why productivity management hasn't been done in your business. But I do know that you should find out why it hasn't been done.

There are a number of identifiable reasons for the failures of productivity management in the 1980s and the early 1990s. The failures were often because productivity management was never tried. Often productivity was never tried because the board and top executives thought that results were good enough. For more and more companies, there will be compelling reasons to do effective productivity management in the 1990s because results will not be good enough.

Productivity management has often failed because the wrong methods were used. Almost always, the error was to rely on a corporate-directed *program*. Outlined here has been a process that will work for you, and it has worked in different ways in many cases.

I think that the potential improvement in productivity of 4 to 6 percent has not been achieved mostly because of the demands of special interest groups (Chapter 10) and responses by the government to those demands. Judge for yourself the virtue and fairness of these matters, but recognize that there is a cost for many of the demands from special interest groups.

The cost of actions resulting from the demands of special interest groups is mostly in terms of less productivity. As this happens, we seem to have failed to achieve the potential improvement in productivity, but, in effect, what has happened, at least in part, is that we have already paid the productivity dividends on changes urged by special interest groups.

Ultimately, of course, those in charge of each operation must accept the responsibility for the low rate of productivity improvement during the past dozen years. This means executive management and their top human resources management advisors—inside and outside the company. Read again the twelve-step productivity management method, and you will see many reasons for the failures in the past. In the future, companies will increasingly have to be effective in productivity management, even if that means getting new executives to manage and new human resources management executives to advise.

There are compelling needs for productivity improvement, and an avalanche of technology is available. Increasingly in the future, productivity management will be seriously undertaken and it will often be successful. We know how to do productivity management well. Almost every company has many reasons for increasing productivity. A company also has to have the *will* to increase productivity. Many companies will increase productivity substantially in the 1990s. They will be the competitive leaders in their field at the beginning of the twenty-first century.

6

Educational Deficiency

You could reasonably rate educational deficiency as the number one human resources management strategic planning item (placing it ahead of productivity management) on the grounds that if there is not a well enough educated workforce, productivity management efforts may not work well anyway. I chose productivity management as number one, partly on the grounds that from a business viewpoint, education *used* is what matters, and that more directly relates to productivity. I also think that during the next few years, the opportunities for productivity will be very great in spite of educational deficiency. Either view is correct, and the point is that educational deficiency is clearly one of the top human resources management strategic planning issues. If there is not effective action with respect to education, then before much longer educational deficiency could clearly become the number one strategic *business* planning issue, let alone number one among strategic *personnel* issues.

The Problems of Educational Deficiency

Don't underestimate the extent of the deficiency in education in this country. It is worse than bad; it is a national tragedy.

The United States has achieved the highest standard of living among major countries in the world because of superior productivity, based mostly on the technological advantage of a well-educated workforce. Technology is sustained by education, and in an increasingly technological world we must maintain technology leadership. Therefore, educational excellence must be maintained, compared to other developed countries in the international economic community if we are to sustain and improve our living standards.

In fact, over the past twenty or thirty years, our knowledge advantage has been eroding, and we are running the risk of becoming second class in education. If current trends continue, the United

States will inevitably become second rate in educational excellence, in productivity, and in living standards.

Historians tell us that every great nation has risen to prominence, then experienced an erosion of its leadership position and declined. Historians have traced the reasons for the rise and then the decline of every great power, hoping, no doubt, that we can learn from this for the future.

Many Americans think that the United States will be the first great power that avoids a decline and that we will somehow maintain our leadership position for as long into the future as it is possible to forecast. If such optimism proves to be wrong, then it could well be that our nation's decline could be largely due to educational deficiency.

For business, educational deficiency is a serious and very practical strategic issue. The deficiency of education in the workforce relative to work requirements becomes worse every year. Educational deficiency is the reason why many operations don't achieve their goals and why many of them fail. Educational deficiency is the reason why many working people lose their jobs.

The seriousness of the problem of educational deficiency is, in fact, a measure of the great economic opportunities that lie ahead. We have it in our power to improve educational excellence enormously—more than the 4 to 6 percent per year rate predicted for productivity improvement. Furthermore, there are actions that business can take: actions that serve business interests directly but that also will help to improve educational excellence.

In fact, there are four distinctly different areas of educational deficiency. These areas are interrelated, but each is also significantly different and has distinct issues.

The four areas of educational deficiency are:

1. Deficiency in grade school education
2. Functional illiteracy
3. Problems of colleges
4. Reeducation needs

Grade Schools

By far, the most urgent and critical area of educational deficiency is the eroding quality of education in the public grade schools in this country. It is a critical strategic problem for business. Educational deficiency in our public schools is getting worse and could prove to be a national tragedy.

There have been so many published reports, news stories, and broadcast specials about educational deficiency that we should all be aware that the problem exists and that it is a very serious matter. Our public schools are not educating our young people nearly well enough. The deficiency from kindergarten through twelfth grade has been documented hundreds of times in the past ten years, but the problems just get worse and worse.

The Problems of Grade School Education

To understand how bad the secondary education is in this country, you need only do recruiting work to fill jobs that require only a high school education. I have talked to many companies about this in recent years and have seen a number of studies. All the information tells the same tragic story.

If you take out the honors students who are going on to college and eliminate the dropouts who are in another labor market anyway, then you have the market of high school graduates. Almost half of these high school graduates do not have the math skills and the verbal ability to perform most entry-level jobs that require no experience. Most of these young people don't have the basic education to advance to a better job.

It will get worse. In the future strategic planning period, many high school graduates will need some remedial education before they are able to perform *any* entry-level jobs that are available.

The educational requirements for high school graduates going into entry-level jobs are increasing at a rapid rate every year because of increased technology. Yet the basic educational achievements of high school graduates entering the labor market are getting worse. More and more young people are being pushed through the system and given some form of a "diploma" even though they have not achieved even basic educational levels.

There has been a twenty-year decline in educational achievement in public schools even though many of the tests to measure achievement have been made easier during that period. Two-thirds of the public gives the schools a flunking grade in every opinion survey that has been published. Employers know that the public schools are not doing the job of education and that educational deficiency at the grade school level is getting worse.

SAT scores are lower now than they were twenty years ago, with combined scores of less than 900. Based on a sample of studies, graduates of public schools who are not going on to college and who are not required to take SATs have an average score that is below 650.

The planning significance of all of this in the practical world of business and the economic welfare of working people is very great. What difference does it make, for example, to have more and better technology if workers are not educated well enough to make the advanced technologies work? Why put PCs in the office if workers can't read simple instructions? Why put computers and communication equipment in delivery trucks if the drivers can't learn to use them?

We have known about the crisis in public school education for a long time—certainly since the 1970s. The educational establishment's answer is to spend more money. For example, the National Education Association, the country's largest teachers' union, suggests $2.2 billion more just to "jump-start" education. In the study titled "A Nation at Risk," teachers' unions and representatives of the educational establishment urged more pay for teachers and making the teaching job more fun as answers to educational deficiency. Predictably, the association of school principals said that the way to improve educational excellence in secondary schools was to increase the pay of principals.

This country has been spending more and more on education and the results are worse and worse. Pay for teachers and principals is generally very competitive, and it is clearly high enough. So more money isn't the answer. The issues are serious, and we need commonsense answers now.

The answers to the problems of public grade school education rest with the students themselves, their parents, the teachers, the school management, and the government. Each must do its part to improve public school education. Employers can also undertake some activities that will improve public education.

Company Actions That Have Been Undertaken

Many companies have tried to do something about public school educational deficiency. Start thinking about future actions by learning from the lessons of the past. Here are representative examples of what companies have actually done in the past ten years.

• The M Corporation gave the community in which it was headquartered $1 million for better education. That amounted to less than 1 percent of the school district's annual budget. That was a lot of money, but it didn't do the M Corporation much good. In fact, 90 percent of the M Corporation's employees are located elsewhere.

• During the past half-dozen years, the P Corporation set up its own school for children who fail in the public school system where corporate headquarters are located. The P Corporation now graduates more students than the public high schools. Few companies could afford this, and most would have simply moved their corporate headquarters.

• Five years ago, the N Corporation made all of its management training programs available to the school principals and administrators in the area in which the company operates. After reviewing these programs last year, N Corporation discontinued the training programs because they hadn't done the company any good. These programs didn't do the school district any good either.

• The K Corporation actually assigned some of its executives to work full-time on the management of the school district in which it has its principal operations. You would have to know the people involved to share my concern about this type of action. Also keep in mind that this is like having consultants who are temporary employees run your company.

These four cases probably represent 80 percent of the types of actions taken by companies with respect to educational deficiency in local public secondary schools. It is time to review company actions to improve public education and identify effective actions for the future strategic human resources management strategic planning period.

Recommendations

I recommend that employers should do three things about the educational deficiency in public school education. First and foremost, I think all employers should recognize that they are *customers* of the public school system. Second, employers should become activists, directly and through their employees, for better public school education. Third, they should use tests to measure the educational achievement of those entering the workforce directly from high school.

Employers should start to act like public school customers. What would your company do if a supplier delivered deficient products or services year after year? The usual response is that a buyer would go to another supplier. You can't do that, except to hire more students from private schools, and there aren't many private school graduates who don't go on to college.

As a customer, you can tell the providers about the deficiencies; be specific about the educational deficiencies of high school graduates. Keep records about key performance information that is relevant to entry-level people. Feed the information back to the school system.

If that doesn't work (and it probably won't), start to feed back the same information to the applicants who are not hired. Feed information about the educational deficiencies of public high school graduates to the community and the media.

As a customer, give more weight to the excellence of the public schools when you locate operations. If necessary, relocate your present facilities to communities where public education is distinctly better.

Your company has a lot at stake in the excellence of public education. So you should also become an organized activist for better public education. Being an organized activist is good for your company, good for your employees, good for the community, and good for the country.

Have your officials talk to community groups about the specific needs for better public education. Give them facts and, where necessary, document your own experiences.

Urge your employees to become activists for better education. Many of your employees are parents, so they have a special interest in improving the quality of public school education. If your employees see a connection between better education and better job opportunities, then they will have a another reason for becoming activists.

Provide help and support to employees who are educational activists. At least provide them with information and encouragement. Time off with pay for work on better education would serve business interests.

We need achievement tests for high school graduates who do not go on to college and for dropouts. Just as SATs and ACTs measure the basic educational qualifications of young people for college-level work, these educational achievement tests (EATs) will measure the ability of high school graduates to do entry-level jobs.

A number of people are working to have national educational achievement tests. Until they are available, a company can use other tests that are available and that roughly measure educational achievement.

Functional Illiteracy

Functional illiteracy refers to the inability to perform work properly because of educational deficiency. Today, functional illiteracy is almost always because of the deficiencies of the public education system. It's not that employees are necessarily uneducated or that they are illiterate. A functionally illiterate worker does not have a *sufficient* education to do an assigned job properly.

The Problems of Functional Illiteracy

Based on a number of studies conducted over the past few years, it is possible to estimate the number of functionally illiterate employees. Probably one of five employees is functionally illiterate, and almost all of them are in low-skilled jobs. No study has shown a company case yet where there were not at least one in ten employees who had some educational deficiencies that materially affected their ability to do assigned work. There have been cases where one of three employees is functionally illiterate.

Sometimes important safety issues are involved in functional illiteracy. Quality of work and customer satisfaction can also be hurt by functional illiteracy. Functional illiteracy seriously detracts from productivity.

Functional illiteracy is a handicap for employees; one that can be particularly frustrating. Often an employee *was* capable of doing a job; then the educational requirements of the work increased and the employee became functionally illiterate one day at a time.

The issue of functional illiteracy is important and it is becoming more important at a rapid rate, somewhat comparable to the rate of increase in technology. The problem of functional illiteracy is not severe yet in many companies but is critically important in others.

Recommended Company Actions

Functional illiteracy is a manageable problem. A number of low-cost actions can be taken to deal with this issue.

I would first suggest that we use a different label. The expression "functional illiteracy" is offensive and inaccurate. Functional illiteracy is incorrect because employees are usually not illiterate—they have educational shortcomings, which are almost always correctable. From now on I refer to the issue as "additional educational requirements."

The first place to act with respect to additional educational requirements is in the employment process. Some companies that have experienced the problem of additional educational requirements found that their employment standards for new employees were inadequate. The simple act of upgrading educational requirements in employment standards to the requirements for a job as it now exists contributes greatly to the solution of the issue of additional educational requirements.

With the critical problems of educational deficiency in public schools, companies must give educational achievement tests (EATs).

Have a battery of tests for high school entry-level jobs and require that all applicants take them.

What is being tested is basic word and math knowledge, not specific know-how for a given job. These are education tests. They are not unlike the standard achievement tests (SATs and ACTs) that are used to test educational capability for college-level work.

Educational achievement tests for entry-level jobs are likely to be critically needed in the next strategic planning period, and they should be widely used by the turn of the century. These tests measure ability to do entry-level work and the ability to learn new tasks and higher-technology work.

In the normal course of your business reviews, you should find out if any of your current employees need additional education. You don't have to give a battery of tests to do this. Your performance appraisal system should indicate the cases where employees are not working as well as they should, and that should trigger actions to determine the cause of performance deficiencies.

When there is a need for additional education, a number of methods can be used. Basic educational skills involve the most fundamental teaching activities. Your company should be able to provide support for those who require additional education.

One way to provide additional education is to send employees to adult education courses at a public school. Correspondence courses are also available, and many of them are on videocassette tapes. Company representatives should provide counseling and mentoring with respect to these additional education activities.

Very often, the way to deal with educational requirements is to restructure the organization. Networking techniques can be very helpful. In fact, all of us need more knowledge than we possess, so access to knowledge by some form of networking is a standard requirement for everyone in all organizations.

Job redesign may be an answer to additional educational requirements in some cases. The educational requirement not possessed may be because of one task or a minor part of a job, and the problem area or areas may then be assigned to another job.

Also consider setting up company-sponsored tutoring programs. Most of the needs for additional education are in basic math and English or for more knowledge about the technologies used in a company. A company has many employees with such knowledge. Why not have some of your employees provide tutoring support for others who need additional education?

All of these are potential methods of dealing with additional educational requirements. Organized efforts by an employer to provide additional education required is a new area of work in human resources management, and professionals in the field will have to develop more know-how and new methods in the future.

College Education

While there is widespread agreement about the problems of grade school education and additional education requirements, you will get different views from employers about the excellence of college education based in part on different experiences. Employers' needs for college-educated people vary a great deal, depending mostly on the type of business and the company's effectiveness in college recruiting, and that's one reason why this experience with the adequacy of a college education varies.

The Problems of Educational Excellence at the College Level

Recognize that colleges vary a great deal with respect to excellence. Graduate schools recognize this. For example, a 2.5 grade point average from one college may be equivalent to 3.5 from another. Companies must also recognize these differences in their recruiting and selection of candidates for jobs requiring a college education.

U.S. News & World Report identifies the best colleges and universities from time to time. Institutions that make this list are superb by any standards, including the standards used by the magazine.

But there are also colleges and universities that are terrible. One indication of just how bad some colleges and universities are is the fact that 40 percent of the math teachers in public schools in some states can't pass an eleventh grade math test; yet all of them are college graduates and some have advanced degrees.

The first problem of educational deficiency at the college level is that public grade schools don't turn out enough qualified graduates to provide a good source of college-caliber people in the first instance. College administrators will tell you that if they had a better quality of secondary school graduates, they would turn out much better graduates.

Actually, the top-tier colleges get the cream of the secondary school crop. These top-caliber colleges receive applications from ten times as many outstanding students as they can admit, even though tuition and room and board are two to four times more than the national average cost of all colleges.

It is the intermediate schools and the poor performing colleges that get the poor quality secondary school graduates as applicants.

For them, the poor quality of public secondary education is a very big problem. Furthermore, to fill the incoming class, these colleges often have to lower entrance standards, and that ensures even fewer well-educated graduates from these colleges.

Deficiencies in education at the college level in all but the top-tier schools are serious and getting worse. But on a scale of one to ten, the problems of educational deficiency at the public schools is eleven (terrible) and at the college level it probably averages five, with a range from magnificent number ones to a lot who could be rated nine or ten.

The top-tier colleges must strive to be even better. The middle-tier colleges need to improve a lot. Many of the bottom-tier colleges should be allowed to fail.

The business stake in improved excellence of college-level work is enormous. Inadequacies in college education relative to need have been one cause for the productivity shortfall and a major reason for the serious decline in technology in the United States versus other developed nations, the alarming decline in the quality of work in this country, and the chronic labor scarcity of knowledge workers.

Recommended Company Actions

Companies have seen the business value of supporting colleges and universities. Many companies have matching grants, where the company makes contributions linked to the donations of an employee. High-tech companies have given a great deal of support to colleges that supply professional employees. High-tech companies also have various special working relationships in activities like research with colleges, particularly colleges near company facilities.

It is time to rethink some aspects of company relations with the college community. Current practices were evolved in a different era under different circumstances. In the next strategic planning period there will be serious shortages of sufficiently well educated college graduates, and new company thinking and actions are needed to deal with the problems of educational excellence at the college level.

Generally, deficiencies in education at the college level are a very manageable issue for a single employer. First of all, there are many colleges, so the individual employer can restrict its recruiting to graduates of colleges that do a good job of college-level education. That simple, direct, commonsense action would do a lot to improve educational excellence at the college level. Make a list of colleges that graduate excellent students who are successful. These become your preferred providers of college graduates.

Companies should similarly have an action program with respect to colleges that turn out poorly educated graduates. The program should involve a number of steps. First, document the inadequacies. Contact the college about these inadequacies. Perhaps a few failures represent mistakes or very special cases. Don't hire graduates from colleges that turn out many poorly educated persons after such feedback and a reasonable period of time.

Employers can consider four additional actions with respect to the problems of educational deficiency at the college level. I have recommended each of these many times and urge every company to consider all of them.

1. Adopt a partnership attitude with respect to a selected number of colleges.
2. Provide management support, particularly in human resources management.
3. Be generous in supporting scholarships for deserving students with financial need. Support colleges financially on an impartial basis, which will tend to support the best performing colleges.
4. Become active in reeducation.

The size of the company and the nature of the business affect the number of colleges where the company can have some type of partnership relationship and the nature of that relationship. Even companies employing only a few hundred employees should consider a partnership relationship of some type with one college or a few colleges.

There are many possibilities in a partnership relationship. Tell your college contacts your interests and ask them theirs. You will find many areas of common interest.

One issue of particular interest to human resources management professionals that I think may emerge in the next strategic planning period is whether business know-how could be of value in college management. Almost two-thirds of college expenses are people costs. So human resources management knowledge should be helpful to colleges and universities.

Consider direct scholarship support. Scholarship support can have a number of advantages. It can provide needed funds for colleges. Scholarships can also reward for student achievement, and thus they represent a form of pay for performance. Finally, scholarships are increasingly necessary to fulfill the American dream of opportunity for everyone.

The cost of a college education is becoming very expensive. The real annual cost averages more than $15,000 a year, and the amount paid by students averages close to $10,000 a year. To become a doctor or a Ph.D. costs more than $100,000 plus living expenses for a number of years. Lower- and middle-income families can't afford these costs without scholarships, and their children are excluded from many lines of work, even though they may have the most talent.

This is a matter that deals with a basic and long-standing American dream. It involves free market choices. And there is the issue of providing the best education for the most talented.

I developed a new type of tuition plan in 1990 to provide direct financial support to the best colleges and for the best students. It is a company-financed plan, which also benefits the company directly. Since it was first reported, many companies have adopted this plan.

In its simplest form, the college tuition plan pays some or all of the college tuition costs for all children of employees. The plan might also pay some or all of the costs of college tuition for grandchildren of employees.

The plan covers four years of undergraduate college work. The plan might also pay tuition for graduate school.

This plan is designed to cover only tuition costs. All other college costs, such as room and board, would not be covered. Two-year colleges, extension courses, evening college courses, and special college courses, whether college credited or not, would be excluded from this particular program. No summer school tuition would be paid, nor would a fifth year's tuition be paid even if the student had not graduated in four years. There are reasons for each of these exclusions, but most of them relate to the simplicity of administration and the management of costs.

The only requirements for payment by the company under this plan would be that the applicant is the legal child of an employee and a full-time student in any accredited college. Tuition bills would be sent to the company, and funds would be paid directly to the college.

Under this plan, the employer makes no judgments about the field of study and has no administrative influence on the college of the employee's choice or whether students are admissible. The company only pays the tuition bills.

Reeducation

In addition to a deficiency in college-level education, there is the problem of the obsolescence of education received at the college level. That directly involves the issue of reeducation. Reeducation basically involves the need to update educational capability from the date of graduation from college.

Different types of reeducation have been conducted in various areas for many years. Medicine, law, and accounting are examples of professions that have well-developed reeducational activities. Some even require certification—a proof that the reeducation activity has taken place and that it has been effective.

Corporate engineering departments have had various types of reeducation for many years. Much of this reeducation has been done on the company's premises.

Reeducation was done in engineering because technology was clearly changing. Even a few years after graduation, there was new technology that had to be learned. In some engineering areas, a scientist's knowledge was obsolete in ten years without reeducation.

In business today, technology obsolescence is occurring in every area of the company. The nature of the specific reeducation needs and the content of the material required for reeducational instruction will vary a great deal between disciplines and departments in each company. But in any field where there is knowledge and the need for a formal education in the first instance, there is then also usually the need for reeducation.

Reeducation for Knowledge Workers

In reeducation we are not improving minds or fulfilling intellectual aspirations. Reeducation is directed at the practical business of teaching discipline knowledge in professional work that is needed because of changes in technology.

The need for reeducation may exist in areas beyond the knowledge of a worker's principal area of study. For some, this multidiscipline knowledge requirement becomes a critical work need. Interdisciplinary knowledge is essential, for example, for some project managers when a person rises to a senior management-level job.

The need for reeducation in no way diminishes the value of continuing education. Reeducation is different from continuing education in that it is related directly to work needs.

Reeducation is not adult education, where people are given a second chance at the education they could have had when they were younger. In a practical business sense, reeducation involves professional teaching of material that is relevant to the field of work that was not taught when the worker was in college.

In the scientific disciplines, the needs for reeducation are specific and clear. For example, reeducation involves teaching chemists who finished college ten years ago the new discipline knowledge of chemistry and related sciences that evolved after graduation. Those needs are obvious in recognized scientific disciplines.

There are also reeducational needs in business disciplines, including human resources management. The needs in the soft sciences are less clear or unclear.

Reeducation is complicated in the soft business discipline areas by a number of other factors. For example, the teaching is not of scientific fact and repeatable experiences but often involves personal opinions and the experiences of the experts who are doing the teaching.

In reeducation there is often a need for unlearning: a purging of disinformation that people have picked up during their years of work. This complicates greatly the curriculum in each field and affects even more the methods of instruction.

The Company College and Other Company Experiences

An early reaction by some firms to the need for reeducation was to set up their own facilities. Some large firms even named these facilities the "company university." They had a "campus" and "faculty." These company universities didn't work very well, and they were among the first casualties of downsizing in the 1980s.

During the last part of the 1980s, some companies assigned the job of reeducation to the training department but gave the department no more staff or money. The thinking was that their central training department could reallocate some time to reeducation. That idea did not work well. The problem was often that the training people didn't want to change or were unable to make progress with work on reeducation because of limits in their own experience.

More recently, there have been discussions with college and university leaders about reeducation, but these have usually been unproductive. It seems that business executives are too prone to say to the college community, ". . . develop your product line and maybe I will buy it." For their part, educators tend to say, "Send us your students and your money and we will do the job." With respect to reeducation, business is saying, "Show me." Educators are saying, "Trust me."

Some lessons have been learned from all of this work on reeducation. For one thing, it seems clear that much of the work of reeducation must be done by educators, preferably in an established college or university.

From the company view, reeducation must be directed by some department in the firm. The human resources management department should take on reeducation, and if the firm is large enough to have a training department, then the role of that group should be enlarged to include efforts in the field of reeducation.

Companies may need technical consultants in the area of reeducation. Even the largest firm is not likely to find sufficient in-house expertise in this area. Such experts are just now emerging.

"The College of Vero Beach"

Some work has been done to develop models of how reeducation might most appropriately be done. I call my model "The College of Vero Beach." The College of Vero Beach is just a paper college, to illustrate what might be done.

The curriculum is developed at the main campus. Lecture series are prepared and also presented at the main campus. The lectures are mostly on closed-circuit television but often include call-ins by telephone and interaction through PCs. Some lectures are on video-cassette tapes.

There are off-campus branches throughout the state, located so that no single student has to travel more than sixty miles to an off-campus facility. Teachers at the branches are part-time and usually now work in an established college, community college, or high school. Students go to the branches for discussion sessions, for help with particular problems, and for examinations.

There is a core reeducation curriculum in humanities. Each of these humanities courses involves briefings on the material up to graduation and the teaching of new material that has evolved in the basic humanities since graduation. Then there are special studies for people in many different fields of knowledge. Programs are available in all the academic disciplines; e.g., physics, psychology, economics, etc. There are also majors in computer science, finance, production methods, marketing, and human resources management.

The courses cover material for fifteen-year time periods. Now would be the time for the reeducation of those who received degrees in approximately 1975, 1960, and 1945.

Each student takes eight credit hours a week, including four hours of lectures. Semesters run for fifteen weeks, and there are three semesters a year. It takes two to three years to graduate. The tuition cost of the college course is less than $500 per student per semester.

The College of Vero Beach is a practical model of things to come in the future planning period. Some may think that the college will not likely happen, but it will be done soon in some manner. When you think about The College of Vero Beach, keep in mind that there is a New England University that now teaches more course sessions in its graduate engineering program by closed-circuit television than in the classroom. And a well-known professor of business on the West Coast has 10,000 students in one course.

Education and Business

It seems logical that in a period of rapid increases in technology, education would be a major strategic human resources management issue. It should have then been obvious that companies had to address this issue and do what they could about the alarming increase in educational deficiency.

Companies of every type and size must be aware of the problems of education, in all of its four main parts. The problems of public school education, additional educational requirements, college education, and reeducation affect every company in some way. Every company that hires employees, regardless of its size and nature, can also do something about educational deficiency.

The need is for action, not more discussion. That's why I have emphasized specific practical actions that each company can take now with respect to each of the four areas of educational deficiency.

I urge you to concentrate particularly on dealing with additional education requirements and reeducation. All four areas of educational deficiency are very important, and there are action steps that are practical with respect to each of these. But additional education and reeducation are required for your employees, and your company has great latitude of action in dealing with these matters.

These are my recommendations. Each reader may find that some of these are useful. Or you may have other ideas that you think are better. If we focus on commonsense answers, we will make progress.

At this point, small accomplishments in each of these four areas of educational deficiency by many companies could mean so very much. Companies can take effective actions, and because that would mean so much, they should take action.

If companies in one community, for example, were to act more like customers and became educational activists, that just might get substantially increased excellence in public school education in that community. If that happened, it would be an example of excellence that could be repeated in many other communities—and I suspect that parents in many other communities would see to it that it did happen.

The tuition-refund plan costs very little and serves business interests directly. This one plan could revitalize college-level education very much.

Give academic achievement tests to applicants for high-school entry jobs in your company. Apply them fairly and with no preference for race, creed, or sex. Identify current employees who need additional education, and start your own company's in-house programs.

I will pursue The College of Vero Beach. Actually, I think there will be widespread reeducation very soon; once it starts, reeducation will become a growth industry with billions of dollars spent on reeducation every year.

In the spring of 1991, the administration in Washington made some dramatic proposals regarding institutional public school educational deficiencies. There have also been some exciting private enterprise activities in the area of public grade school education.

We can hope for the best, but keep in mind that powerful forces are opposed to many of these proposals. State governments, the educational establishment, and teachers' unions are particularly committed to the status quo.

In spite of the opposition, I think there is reason for great optimism. I forecast that three things will happen in the 1990s—we are seeing them start to happen now. First, many employers will take actions, particularly in areas where they have full authority. Second, parents will rise up and demand educational excellence. Third, some dramatic successes in the early and mid–1990s will start an avalanche of actions for and cases of much better educational achievement in the public grade schools.

7

Delegative Management

A fundamental strategic human resources management issue of the 1990s that will continue into the twenty-first century will involve the correct style of management. In essence, business is in the process of shifting from a rather programmatic style of management to a more delegative style. This involves a shift toward more management by people and less management by programs and rules. This change will affect all areas of an operation, including human resources management.

Delegative management is not a new idea. In fact, I wrote about it in a lengthy feature section in the fall 1982 issue of *The Sibson Report.* It has been on the agenda of many conferences I have held, particularly in 1981 and 1982.

In those days, there was an interest in the subject, but the top people in most large companies thought that their companies were doing well and there was no need to change their style of management. In the 1990s, many companies are doing less well and are moving to delegative management because they know they must change. The old ways are not working or they are not sufficient.

This is delegative management, not just decentralization. Decentralization means granting some authority to the management level below the corporate office to apply programs—mostly corporate programs. Delegation means granting authority to act at every level of the organization, and that authority often includes the right to use or not use programs and to determine which programs to use.

In the 1990s, observed trends and issues plus reasonable extrapolations make delegative management an extremely important strategic human resources management planning item. By my weighting system, it is third in importance among the strategic personnel planning items and involves many complex issues.

The Planning Issue: Changing Management Style

Delegation in business means granting authority to others to act. The change in management style means that more authority to do more things is granted to more people.

Authority that had been encased in programs, rules, and requirements is often granted to people under delegative management. Authority flows downward much more now than in the past. Authority also flows from rules and programs to managers and through them to every worker.

Delegative management isn't happening because of some grand scheme or a brilliant plan. Delegative management is occurring because it is necessary, mostly because of rapidly increasing technology.

No company I know sets out to become more delegative. Companies have problems with programs, or productivity isn't improving, or there is a failure to react quickly. Then it becomes apparent that the style of management is at least part of the problem. Some adjustment is made, and then the company has taken a step toward more delegative management.

When a company has made many adjustments, it will reach a point where more patches to the style of management won't work. Then work must be done to have a formal delegative management system installed. This usually means incorporating past changes and adjustments and some additional changes in management style at some point in time. The change to delegative management is often very painful and very difficult.

Companies are visibly changing to a more delegative management style. These changes are occurring at a different pace and in a different way in various businesses.

It is mostly the new technologies that are forcing high-level managers to give up centralized decision making and control and delegate work decisions of all types. When the technology required for decision making resides down in the organization, the decisions must be made down in the organization, not at the top.

Competitive pressures and the need to lower costs have also influenced the change in management style. Fewer highly paid people are required with delegative management.

Some companies have also found it necessary to be able to react more quickly to business changes. A more delegative style helps companies react more quickly because there are fewer levels of higher authority to review the decisions.

Strategic planning issues always represent cross currents, with some running counter to others. Special interest groups, for example, consciously attempt to restrict the latitude of action by managers and establish their own chosen order by rigid rules and quotas. But on balance, the movement toward more delegative management is clear and, I think, inevitable.

Recognize that more delegative management is a fundamental change in operations, requiring new methods of working and new skills by those who manage. Moving to a delegative management style also means eliminating jobs, sometimes many jobs.

Also remember that managers in charge were trained to manage in a programmatic manner. They must change from what they know and do well (or think they do well) to new systems that they must learn and that involve unknowns.

To move to a programmatic style of management required a lot of formal training and the establishment of institutions. For example, graduate business schools grew and flourished, based mostly on the need to teach a programmatic style of management. Now we need to purge all of that and teach the new methods.

Under such conditions, the evolution to delegative management is often difficult and painful. Expect to encounter substantial resistance to this change—sometimes by very high-level managers.

The change from essentially programmatic styles of managing people to essentially delegative styles must happen. It must happen because the centralized programmatic styles don't work as well in an era of technology.

Linking the Future to the Past

To see where we are and have a proper vision of where we are going often requires some looking back. I think this is the case with respect to changing styles of management.

During most of the twentieth century, the style of managing was generally programmatic. Looking back even further, the management style was highly discretionary.

Early in the twentieth century, the growth in the size of businesses and the increasing dominance of companies that were not privately owned led to the evolution of less discretion in management and to a far more programmatic style of management. The style of management became more and more programmatic throughout the 1900s and into the 1970s.

There has never been one management style, and there never will be. If you illustrated the change in management style by colors, you could say that discretionary management is yellow, programmatic management is red, and delegative management is blue. The management style in organizations generally then went from an off-shade of yellow to orange and is now going toward purple.

Also recognize that in the future strategic period there will still be many companies that have different degrees and types of delegative styles. Furthermore, many organizations (typically small companies) will be managed in a highly discretionary manner, and many other organizations (government and utilities) will still be mostly programmatic in their management style.

There are many personnel programs under programmatic management. The programs vary greatly and, in fact, during the last fifty years many professional debates in the personnel field were about which program in each area of personnel was the best. Until recently, few voices raised the question of whether the programmatic system of personnel management itself was flawed.

The process of programmatic management was always essentially the same. Top-level people developed the programs. The programs that were developed were the best answer—or the way to get the best answer. Managers required people to follow the programs developed by top management or their experts. Therefore, everyone worked correctly and effectively using the company way.

To design and implement the programs, an army of experts emerged. These experts designed and developed systems and methods in every area of the business. In fact, during the era of programmatic work, the value of staff work was largely related to the ability to develop new programs, understand them, explain them to others, and then make certain that the programs were applied the same way.

Sometimes there were very analytic methods of developing the new programs. This was the era of scientific management.

Scientific methods in personnel were used a great deal. Scientific methods were used to develop the best programs for employment, pay, training, career pathing, organization, and manpower management. Then personnel people implemented these programs in a consistent manner. In this way, the best programs (the company way) were carried out the same way throughout the organization. To a large degree, the programs then made the decisions.

Now we are moving to delegative management. This involves more management by people rather than by programs.

One advantage claimed for the programmatic management of people was that decisions were consistent and therefore fair. But "same" isn't fair when circumstances differ. Furthermore, what consistent sometimes meant was that bias and error became institutionalized.

In the programmatic systems of management, recognize that power is vested in a few hands. Senior management directs many programs. Staff people are the chief assistants of executives and are often the enforcers as well. Senior managers and staff people often like that system, so not all executives and personnel professionals support changing to a more delegative management system.

Today, it seems clear that programmatic systems often don't fit anymore. Companies are finding that the programs are becoming more costly and more complex. There are too many programs and a need for too many variations and exceptions to most of the programs. Under programmatic management, the reaction to new issues in this changing environment is too slow. Innovation is smothered, and productivity is retarded. Management style must be less programmatic; it must be more delegative.

Delegative Management

Simply stated, delegative management means the granting of authority to managers. More specifically, in this strategic personnel planning period, delegative management means:

- Much more authority is granted to managers.
- Authority is granted to all levels of the organization.
- The authority granted is to decide and act.
- There is somewhat equivalent authority to decide and act at every level of the organization.

I think the key to delegative management is that there is equivalent authority, which is granted at every level of the organization, from the chief executive officer to the first-level manager. That first-level manager also has about equivalent authority in the management of people as does his counterpart in independent firms.

Delegation today is not simply involvement or participation. Delegation is the authority to act, not just permission to suggest. Delegation must always include accountability and authority.

Under delegative management, every manager is much more accountable for the effectiveness of work. A manager's performance is largely judged by the effectiveness of the work in the organization he manages.

To appreciate what delegative management means, you need to think in terms of cases. Here are a few examples of delegation in the area of personnel.

- A manager determines the training requirements for each employee. The training department becomes mostly a facilitator of training activities that managers determine are needed.

- With respect to jobs that are not priced in the marketplace, the manager determines the proper salary grade without prior review and approval.
- The manager also determines performance pay increases, not retarded by pay increase budgets or administrative controls.
- A manager has the authority to select people for promotion to a job in his unit, provided that the decision is based on past performance and qualifications to do the work.

Experts may make studies or suggestions about work methods and systems. But each manager has authority for work and may or may not accept the suggestions of experts.

Don't be misled into thinking that delegation means anarchy or chaos. It may seem like that to those who don't understand operations, but a delegative style *is* management. The management is simply different—very different.

Delegation today is not group work or group think. Delegation is to individuals, each individual worker-manager and through each of them to each employee. Delegation is to a group only when they work in a totally interdependent manner. Then the delegation is only to their manager or to the project leader, but never to a group for consensus management.

Delegative management is a powerful idea. Unleashing the combined knowledge of all managers about how to work more effectively contributes greatly to higher productivity. The accountability for work methods and work effectiveness makes productivity every manager's job. It also encourages entrepreneurship.

The delegative management style uniquely fits the American culture. This is one reason why I have urged companies for many years to increase productivity "the American way." The Japanese, for example, have great difficulty with delegation; it is not part of their culture, and so things like quality circles are right for them. For Americans, the personal attributes required by accountability are part of our culture; traits such as initiative, self-reliance, comfort with free choice, and generous measures of independence.

As a more delegative method of managing evolves in a company, a very different management job also evolves. In the past, the manager had something to do with how to organize work, assign people to work, communicate, make pay decisions, train, applaud, and discipline. But under programmatic management, much of the authority was in the programs, and supervisory managers mostly participated in program development and suggested how the programs should be applied. Under delegative management, the managers of people will have authority to decide many more work matters; they will often develop their own programs and have a great deal of authority about which programs will apply and how they will be used.

The job of the human resources management professional also changes under delegative management because so much of the decision making shifts from an emphasis on programs to supporting the managers of people. Therefore, the time and attention of the personnel professionals must shift from a focus on technical specialization to a broader professional knowledge. The skills of the personnel professional must be relatively greater with respect to the skills of working with the people who manage and with individual cases. Under a delegative management style, personnel professionals spend relatively less time on program administration and more time on operations matters.

There will still be a great need for excellence of specialized professional knowledge in human resources management. But a great deal of the specialized knowledge will increasingly reside in computers and with consultants. In the future, then, the key job in the field of personnel will be the personnel generalist, who assists, guides, and supports the managers of personnel with their greater authority under a delegative management style.

Empowerment

Delegative management specifically refers to the granting of authority for decisions to the managers of people. Empowerment refers to the delegation of authority to act by the managers to each worker. Then workers and managers at every level are empowered to act, not just follow someone else's procedures or make suggestions.

Some say that empowerment is the right to participate. That is the mother of all oxymorons.

Delegation of authority from the manager of personnel to each worker empowers each worker to determine work methods and practices that are best for his job. The worker then has the basic authority to determine the best way to do the job that has been assigned, consistent with objectives that have been set. Each worker is expected to determine the best way to do work that has been assigned and achieve optimum productivity and the highest excellence in his work.

Each worker, of course, must comply with existing laws, work within policy, follow the rules, and work safely. Every employee must only do work that is needed and relevant to the mission of the organization and must work within the scope of an assigned job. Each worker must also consider the effect of his work on others.

The immediate manager of each person assures compliance with laws, policies, safety requirements, operational integrity, and other requirements. It is the immediate manager who should empower the employee. Managers must always have the authority to take back authority and require an individual to modify his work practices to achieve the unit's goals and objectives, which, of course, are broader than one job.

From the time of initiating organized efforts at empowerment to completing the change takes at least three years. Thus it will be in the early or mid-1990s before plans initiated so far result in greater empowerment and a number of years after that before they visibly show up in productivity figures.

If many of these efforts are successful, then you can expect many others to follow quickly. Experience suggests that a high percentage of efforts at empowerment will, in fact, be successful—often beyond anything imaginable or planned at the initiation of such efforts. By the end of the decade, the employees in many companies will have been empowered—and the productivity of many companies will have increased greatly as a result of empowerment.

Empowerment is such a simple idea. It means granting latitude of action for how the work is done to those who do the work. The employee will always know something about the work and how it can best be done that no one else knows. Empowerment uses that knowledge to optimize productivity and work excellence.

Obviously, empowerment works better in some jobs than in others. Empowerment contributes to greater productivity the most when worker knowledge is important to the work, when machines used in the work are worker-controlled, and when work methods are not inherently prescribed. These conditions exist in more and more jobs in an era of technology, and except in highly automated plants, they exist to some degree in all jobs.

Recognize that empowerment changes a job dramatically. For example, every job that has authority to determine work methods has at least the elements of management. Empowerment pushes the first level of management all the way down to those who do the work.

Don't ever think that empowerment dilutes or diminishes the job of the manager of people anymore than delegation to managers diluted or diminished the job of executive management. Clearly, however, empowerment changes the jobs of employees, managers, and executives in terms of what is done and how it is done.

Delegation to managers of personnel has proven to be the most difficult job. Delegation requires many basic institutional changes. For example, delegative management requires dramatic changes in organization. Delegative management also requires changes in many personnel practices.

It is natural for an operating manager to delegate work-related actions to workers. Companies that have succeeded in delegating more authority to managers have found that most managers automatically empowered their subordinates more.

In fact, even in the most programmatic and bureaucratic company, some empowerment to employees actually occurs. For the effective manager, empowerment is the commonsense thing to do and is often necessary. Formal empowerment means much more delegation to each worker, and it is the right of each employee to act rather than a right to ask or suggest.

Empowerment places a burden on every employee, an obligation to act and a responsibility to do their best. Not all employees are equally comfortable with such a condition or capable of such responsibilities. The acceptance of authority by employees under empowerment is thus a critical issue that must be dealt with.

The consequences of empowerment are very great—almost revolutionary. Empowerment changes the culture of a company and will require changes in most personnel practices.

For those who look for the deeper meaning of basic change, empowerment is deregulation in the workplace and a great leap forward into a new level of democracy at work. With delegation and empowerment, I think we are starting a revolution in the workplace. The first consequence will be much greater productivity, but longer term results will likely be very great and profound in a number of respects.

Problems of Delegative Management

There are issues and problems with respect to delegative management. One of the key issues is that with delegation there are many more people who manage personnel. Management by people means management by more people—by many more people.

Some wonder where all the new true managers of personnel will come from. The key to answering this question is that the span of management is increased under delegative management. Then fewer managers of personnel are needed, about one-third as many. For most companies, this means that one true manager of personnel will be needed for each three current supervisors. A company can then select those who would most likely become effective managers of personnel, and that's where all the true managers of personnel will come from.

You may be surprised by how effective the managers of people are when they are given the true manager's job. As a matter of fact, some can manage people better than they can administer programs.

This process of selecting managers of personnel from among current supervisors is an issue, because many former supervisors will have to be replaced or outplaced. Selections will have to be made, and it will be necessary to consider how well the new jobs will be performed as well as how well the old jobs were performed.

Managers will have to learn new ways, and this will require work and effort. Mistakes will be made in the)learning process. This is part of the cost of implementing delegative management. Greater effectiveness of work from delegative management will more than cover the cost of the mistakes made during implementation.

In the immediate future, there will also be questions about the ability of employees throughout the organization to assume accountability for work methods and work excellence. This will particularly be a concern in unionized work groups and where there is educational deficiency.

Some people think that many different practices under delegative management will cause problems and that the managers of personnel will make mistakes if they are given latitude of action to make personnel decisions. In fact, what you find under delegative management is that some managers' actions are better than the company way and others are worse. But, on balance, productivity and worker satisfaction are much higher under delegative management practices.

It is important to make sure that managers' differences reflect different circumstances and methods, not arbitrary judgments. As a company evolves into a more delegative management style, there must be safeguards against discretionary judgments that reflect bias or favoritism.

Regardless of systems to safeguard against arbitrary actions, under delegative management there will be instances of improper exercise of power, prejudice, and favoritism in any company. The company must have effective monitoring and auditing systems plus the ability and inclination to move quickly to correct such cases.

Under delegative management, it would seem likely that there might be more incidents of EEO problems. Some EEO problems would be because of errors by individual managers, and some would be due to more differences in practices. Under delegative management, however, EEO cases tend to be individual cases. Under pro-grammatic management, EEO cases are often class-action cases.

No problem of delegative management will be more difficult to deal with than the issue of management confidence. Will high-level executives have the confidence to delegate decisions and actions to division executives? They probably will, in most situations. Will high-level executives and division executives delegate to front-line managers and individual workers? Probably not, or with great reluctance.

The reluctance to delegate deep into the organization is largely due to a belief that high-level executives are more effective and more trustworthy than others. Of course, this isn't true, but that thinking will be a big problem in achieving delegative management and empowerment.

As delegative management occurs in your company, also recognize that there will be those who oppose the change for personal reasons. Some will oppose delegative management because they cling to the old ways; others because they *believe* in the old ways, and others will oppose a change to more delegative practices because they think that change will diminish their status. Some who oppose the change to delegative management are in high places.

Regardless of any opposition, however, more delegative management styles and more management by many more people will occur. With technology, the change to a more delegative style of management is inevitable.

As you work on the problems of delegative management and empowerment, remember the advantages. Delegative management is a key part of productivity management because such a management style makes every manager of people accountable for productivity. There are then as many productivity managers in an organization as there are managers of people. With empowerment, every worker is also managing productivity.

Personnel Management and the Management of Personnel

As there is more delegation to the managers of workers and to the workers themselves, the work of those in the field of human resources management will necessarily also change. Work in the personnel field is changing because of delegative management—and it is changing dramatically.

One type of change involves programs. As we delegate work, there will still be programs and practices of various types, but there will be fewer companywide programs, and those that exist will be different in the future than they were in the past.

Those who work in personnel will have to develop know-how and skill in the new and different programs and practices of the field. Based on past performance in dealing with programs, there should be great confidence that those in the field will do well with the new types of programs.

There is another change in the work of personnel professionals, and there is little past history to help us judge how well those who work in the field will adjust. This involves support to the managers of personnel in *managing*.

As delegative management shifts emphasis from management by programs to management by people, there will be a great need for advice and counsel for managers about how to manage people. That would logically seem to be a job for those in human resources management.

Who in the field of human resources management is really expert in managing people? Personnel hasn't dealt with this very much in the past. In fact, management of personnel in the personnel department has been much less than great in most companies.

For example, people in personnel know how to develop performance appraisal systems, or they think they do. But few I know in personnel do good work in appraising performance. You can find similar examples in every aspect of human resources management. The fact is that personnel management people don't know anything special about the management of people. In fact, only a minority of those in the field have ever been managers of personnel.

Those in personnel are not perceived to be expert in the management of people. For a number of reasons, for the past fifteen years I have asked hundreds of personnel people what questions operating managers ask them. Rarely are there questions about managing people.

The role of the personnel function is changing, and it is changing rapidly. In the future, those in the field will be expected to be expert in the management of people. That will mean very different career paths, training, and activities for those in the field.

Recommended Actions

There is a proven process of implementing a delegative management style, and any company can follow this general system. This system involves:

- *Policy management actions.* Policies must be detailed more clearly under delegative management.
- *Availability of information and guidelines.* Managers need good information and advice to assume accountability.
- *Delegative actions.* Steps to actually *delegate.*
- *Quality management.* Some system of monitoring and auditing the decisions of managers.

Of these, the most difficult action involves the actual granting of authority. It isn't just a simple matter of saying "Do it."

Briefly, I think that a half-dozen actions are required to actually grant authority to managers. Each in itself is a complex issue. Here are the steps I follow to actually cause delegation.

First of all, delegation and empowerment should be recognized as being a productivity improvement step. In the twelve-step productivity management process outlined in Chapter 5, delegative management is fiftl on that list and empowerment is eighth. Greater productivity is a driving force for delegative management, so start by linking actions in the area of delegative management to needs for productivity management.

As a second general recommendation, focus your attention on changing the management style in the high-technology parts of the operation. High-tech operations in particular require a more delegative managerial style for many reasons. So emphasize delegation and empowerment first in high-tech areas. Later on, successful experiences in high-tech areas will facilitate work in other areas of the operation.

Four additional, specific, affirmative actions can then be taken to move a company quickly into a much more delegative management style. These actions are:

1. Eliminate at least one organizational level and therefore increase the span of management.
2. Establish operating units deeper in the organization.
3. Off-load personnel decisions to the managers of the performance units.
4. Have a computer-aided general purpose human resources management data system to monitor results.

Each of these actions has substantial values in its own right. These actions also make the movement to a far more delegative management style happen.

First, eliminate at least one organizational level. Most companies have organizations that are far too hierarchal anyway, and many companies could eliminate up to three organizational levels. Some larger companies have already taken this first step, and by the end of this strategic human resources management planning period, most operations with more than two hundred employees will have eliminated at least one level of organization.

The elimination of organizational levels does a great deal for a company. It reduces payroll costs substantially, streamlines the organization, increases the effectiveness of communications, and helps the company react more quickly to emergencies and opportunities. Reducing the number of organizational levels is also an essential step in achieving a more delegative management style.

When the number of organizational levels is reduced, then the span of management increases. The effective management of people requires that a manager has at least ten subordinates. To do this requires the elimination of organizational levels. You can then select from among all former managers those who are most effective in the management of people.

The second action step for implementing delegative management is to establish organizational unit performance measures in the operating units, as deep in the organization as possible. It is best to have profit and loss statements as the performance measures. Companies will be working to push P&L accounting further down in the organization, and with computer technology they will very likely have many successes.

When it is not possible to establish unit P&L measures, it may be possible to establish statistical measures for units below P&L centers. These statistical measures are often only part of a P&L statement, such as office expenses or payroll. Such measures have been used in factories, warehouses, and sales offices.

Some unit performance measures may be personnel measures. Productivity measures, turnover, and the cost of hires would be examples. Expect the concept of unit performance to be extended in the future for various reasons, and as this happens, there will be operations with performance measures. It is more practical for executive management to delegate to operating units with performance measures than it is to delegate activities to individuals or groups without performance measures. The issue of organizational restructuring is itself a strategic human resources management planning item and is covered in Chapter 17.

The third recommended action is to off-load personnel work and personnel decisions to the P&L centers and the operating unit centers. Delegate human resources management decisions to the managers of the units as deep in the organization as possible, provided they have at least ten people working in their unit. This off-loads management work to managers, and it *is* delegation. Outplacing personnel work to operating managers also frees up the time of human resources management professionals for other work; or it makes possible the downsizing of the personnel function.

A company can off-load personnel work to the managers of personnel just by letting them make decisions that were formerly administered in the personnel department or by cutting the size of the personnel department. Downsizing in the personnel department is what most companies have done so far. But letting managers manage is the more orderly and humane way to achieve delegation.

As a final recommendation, have in place a sound system for monitoring management decisions. This should be computerized, with information accessible from your human resources management department's PCs. Executive management will not likely delegate decisions unless such a monitoring system is in place. Computer-aided personnel systems will do this job well.

The Manager Difference

It has always been true that an effective manager of people will usually have a more effective work group. This will probably be much more true in the next decade because of the evolution of a more delegative management style.

There haven't been good, definitive studies that would tell us in an objective manner just how much of a difference a good manager makes with respect to employee productivity. The studies I have seen suggest that the manager makes a difference in the effectiveness of work of at least 25 percent and occasionally as much as 50 percent.

The models in these studies, however, have been the large companies in a traditional smokestack or service industry that had a high degree of programmatic management and structured practices. In this environment, the manager difference is confined and restricted. The machines set the pace of work, and the company's programs controlled the methods. Managers of people were largely administrators, schedulers, and sometimes spokespeople. Output was limited by facilities. The manager of personnel helped keep it running at full speed or whatever level of capacity was called for. More work or less work meant building more facilities or idling facilities, and increasing or decreasing employee count proportionately.

Perhaps the best insight into the manager difference is in chain businesses where there are many identical business units, some of which are owned by the company and some of which are franchised. Motels, restaurants, and convenience stores are all examples.

In cases I have known, the operations were run in a traditional programmatic manner in company-owned facilities. Differences in results in the company-owned and operated facilities were small.

The franchised operations in these types of businesses were privately owner-managed. The management of people was not controlled. In the franchised operations, *managers* managed people, not company programs.

In every case I know, the results of franchised operations varied greatly. Some of the franchised operations had much higher productivity and better operating results than the company-operated facilities. Some of the franchised operations had much lower productivity and did much worse than the company-operated facilities, and many of them failed.

Company programs bred mediocrity in company-run operations. Management made a big difference, for better or worse, in franchised operations, mostly because there were differences in management and the management was by people.

Company programs in human resources often tend to breed mediocrity. The programs are *designed* for the average manager and the least talented employee. Programs prop up or tolerate the poor manager but retard and restrain the effectiveness of the outstanding manager. With programs, there are fewer individual errors, but the programs insulate the organization from excellence. There should be less breeding of mediocrity in the future under a more delegative management style.

In some operations, particularly where there are high capital investments, it may be that mediocrity in the management of personnel is a price worth paying to avoid worrying about costly errors affecting the use of big dollar assets. That is surely not the case in high-technology businesses and, for that matter, in any organization in which a high percentage of the cost is payroll costs and most of the assets are people. In the future strategic planning period, much of the employment growth will occur in people-intensive businesses, and all companies will become somewhat more people-intensive because of technology.

The era of technology limits more and more the ability to manage by programs and thereby to manage to levels of mediocrity. In the 1990s, people, not programs, will manage more and more. Then the effectiveness of management will impact the results of operations much more under a delegative management style and with empowerment.

In a delegative management culture, those managers of personnel will also be exercising leadership. Leadership will become a major factor in productivity management throughout the company and at every level of the organization.

By the end of the 1990s, it seems likely that the manager difference in work effectiveness will be more like 250 to 500 percent rather than 25 to 50 percent. The differences in business results from the management of people will be potentially very great when there is management by people.

8

Fairness

Issues concerning fairness will be important in human resources management in the forthcoming period. Fairness issues will cause a great deal of controversy and involve many contentious questions. The importance of the fairness issue, plus the considerable amount of disagreement on specific fairness issues, makes this the fourth most important strategic human resources management planning item in my judgment.

Notes About Fairness

Fairness at work relates to how employees meet their work obligations and how they treat others. Fairness at work relates equally to how the employer and those who represent the employer (the managers) behave in matters of employee-employer relations.

Fairness means that decisions and actions are free from bias, prejudice, and injustice. Fairness means that personal values are applied at work.

Many different practices may cause unfairness at work, including those of the employer, the employees, the government, unions, or some activist group. However, if pressure felt by any group results in unfairness, then employees think that the employer is at least partially accountable.

Fairness for employees means three things. There must be equal opportunity, equal treatment, and high values in personnel relations.

There must be *equal opportunity* for everyone with respect to jobs, pay, and conditions. There must be a complete commitment to equal opportunity and affirmative action to achieve that goal when it is required.

Equal opportunity must be achieved with *equal treatment*. This means no prejudice *against* anyone or any group and no preferential treatment *for* anyone or any group. The equal treatment facet of fairness may prove to be one of the most contentious issues in the history of employee-employer relations because of the insistence on preferential treatment for their constituents by some special interest groups.

Fairness also means the application of *personal values* in relationships between all employees and between each employee and the employer. Of course, values can be what you choose them to be. In the workplace today and tomorrow, the values seem to be more and more the traditional values.

Fairness must be for everyone. You can't have fairness for some at the cost of unfairness for others. You can't have more fairness for some if that means less fairness for others. Fairness must mean equal opportunity *and* equal treatment *and* personal values at work for every group and every individual.

The concept and expression of fairness are so simple. But at work, they appear to be something else. For example, employees don't think much about equal opportunity in the abstract, but rather in specific cases, such as their chance to get ahead and whether they receive fair treatment when a promotion is available. Fairness at work in such practical ways is experienced every hour of every day in many specific incidents.

Fairness is sometimes opinion and perception as well as fact. Opinions and perceptions about fairness will differ greatly, not only with each person but in different locations and facilities.

Fairness at work is based much more on what people experience rather than what they hear. A company can say it promotes from within, but employees think otherwise when a high-level job is filled by outside recruiting.

Perceptions of fairness are based on what people read and hear away from the job as well as what they experience on the job. Fairness is what is reported in the media. Actually, unfairness is what is mostly reported in the media because that's what sells, and that's part of the problem of fairness.

The employer has the authority to set conditions of work and should, therefore, be held accountable for fairness or unfairness. Even if union contracts or government regulations compel unfairness, the employer is accountable for unfairness unless that employer informs employees about how others compel unfairness.

Unfairness rather than fairness is really the issue most of the time, and that in itself may seem to be unfair to some. You can have many cases of fairness, but they are unreported and not noted. One case of unfairness, however, can be headline news throughout the organization for a long time.

Fairness is often a personal matter, and that can also be an issue.

For example, top executives may think it is fair or even necessary to cut health-care benefits for employees when the costs of benefits are rising and profits are falling. Employees may see the same circumstances as being very unfair, particularly if special executive benefits and perquisites are preserved.

Don't confuse fairness and niceness. It's always nice to be fair, but some actions that are taken to be nice may be unfair.

There is a great reluctance to speak the truth and be candid on matters of fairness. There is a tendency to avoid issues of fairness.

Special interest groups (Chapter 10) speak out, often with great emotion and in a language all of their own. Others want to avoid the issue because it is so contentious and divisive. But it will not be possible to avoid the issues of fairness at work in the forthcoming strategic planning period.

The Importance of Fairness

These fairness issues are one of the more important strategic human resources management planning items, partly because fairness and productivity are closely linked in today's work environment. The greater the application of worker-controlled technology and the greater the delegative management style that is in existence, the more important the worker commitment to achieve high productivity and excellence of work. Worker attitudes are more directly linked to productivity when workers determine how they spend their time and control or influence how the machines are used.

With delegative management, employees make decisions about work—and how to get things done the best way. Such decisions impact the effectiveness of work. There is greater latitude of action under delegative management, and the degree to which employees are committed to excellence of work is, in part, a matter of the desire for excellence. Those attitudes must be affected by fairness, or the employees' perception of employer fairness.

It's not that people do their worst if there is unfairness. More likely the existence of any degree of unfairness will result in people doing less than their best or what is required rather than their best. Those differences among all employees, accumulated over time, can make huge differences in productivity.

Fairness is important as a strategic personnel issue for another reason. Values are linked with economic welfare, and as living standards improve, fairness is more and more important.

The world is divided into undeveloped nations, developing economies, and developed countries. In undeveloped countries, the economic focus is on survival, avoiding starvation. In developing countries, the economic focus is on accumulating things: cars, homes, clothes, and television sets. In the developed economies, many people have already accumulated many things, and the society focuses more on fairness.

Fairness is always right. First, it is fair to survive, then it is fair to accumulate things for reasonable comfort and satisfaction. Then comes the time when there is latitude to just be more fair.

There are parallels with those who work in organizations. First, it is fair to get a job and earn enough to live above the poverty level. Then it is fair to have a chance to get ahead and earn money for cars, homes, and education. Then it is fair to have a chance to be successful.

The impact of fairness on the effectiveness of work is usually unprovable. There has never been much information about this important issue.

The perception of most practicing human resources management professionals I know is that actual or perceived unfairness will inevitably result in substantially lower levels of effectiveness than are reasonably achievable and endless trouble. The view has been that fairness facilitates productivity, that high degrees of presumed fairness create an environment that makes possible a high level of work effectiveness.

In today's jobs, the margin between the best that is possible and what is acceptable is not related only to physical effort and it is not restricted by the physical power of machines. Output is leveraged by technology, and effectiveness is partly a matter of the productivity of minds. Under these conditions, the spread in work excellence that is possible when fairness exists would seem to be much greater in the future than it was in the past.

Fairness is a more important legal matter now and will continue to be in the foreseeable future. It was sometimes illegal to be unfair, and it still is. Now, however, it is also sometimes illegal to be fair, at least fair in the perceptions of the overwhelming majority of employees.

The issues of legality and fairness at work will probably go through a critical state during the next strategic planning period. However it turns out in the courts and in the legislatures, employers will be at risk, productivity will suffer, and many employees will be deeply and emotionally involved with struggles against legally required unfairness as much as unfairness not touched by laws.

Many operating managers and personnel professionals would not rate fairness highly at all, not as a planning issue and not as an item on the work agenda. Many executives, for example, consider the subject of fairness as a discussion of philosophy: niceness at work and the golden rule. No doubt, many of the programs and a lot of the words of the past made fairness obscure and philosophical. I think fairness is an important *practical* business matter now and that it must be handled as such.

We all want to be fair and like to be thought of as being fair. In the next strategic human resources management planning period, fairness will also be a hard productivity matter, not a philosophical matter. Fairness will also receive a great deal of attention because it will be a major political and social issue that will naturally flow over into the world of work.

Fairness in the News

Fairness has been a major political, social, and religious issue for some time. The term "fairness" was coined as a slogan in presidential elections as early as the 1970s, and in different ways we have heard about fairness from both political parties.

If you look for them, you will see fairness issues in the newspapers almost every day. The media report actual or perceived unfairness on almost every conceivable issue. It would not be possible to have such pervasive and persistent reporting and preaching on the subject of fairness for such a long time without finding that it becomes a major strategic planning issue at work.

There are many indications that there is more focus on fairness at work. For example, there has been a steady rise in the adoption and use of grievance systems of various types in nonunion organizations. That is a sign that managers are conscious of the importance of fairness at work. A high percentage of grievances submitted in both nonunion and union situations are related to fairness every year.

The issue of the working poor (covered in detail in Chapter 19) is another observable current human resources trend issue with strategic importance that relates to fairness. Many people think it's unfair that an employee works all year and has an income below the poverty threshold that was determined by the government.

Plant closing notifications were a fairness issue. Workers wanted something more in the way of job security.

There were the Civil Rights bills of 1990 and 1991, and they dealt directly with fairness in the workplace. There was the related issue of upward mobility, which proved to be an unsolvable problem for many companies. Upward mobility is a fairness issue.

Deep divisions and strong feelings have emerged in the workplace about quotas of all types. Special treatment for some groups is a related fairness issue.

The cases of fairness reported by the media and experienced in the workplace are endless and a daily event. Just the sheer volume of fairness-related cases suggests that it is an important strategic human resources management planning issue.

Employee Fairness

Fairness at work is double-edged. There must be fairness by the employer and there must be fairness by all the employees who work in the company. Employees must be fair to each other and they must be fair to the company.

All employees must follow reasonable rules, and that includes executive employees. With greater delegative management styles, there are fewer rules, but those that exist must be more rigorously followed. Whether employees follow reasonable rules is an employee fairness issue. The proper and prudent use of company property is an employee fairness issue. The proper use of benefits and perquisites is another employee fairness issue.

The most important issue of employee fairness to the employer and his fellow employees has to do with the employee doing his best. When employees work less than their best, that's unfair to the company; it's also unfair to fellow employees, the stockholders, the economy, and to the person himself.

Workers generally have not been doing their best. Every study that has ever been made on the subject shows clearly that workers are doing about a third less than their best, and we know why. Of course, the results vary between different groups and depending on the circumstances that exist at the time each study was conducted. But here are seven reasons why workers don't do their best that have been mentioned in many studies.

1. Many employees don't think that they are really a part of the business. This is the "them" and "us" syndrome.
2. Employees don't always feel that as individuals or as a group what they do or how well they do it makes a difference.
3. Employees report that they are prevented from doing their best by the programs and rules in effect. This is the "company way" syndrome.
4. Employees think that excellence is not rewarded as much or as consistently as it should be.
5. Over the past fifty years, workers have generally been lulled into thinking that they don't have to do their best, that we can all be successful by doing less than our best.

6. Many people have become dispirited by the preferential treatment for some and by the number of nonworkers who must be supported by workers.
7. In varying degrees, people either don't like the work they do or they don't like to work at all, so they only do what is required.

Managers must work to reduce if not eliminate these attitudes and get workers to do their reasonable best. That would be a productivity dividend from fairness. Here are examples of how to deal with the issues just listed (the number for the recommendation matches the number of the issue listed above):

1. As for the "them and us" syndrome, many actions can be taken. For example, employee stock ownership should be considered. This will create more of a partnership environment. When you are an employee partner, you are much more a part of the business.

2. As more and more people work in small businesses or small units of large businesses that have performance unit measures, people will see more and more that their effectiveness makes a difference in results. So establish organizational units as deep in the organization as possible, each with performance measures. This will make much clearer the relationship between a person's work and enterprise results.

3. The rules and regulations of programmatic management are being eliminated. The result will be that workers' attention will be focused on the effective way rather than the company way. Deregulate the company as much as possible.

4. Most managers don't think that excellence is sufficiently rewarded, and reward for performance is itself a strategic human resources management issue. Reward for performance is also a central part of productivity management.

5. People in more and more jobs will be managers—at least the managers of knowledge. Then by the nature of their work, more people will be "bottom-line" oriented.

6. Equal treatment in all matters will be the high moral ground at work, and employers must work to end preferential treatment. When you are compelled to give preferential treatment, communicate the details of what and why to all employees.

7. We are all less than perfect, and it must be part of the manager's job to set requirements.

Deal with the issues of employee fairness by effective communications. Make sure that your employment selection systems evaluate each person's propensity to do his best. Above all else, recognize that each employee is a unique case, a productive human business unit. The effective manager knows each person and how to get each person to work closer to his best.

Employer Fairness

In the 1990s, the major focus of the fairness issue will be about employer fairness. That is the other side of the double-edged fairness issue.

Greater fairness by the employer will be hard to sell in many companies. The problem of executive perception has been aggravated over the years by the fact that companies have not had good experience with proposals relating to fairness. Too often fairness programs were sold on the basis that being more fair to employees would mean that workers would be happier people and the quality of work life would be enhanced. This condition was somehow to result in greater productivity. These prophecies never worked out.

Most of the fairness-related programs of the past were based on psychological studies. For example, some people observed that effectiveness was reduced when interpersonal and intergroup relationships deteriorated. The result was various forms of organizational development programs. On balance, organizational development programs didn't do much harm, but they cost a lot. Organizational development failed because it was a program—and very likely the wrong program for the observed problem. Such experiences are part of the future problem of getting approval for actions needed to assure fairness.

Employer fairness in the 1990s will be productivity driven, not geared to happiness, well-adjusted persons, good relations, or tranquility. Employer fairness is a business opportunity in the forthcoming strategic human resources management planning period.

Employer fairness must be in the areas already identified: equal opportunity, equal treatment, and personal values. Executive managers cannot guarantee equal results and they should not attempt to change people.

Equal Opportunity

Equal opportunity is the first crucial element of fairness. Equality of opportunity is guaranteed for all of us by the Constitution and the laws of the United States, supplemented by the laws of the states and localities. You can't make equal opportunity more official than that.

Equal opportunity is also sound business. For example, the rational businessperson will always hire the most qualified worker. To do otherwise would be poor business, because at a given job salary, the most effective person is always the best "buy."

Employers' groups claim that there is now net equality of opportunity, at least in companies employing more than two hundred people. Studies I have seen and the experiences I have had would support that conclusion absolutely. In general, my experience suggests that it is now correct to say that bias against some people in a group is roughly offset by preferential treatment for others in the same group.

From reports in the media and from "studies" by advocates as well as from statements by spokespersons, you could get the impression that business has not achieved equal opportunity. Most of these "studies" are biased.

The only way to test equal opportunity is to look at a *job* and evaluate qualifications. There have been dozens of companies that tested equal opportunity by job, and each case clearly shows two things:

- There is bias in favor of minorities in hiring.
- In all other matters of work, there is relatively equal opportunity.

The questionnaire used by thirty-one companies is shown in Exhibit 8-1. In each of these studies, data for each person in a job was listed along with:

- Their current salary
- Their race: white, black, Hispanic, Asian, and other
- Whether male or female
- Age
- Full months on the job
- Performance

All of these data must be evaluated to see if there is equality of opportunity. You can use this method to test equality of employment and pay in your own firm.

Even though bias, in fact, is offset by preferential treatment, net mathematic justice in equal opportunity won't do in the 1990s. Employees will expect equal opportunity in every case, without offsets.

The issue of fairness is human values, not bookkeeping. It isn't possible to offset bias of one type by instances of opposite bias.

It is absolutely possible to achieve equal opportunity in employ-

Exhibit 8-1. Equal pay treatment questionnaire.

Case #	Salary*	White	Black	Hispanic	Asian	Other	M	F	Age	Full Months in Job	High	Std.	Low
1													
2													
3													
4													
5													
6													
7													
8													
9													
10													
11													
12													
13													
14													
15													
16													
17													
18													
19													
20													
21													
22													
23													
24													
25													

(Columns grouped: Race = White, Black, Hispanic, Asian, Other; Sex = M, F; Performance† = High, Std., Low)

*Salary rate for each person. Record whatever figure you use—hourly, weekly, monthly, or annual.

†Check one column only. Use only if you have a performance appraisal system that shows highest and lowest. If you have more than three-gradient ratings, show only high and low separately and all in-between ratios as standard. For example, if you had a five-gradient system, you would show 1 for low, 5 for high, and 2, 3, and 4 ratings in column labeled standard (std).

Exhibit 8-1. Equal pay treatment questionnaire.

Case #	Salary*	Race					Sex		Age	Full Months in Job	Performance†		
		White	Black	Hispanic	Asian	Other	M	F			High	Std.	Low
26	——	——	——	——	——	——	——	——	——	——	——	——	——
27	——	——	——	——	——	——	——	——	——	——	——	——	——
28	——	——	——	——	——	——	——	——	——	——	——	——	——
29	——	——	——	——	——	——	——	——	——	——	——	——	——
30	——	——	——	——	——	——	——	——	——	——	——	——	——
31	——	——	——	——	——	——	——	——	——	——	——	——	——
32	——	——	——	——	——	——	——	——	——	——	——	——	——
33	——	——	——	——	——	——	——	——	——	——	——	——	——
34	——	——	——	——	——	——	——	——	——	——	——	——	——
35	——	——	——	——	——	——	——	——	——	——	——	——	——

ment and in all matters of pay, benefits, job assignments, and conditions. To achieve equal opportunity, a company must first have a *commitment*, a true commitment to equal opportunity that is based on personal values and commonsense business views.

Even with a commitment, a period of affirmative action may be required to achieve equal opportunity. Affirmative action means special efforts to achieve equal opportunity—without preferential treatment and without quotas. With the experience of the past dozen years, there is plenty of know-how about how to purge prejudice to ensure equal opportunity.

There are no perfect and scientific methods for determining equality in all personal judgments. But the employer who is committed to fairness will succeed in having plainly fair processes for making decisions and will never make plainly unfair decisions. There is more than sufficient know-how in personnel to make equal opportunity a reality in every case, and there are auditing methods to make sure that there is equal opportunity in every case.

Some new answers to the issue of equality of opportunity will also be needed in the future. For example, how does a company choose between equally qualified persons for job openings? Seniority was often the answer in the past. But that will be less possible in the future because seniority involves age discrimination. Random selections would not be acceptable because that would seem to invite new prejudices or preferences. Perhaps quotas are the answer, and this may prove to be one of the few instances where the use of quotas of any type is reasonable and fair.

In the past, equal opportunity questions have been centered on large companies, mostly because compliance enforcement was more cost effective. In the future strategic human resources management planning period, the attention will shift to small companies, partly because they haven't had as much enforcement attention and partly because most of the growth in employment is occurring in small companies.

To achieve equal opportunity, I recommend first that each company recognizes that equal opportunity for all employees is good business and that the company establishes a strong equal opportunity policy.

Of course, equal opportunity is fair; and it is the law. But rather than preaching or threatening, I find that the best results are most often achieved by emphasizing the business value of equal opportunity. It is always good business to make personnel actions that are based only on capability and performance.

Second, every company should have affirmative action programs. The affirmative action programs that I think have been most effective and will be used more and more in the future focus on the process, not the results. If your company truly makes personnel decisions based only on talent and effectiveness, then that *is* equal opportunity, and unless you believe that some group is inferior in talent or capability, then equal opportunity will achieve results that would be acceptable to any reasonable person.

There must be monitoring of opportunities and, as required, investigation and auditing. The monitoring process must be based on information, and with computer-aided personnel information systems, even the largest organization can be continuously scanned to ensure equal opportunity.

The monitoring system should be diagnostic: identifying instances of possible failure. Then there should be investigation to determine the facts. Once problem areas are uncovered, then audits may be needed.

Equal opportunity is difficult and contentious work. But the methods of doing this work are clear and simple: policy, process, auditing, and, when required, strong corrective action.

Your work must be aimed at ensuring true equality of opportunity, not just compliance with laws and regulations. There are cases of legal compliance that involve unequal opportunity. That is one of the issues of equal treatment.

Equal Treatment

The newest component of fairness is equal treatment. In fact, equal opportunity plus the absence of preferential treatment amounts to equal treatment.

Equal opportunity means no bias. Equal treatment means no preferential treatment. They both mean no discrimination, but there is a big difference. Equal opportunity means no discrimination *against* any group. Equal treatment means no discrimination *in favor of* any group.

There are many specific issues relating to equal treatment. One involves upward mobility. This issue essentially relates to equal opportunities for promotion.

There can be neither unequal opportunity nor preferential treatment with respect to promotion. These cases would be highly visible to employees, and discrimination of any type would be considered grossly unfair by all employees.

Employers can set quotas on hiring and engage in preferential treatment in the employment process for some to the detriment of others. Those discriminated against probably won't know about the bias, and they are not the company's employees. In fact, it is my opinion that the regulators of the law and the courts support such discrimination. In many cases such discrimination is required in order to meet quotas and avoid EEO court action.

If a company gives preferential treatment in promotions, however, it is known to be discriminatory by other employees. Employee reaction is always direct and strong. Employees will always consider preferential treatment or bias in promotions as being grossly unfair.

Employees also learn about preferential treatment in pay matters. Pay based on bias of any type is a bread-and-butter issue to employees and always brings strong resentment and reaction. Also remember that overpayments based on preferential treatment may have to come from money that should have gone to others, and many of them may be high performers who earned it.

Employees also know when fairness is ordered by the courts or required by government regulators. It is hard to find any employee who does not know some poor performer who was given preferential treatment by the courts or by some government agency at the expense of good performers.

This crisis of what's thought to be legally right versus what's judged to be right in the workplace will likely reach a critical point in the near future. Employers are between a hammer and an anvil; they cannot be illegal or the courts will get them, but they cannot be unfair or their employees will react—and at times the reaction will be very strong.

Remember that employees know the real facts about pay, promotions, benefits, and conditions, not the theoretical, legal, or social version of right or wrong. It is the area of equal treatment at work where the great issues of fairness will be battled in the 1990s. Employees of any nationality, race, sex, and age will never accept anything but equal treatment.

Equal treatment is a highly sensitive and contentious issue. We really don't find many who would clamor for *unequal* treatment, but you do find leaders of groups who claim the need for and the right to preferential treatment, and that is unequal treatment. Working people in general will never accept preferential treatment in the 1990s; not for any group and not in response to any pressure.

Management by Quotas

Some people would like to have at least some personnel actions based in whole or in part on quotas. Management by quotas is based on the idea that there should be equal *results*, not just equal opportunity and equal treatment.

Equal opportunity and equal treatment for any class or group should cause equal results, given a reasonably large group, enough time, and no interference in the process. But equal results are not *assured*, and equal results, in my opinion, should never be imposed by quotas.

We must forget about quotas, which are results. We must concentrate on equal opportunity and no preferential treatment.

Selecting people for work, promotions, and performance pay increases must be based only on competency and performance. The only bias in personnel decisions must be a bias in favor of high performers. Any other basis for job selection or any other personnel action is economic foolishness that everyone pays for and is grossly unfair.

Those who argue equal results by quotas sometimes argue that the end justifies the means, the argument for tyranny of all types from the beginning of time. If they then argue that quotas are to correct former injustices, then they argue that two wrongs make a right.

If any group, whether it is based on race, sex, religion, age, or any other category, cannot compete for jobs, promotions, and pay when there is an even playing field, then they will do less well than others. But so far, every group has competed successfully, given an even playing field and an equal opportunity.

To argue that the playing field should be tilted so that the less able members of some group come out equal with more able people in other groups is gross injustice. That course is not only wrong, but it almost guarantees more future injustices and more, not less, bigotry.

Management by quotas is now getting to the point where the playing field is being tilted in many directions. That results in chaos and will be the cause of many injustices.

We must all be constantly alert and vigorous about protecting against bias of all types, recognizing that minorities of any type may be particularly vulnerable to unequal treatment. But the answer to bias cannot be the institutionalization of bias in quotas.

We are, I fear, heading for a confrontation of monumental proportions in the workplace with respect to the use of quotas during the forthcoming strategic personnel planning period. On the one side, politicians and spokespersons for special interest groups want more quotas and stronger quotas for more groups. On the other side of the battle line, you have the great majority of working men and women who say *enough*—no more preferential treatment for anyone.

We see very plainly many cases of reactions to quotas and preferential treatment. These reactions are mostly in the workplace, but they have spilled over to college campuses and voting booths. The reactions are often as ugly as the preferential treatment and quotas that spawned them.

No doubt quotas will be a major part of the fairness issue during the next strategic human resources management planning period. Quotas must be recognized as unequal treatment by design.

Personal Values

There is one other important component of fairness. It involves the application of personal values at work. In the technology-dominated economy of today and in the foreseeable future, it may not be possible to have high productivity without a high level of personal values on the part of all employees and their employers.

I have written more than once about personal values. Briefly summarized, here are the criteria of personal values that I believe should be followed by all employers.

1. The company and all its spokespeople must always tell employees the truth.

2. The company should always respect every single employee; not just in the sense of the acceptance of each person, but on the assumption that each employee will do his best and that each employee is trustworthy and responsible.
3. There must be equivalency of treatment for every person in the company. There can be no preferential treatment and no favorites. There can be no bias and no quotas.
4. There must be a commitment to each employee. If the employees do their best, the employer will commit resources to help them be successful as long as there is work to be done.
5. There must be a concern for each employee, including recognition that there are times when an employee cannot do his best because of personal circumstances.
6. There must be justice in all matters. It is never sufficient to say that it is a company rule.

There will be an increasing need for such personal values at work in the future. Employees of the future will be just as forgiving as ever about mistakes, but these same employees will be less and less inclined to accept any action by employers or their representatives that does not reflect high personal values.

Special Problems of Fairness

Fairness is about equal opportunity, equal treatment, and personal values. Fairness at work, however, is not a guarantee that any employee or any group or class of employees will achieve equal *results*.

That view of fairness is not shared by many. Some people think that fairness means equal status and equal results. Their view is that unless there are equal results for each group, then there has presumably been bias. That's the rationale for quotas and for comparable worth.

The theory of fairness is that given equal opportunity, equal treatment, and personal values, people from every group will have a free choice and an even chance. Then the results will be the choice of each person.

Those who believe in equal opportunity, equal treatment, and personal values think that people of any race, sex, age group, religion, and ethic background have an inherently comparable personal worth and capability. Given fairness and an equal playing field, any group can compete—and success from every different conceivable group proves that to be correct.

Fairness at work versus quotas and equal results will be a major difference in the 1990s. My view is that employers should always be monitoring the equality of results. If results are unequal, then the equality of opportunity and equal treatment must be audited carefully.

With available computer technology, those in the human resources management department can monitor the status and personnel actions for every group and every job on the department's own PCs. By the twenty-first century, there will be expert systems, so the computers will be monitoring this data and will immediately flag possible deviations from fairness for review. That will be fairness compliance at its optimum. But state-of-the-art monitoring won't guarantee equality of results either, just an equal chance.

Every person should have an equal opportunity and equal treatment. There should be no preferential treatment with respect to job, pay, benefits, or conditions for any group or any person. Talent, capability, and performance should be the only basis for personnel actions of any type.

9

Managing Differences

As you think about strategic human resources management issues, there are a number of ways in which you can categorize or group the subjects. The subjects in this chapter (managing differences) and the next (demands of special-interest groups) are cases where I tend to group closely related planning items, but others could just as logically treat each subject individually.

The subjects I group into the category of managing differences are:

- Managing work differences
- Managing different programs
- Organizational unit management
- Multinational management
- Multicultural management

Each of these is a strategic human resources management planning issue of some importance. In combination, they represent a very important strategic human resources management planning matter.

I tend to group these items because all of them involve managing differences of some sort, are closely interrelated in some cases in some way, and because some business practices are applicable to more than one area. It was also useful in organizing material for this book, because each of the separate items of managing differences would make a very short chapter.

Managing differences is a very important strategic human resources management issue, mostly because the number of differences facing management are growing rapidly. Furthermore, there is reason to have considerable doubt about how successful operations of all types will be in managing differences generally or in dealing with any of the specific items of differences. The fact is that there will plainly be many more differences in the future strategic planning period, and management will probably have to become much better at managing these differences.

Managing Differences at Work

The most important and pervasive differences to be managed will be with respect to differences at work. This will mostly involve differences in how work is done.

There have been different ways of doing work in the past, but management methods sought to neutralize them and create sameness—the one best way. Now the trend is away from sameness, and the strategic issue will be effectively managing more differences at work.

In the future strategic planning period, the need will increasingly be to recognize many different circumstances at work and fashion different practices for each truly unique situation. Technology, worker control of machines, shorter typical product runs, faster obsolescence of products and services, and reliance on the unique knowledge of people require a fast and skilled fashioning of a best method of work for each different work situation, and that will usually be done close to where the work is conducted when there is a delegative management style.

Of course, there will be pockets of sameness, operations with programmed methods and everyone working to standard systems—just as there were pockets of differences in the programmatic era of sameness. In a delegative work environment, the emphasis will shift dramatically from managing programs and achieving uniformity and sameness to a focus on utilizing unique capabilities in each different work situation. That shift means managing more different work situations.

In managing differences at work, there will be much more emphasis on areas of management that are closely related to human resources management. Five such areas should be sufficient to illustrate this change in managing differences.

1. Managing knowledge
2. Managing capability
3. Managing time
4. Managing choices
5. Managing change

Here are a few notes about each of these areas of managing people. Each is a challenging area of management and is more important in an era of technology. Each also involves issues related to managing differences.

Managing Knowledge

Managing knowledge involves managing more differences because there is an increasing amount of knowledge as well as more types of knowledge. In addition, which knowledge is used, when different knowledge is used, and how knowledge should be used are different in many cases.

The management of knowledge involves the use of knowledge and the management of knowledge workers. Both are important in managing knowledge.

In the use of knowledge, the know-how required, the accessing of information, and evaluating knowledge are the three principal management issues. Each of these elements will be somewhat different in each case. In managing knowledge, therefore, there are many differences to manage.

With respect to know-how, recognize that managers can't know everything today. They must have a broad education and a sampling of knowledge, the intelligence to identify what additional knowledge is required, and then the ability to locate and access that needed knowledge. Different people have different knowledge gaps, and there are many different ways of accessing knowledge. These are issues of managing differences.

In the soft sciences, which represent an increasing part of total knowledge in business, there is no true wisdom, facts, or scientifically reported theories, so the manager must also have the ability to evaluate the sources of the information and judge the usability of information that is forthcoming. All of this requires managing different knowledge sources.

The management of knowledge workers involves special areas of expertise that relate to managing differences. In knowledge work, for example, it is particularly critical for knowledge workers to focus on the specific needs of the business and the objectives of the firm. It isn't just knowledge but knowledge used that matters. Knowledge must be focused specifically on the company's needs. This is a facet of managing knowledge which may be done differently for each project and in each group.

Recognize that knowledge and capability are general-purpose assets that can be used in many ways. The manager must orchestrate these many differences to achieve enterprise goals.

There are many different ways to do knowledge work, and managers must help individuals and groups find the best ways in a variety of situations. In fact, if the manager of knowledge workers has one area of knowledge greater than any of the professionals who work for him, it would be with respect to work processes and assuring that the correct processes are used from among the many different methods that are available.

Another increasingly important skill of managing knowledge workers involves interdisciplinary management. With more technology and more disciplines, many more different categories of technology must be managed. The effective manager will increasingly have to integrate different technologies to gain organizational goals. The number of different combinations of disciplines is almost endless.

The managers of knowledge workers also exercise quality control. Quality is correct work and relevant work in many different situations. Relevant means appropriate to that unit at that time. Quality means correct the first time. Only the manager with discipline know-how can check the quality of knowledge used. What is checked and the process of quality management will be different in many cases.

Capability Management

Capability management is an integral part of productivity management. Capability management is an important part of managing differences, mostly because people's capabilities differ as much as personalities or fingerprints.

Capability is a broader concept than performance. Capability includes the performance of current work *and* the ability to perform other tasks that might be required in the job assigned. Performance relates to how well a worker does the work being performed. Capability relates to a proven ability to do work that has been done and work that might be required in the future.

It's important to know about and focus on capability management, and it should receive a lot of attention during the next decade. Part of the job of the managers of personnel will be to utilize the unique capabilities of each person to achieve group and enterprise goals to the extent possible.

It was always management's job to utilize physical assets: use factory space well, have an efficient process and work flow, and keep all the machines running. In technology work, it is just as important to utilize human assets. Productive work always requires that each knowledge worker is kept busy doing the most important tasks.

There are clearly many types and combinations of capability. That requires managing many differences.

Little work has been done on capability management or the issue of managing differences in capability. Some capability pay plans have been proposed, but there has been no capability management work, which seems to be out of order.

I have my own view of capability management, but it isn't relevant here, other than that capability management involves managing the many differences in capability in a work group or a workforce, and this is a matter of some unknown importance in the future strategic personnel planning period.

The Management of Time

A knowledge worker could be considered to be a knowledge machine. If you think of it that way, it is inconceivable for the machine to be idle during working hours or used in unproductive ways. It is just as uneconomic to have knowledge workers idle—or not spending time on matters of value to the organization. The management of time is thus an increasingly important part of management and evolves in many differences.

Employees are general-purpose machines, and their time can be used in different ways. It is in that sense that the management of time is an important component of managing differences.

Most employees are paid for their time, so much an hour, a week, or a month. This theory of pay then assumes that it is the job of management to use time and knowledge effectively. This *is* the management of time, and there are many different ways to use the time available in a work group.

Companies have not focused much in the past on the question of the management of time, partly because standard bookkeeping practices do not call for an accounting of time. In addition, much of the thinking about operations assumes that equipment, work procedures, and supervisory oversight assure the proper use of time. Such thinking does not apply or does not apply as much to knowledge work. You can't visibly overview mental processes, for example. And there is at least less of the traditional control of time for those who use equipment like PCs.

We have moved from a work environment where time was largely controlled to one dominated by work where there is great latitude in the use of time. There is latitude with respect to doing the right thing and the process or sequence of doing the right thing. Management of the use of time directly affects productivity.

With respect to different people, different groups, different times, and different circumstances, latitude in what to do and how to proceed is highly individual. Thus the differences are virtually infinite, and the management of time has a heavy flavor of managing differences.

In the next strategic human resources management planning period, there will be a great need for human resources management professionals to acquire know-how in the management of time. Also expect to see an emergence of time management practices, such as time accounting and activity value analysis.

Managing Choices

With latitude of action in what to do and how to proceed, more people at work will have more choices. Making the correct choices (including choices with respect to the use of time) relates to managing differences and will be a major problem of productivity management. Expect management of choices to be a major management issue in the 1990s.

It isn't managing choices but managing each choice, and there are many choices in knowledge work. Under delegative management, the true manager will have a big challenge in managing the choices of subordinates who will also have much more accountability for making correct choices about work methods in the future as empowerment becomes more prevalent.

There are simply so many more choices in work today, and the trend seems to be for even more. That makes managing choices a special category of managing differences.

I don't know if you can really manage choices or direct good judgment or if people must be managed so more good choices are made. But I think we can be sure that the issue will be a major one and that choice is an important part of managing differences at work.

Managing Change

A great deal has been said and written about managing effectively in an environment of change. Change means different. The fact that there is more change means that there is management in an environment of more differences.

We have always lived and worked in a climate of change. Change is now more varied (different) and it is more rapid. That's why managing change also affects managing differences.

Some teach very formal methods for managing in a climate of change. But the changes are so varied and they are happening so rapidly that formal systems haven't worked very well.

We have learned some practical things about managing in an environment of rapid change. But most of what has been learned applies to companywide changes. Yet the overwhelming amount of change that is occurring is down in the organization. Today, many different changes and many different types of changes are occurring every day in every part of every company. Cumulatively, these different changes are much more profound than the visible changes seen by top executives and reported in the media.

Managing Different Programs

There will be less programmatic management in the future, but there might be more programs. What may seem like a contradiction is because, while there will be fewer programs at the corporate level, there will be latitude of action to use programs at all levels. As a result, there will be many different programs down in the organization. These many different programs are another facet of managing differences.

In the future planning period, in fact, there will often be very different approaches to program development. Companies will more often develop essential policy guidelines and have some essential companywide programs. Then most programs will be developed from the bottom up instead of from the top down. The focus of the development will be on the lowest practical levels of the organization.

Specifically, the focus of a great deal of the development of programs and practices will be on the organizational unit. There are many organizational units in companies, and that means many different programs.

Managers of divisions, P&L centers, and organizational units below the P&L center will initiate the development of programs. Programs will almost always be developed in response to a need or a problem. The needs of each unit will be very different, so there will be many different programs.

Programs at the organizational unit level will typically be for the specific use of rather small units. The programs will tend to be much simpler than the programs developed by the corporate staff or by consultants for the entire company. The life span of these programs for organizational units will be rather short. Those factors will also contribute to more and different programs.

Managing different programs will bring special problems of its own. Managers will have to be expert in many more ways of operation and many more types of programs. For example, managers are moved from time to time, and each move may mean the use of different programs.

Companies will have to be careful that they don't have more different types of programs than are necessary. Differences for the sake of differences or differences based on personal preferences rather than operational needs cannot be tolerated.

Operating managers in organizational units will usually be assisted in developing needed human resources management programs and practices by the personnel support generalists in their organizations. These field personnel generalists may get needed support from the central personnel staff or directly from outside consultants. However it is done, each field personnel generalist will have some latitude in the programs and practices he recommends. This will also add to the differences.

Organizational Management

The focus of organization now is the profit center. Each business or business area may have a number of profit centers. Organizations will not only tolerate differences in profit centers more in the future, they will encourage differences, if that's what is required to improve results.

There is no data on the number of profit centers now in existence in business, but as profit centers were established within a company, the number of organizational units increased greatly. Differences in work methods and practices at the profit-center level were often permitted, and this meant that the management of differences was a more important part of the management job as organizations established more profits centers (or cost centers) within the operation.

Expect companies to continue work to develop more profit centers and in some cases develop profit centers at the next lower level of the organization. In addition, there has been a great deal of work on developing statistical measures for operating units below the P&L level.

As companies move to more P&L centers, the number of managed organizations may double. As a company moves to organizational unit management, the number of managed organizations may increase tenfold.

With greater technology and the need to delegate decisions, there will be a logical tendency to delegate management to more organizational units deeper in the organization. Top management will often not understand operations even a few levels down in the organization, but they understand results and often feel comfortable running organizations even when they don't have a detailed understanding about the work being done or the specific activities that are involved, provided there are satisfactory organizational results measurements.

Many companies now have multiple business areas and operate each area as a separate business with a separate income statement. Organizational management is the same basic style, but it is applied much deeper in the organization and often with partial accounting measures or statistical measures rather than complete P&L measures of results.

Computer technology will facilitate the delegation of management to organizational units by making it possible to have more statistical measures at the unit level. It is also important for those who work in the human resources management area to understand that many of the statistical measures at the organizational unit level will be human resources management measures, such as employment effectiveness and productivity.

The trend toward organizational management is a basic business trend that is affecting all areas of operations. The implications of the evolution of organizational management on human resources management are very great, partly because businesses will be creating many more organizational units run by general managers.

The organization of the human resources management department will have to be geared to service the organizational managers. Essentially, these general managers at the unit level will need the support of personnel generalists. The personnel generalist's job, therefore, is likely to become the key job in human resources management at every level—from the first level right up to the vice president of human resources management.

As there are more units, there will certainly be more differences. Therefore, this trend toward more organizational units, many of which are deeper down in the operation, also creates more differences and is another important area of managing differences.

Multinational Management

An increasing number of American companies have been purchased by foreign companies, and in many of these cases the management practices of the foreign owners affect the human resources management practices of the domestic operation. This represents another difference in management. Actually, there are a lot of differences because many different countries have bought American operations in recent years.

When there is a foreign purchase, the managers of personnel

don't change but the top decision makers do. Then top-level policies and basic thinking change, and sooner or later that trickles down and affects the practices and thinking of the operating managers.

The most direct effect of ownership by foreign companies is with respect to the personnel practices of the companies that have been purchased. However, there is a secondary effect. As foreign-owner induced practices are adopted in the companies they purchased, the practices become more a part of the experiences of the labor market. In many thousands of experiences by many people, foreign cultures and foreign experiences become part of the American experience, and this is an increasingly important facet of managing differences in personnel.

There will also be a continued growth in American investments abroad and more American-owned operations in foreign countries, and that will also mean more differences. As Americans operate abroad, they absorb the work cultures and practices of the countries where they are the owners. Those experiences filter back and tend to trickle into practices. This also contributes to more differences.

There isn't one big difference in a foreign way of managing; there are many specific differences. The cumulative result will be a greater diversity of practices and more differences.

Some people include the influence of foreign practices on American business practices as a separate strategic issue. This seems to be a natural part of multinational business. But I don't think it is a big issue in human resources management, other than the fact that the influence of foreign human resources management practices is resulting in more differences and adds to the problem of managing differences.

Multicultural Differences

There are now those who talk about multicultural differences. They say that this is also an important part of managing differences.

The exact view may vary with different practitioners, but generally the thinking is that there are great differences in the culture of different groups and that these differences must be factored into management practices. This argument is often applied to all cultures and backgrounds, although some have the impression that the focus has mostly been on blacks in the workplace.

The general arguments relating to multicultural differences start with an emphasis on the differences in culture. Then there is a demonstration about how the differences in culture require different management practices for those with that cultural background.

As one example, there is an assumption that the culture of some societies or races is more tribal and is based more on group cooperation than competition. From that, it seems to some that performance must be defined differently for workers with that cultural background or that personnel actions for one group should not be based on performance but on some other quality that is more compatible with their cultural background.

Others only urge that multicultural considerations should be factored into management by a better understanding of the different cultures. This view suggests that cultural factors are to be understood and should be weighed in decisions. Sometimes when specific actions are discussed, however, this means preferential treatment to offset alleged cultural handicaps.

Some who work in this area say that work on multicultural differences has particular relevance in lower-level and unskilled jobs. It has been said that these jobs claim the greatest need for multicultural differences among those who come from a culture where there has not been a work ethic. For example, some argue that multicultural practices may have a particular value in work areas located in inner city locations where many people have been on welfare for generations.

Multicultural arguments almost always end up with claimed needs for different treatment. The failure of the group is said to be cultural, even when a majority of the culture has been successful and many, in fact, have risen to the top.

The field of multicultural differences is relatively new. To the best of my knowledge, work in the area as it relates to managing is only a few years old. As in all new areas of work, more work and some patience are needed.

The notion of multicultural management seems to be directly in conflict with our national culture. We are all foreigners in this land. Our workforce has always been composed of many cultures, and each has its own distinct character. The competition, individual initiative, and freedom of choice in our work system tended to capitalize on the best attributes and talents of each culture for the benefit of all cultures. We have had many races and cultures for two hundred years, and only in the past few years has the question of multicultural issues been raised.

Whatever your views on multicultural differences, this area is now part of our work vocabulary and has become part of the agenda, at least for the 1990s. You should be informed about the views and recommendations of those who support multicultural practices. It has been included as an item of strategic human resources management for the future, and multicultural differences factored into management practices would mean still more differences to manage.

Guidelines and Recommendations for Managing Differences

The first essential step in effectively managing differences must be a recognition of this important strategic human resources management issue. That is often difficult, partly because the changes are evolving a day at a time and there are no dramatic or identifiable indications of when action is needed. In fact, some people would argue that such matters as managing differences are in the future and do not have to be dealt with today, and that argument can be used every day.

To manage differences without anarchy at work, it will likely be necessary to evolve key principles for effective management that will get the results required in the face of more differences. Here are eight basic guidelines that I recommend for management in the 1990s for work excellence in the face of many differences.

1. It is essential to maintain a high degree of free choice at work—free choice for those who work and free choice for the employer.

It seems obvious to me that with more and more differences there must be more and more latitude to deal with these differences. More programs can't be the answer: it would soon lead to an administrative gridlock.

Essentially, we must deregulate the workplace to make more free choice possible. Only in this way can actions reflect more and more differences.

There are many methods of deregulating the workforce. Deregulate one step at a time, and be sure you factor in risks.

The key to deregulation is usually the excellence of operating management and the auditing systems that are in place, e.g., computer-aided personnel.

2. Practices must be geared to our American traditions and our national values and built on the culture that exists in this country. Your company can change its culture, but not the national culture. So manage the American way in America, and manage the Japanese way in Japan.

3. The focus must constantly be on performance and productivity. Create a productivity culture in your organization. Recognize that the greater number of differences create an opportunity for higher or lower productivity.

4. A very different type of "organization man" is emerging, and your policies and practices must reflect this. The new organizational people are men and women, and there are many different types of people. The new styles involve utilizing people's unique talents—utilizing the unique talents of unique people.

5. Excellence in communications will be needed in order to manage differences effectively. With so much knowledge and so many differences, no manager can know enough about everything that is needed to manage effectively in many situations. There must be selective communication and learning in key areas. Then there must be quick access to the specific know-how and information required in actual work cases.

Worknetworking is a word you will often hear in the future strategic human resources management planning period. Worknetworking refers to the act of contacting others known to have experience or special know-how that will be helpful with respect to specific problems and situations.

Information resources will act more as transponders. The experts will have accumulated a great deal of relevant information, and then when a question or inquiry comes from a manager, the experts will respond quickly, helpfully, and responsibly.

6. The key to managing differences effectively is in managing organizational units effectively. When P&L centers are established lower in the organization and operating units are established below the P&L level, each must be headed by a manager; a general manager in many respects. Each of these general managers will be running a business and in a sense will deal with the same issues and differences that are dealt with by very senior general management executives.

7. The key to managing differences is the managers. They are the key to effective delegative management and empowerment. In a deregulated unit, the authority of the manager will be somewhat equivalent to that of his counterpart in small independent firms.

There will be a number of reasons why the managers of people will be the centerpiece of management in the future, and we have covered most of them. Differences can *only* be managed effectively by each manager of personnel.

Under these conditions, the organization of the future will focus on management rather than administration, programs, and bureaucracy. This should lead to much higher levels of excellence in management; management that is good enough to manage many differences.

In the organization of the future, a company with 10,000 employees will typically have five hundred or more true managers. People will assume general manager responsibilities earlier in their careers, and those who manage the units well will move up the management ladder. Managing differences will be a critical element in determining who manages well. Then we will be selecting competency in managing differences as well as developing that competency.

8. A final key to managing differences is knowing when to do nothing. Not all differences need to be managed, e.g., some people are taller than others. Some differences can't be managed, e.g., some people are brighter than others. There will be many differences in the future that must be managed, and the ability to do this depends in part on not managing differences that don't need managing.

I know of no other actions that would relate just to managing differences, and there is no one way or one single program that will deal with differences. No doubt someone will come out with a uniform way of dealing with differences.

Addendum

As you reflect on the issue of managing differences, recognize how much of it is interrelated to the four strategic personnel issues covered in Chapters 5 through 8: productivity, education, delegation, and fairness. Each of these five strategic issues is an integral part of each of the others.

For example, there are reasons to think that the establishment of organizational units will create more differences, but at the same time this is a key method of increasing productivity. Managers must be successful in managing work differences or productivity improvement will suffer.

Without a better education, managers and workers will never to able to manage differences. More differences means more complexities, and more complexities generally require a better educated workforce.

Delegative management is listed as one of the essentials for the effective management of differences. It is the manager alone who can manage all of the emerging differences.

Differences create more opportunities of one sort or another. Thus there are more cases for equal opportunity or a lack of equal opportunity. I think those who advocate preferential treatment and quotas are wrong, partly because they have not considered the increasing number of differences and the compelling need to manage differences.

Companies will thus deal mostly with more differences by better management. That seems glib, but in my opinion it is the only way to do it.

10

Special Interest Groups

The demands of special interest groups are a major human resources management planning item because they take so much time and often impact conditions of work. Each special interest group would also tell you that what they represent, seek, or advocate is important, and this is why *they* are important.

You could identify each of the special interest groups and treat each one of them as a separate human resources management planning item. My preference is to lump them together, mostly because there are so many. New special interest groups spring up all the time, the old special interest groups change their demands or expectations, and you never really know from week to week which special interest group is going to be the center of attention.

It is very difficult if not impossible to anticipate the next demand of most special interest groups, let alone their strategic impact. Therefore, the strategic issue for human resources management is basically that these groups will certainly take a lot of time and that many of the issues they raise will be contentious and likely detract from the effectiveness of work and the conditions of work for many people.

About Special Interest Groups

There are many special interest groups. In fact, we are becoming a society of groups as well as individuals. By actual count, I am part of seven groups, and I didn't join any of them. I don't support much of what each of these groups advocates, and I have never given money to any of them. Yet each of them claims me as part of their constituency.

To deal with special interest groups or the issues generated by these groups, it is important that we understand them and how they operate. Here are a few notes about special interest groups that have relevance to management and personnel professionals.

One study by a local personnel association identified two hundred and fifteen special interest groups that impacted in some significant manner the employee-employer relations of companies in that group (but the association forgot to count itself, so make that count two hundred and sixteen).

There are, of course, various unions, and they are the only special interest group that has direct authority to represent your employees. The others must work through the government, unions, or directly with the employees who are in their constituencies.

There are various groups representing blacks, a number of women's groups (including women without children and women with young children), the young and the old, minorities, the handicapped, religious groups, alcoholics, nondrinkers, nonsmokers, overweight people, lefthanded people, veterans, homosexuals, drug users, religions, and almost as many nationalities as there are nations. There are many special interest groups that affect the employer-employee relationship in some way.

I don't know of anyone who has counted the number of personnel issues that have resulted from the demands of special interest groups that are active at any one time. From scanning human resources management planning items, the number is probably more than a hundred.

Those who did labor relations work would say that it was necessary to understand unions. Similarly, in today's work environment it is important to at least understand something about special interest groups other than the fact that there are many of them and they present a lot of issues.

A special interest group is an organization that represents the interests of some category of persons. The three operative words are "organization," "represents," and "category."

The special interest groups we are concerned about in business are organizations of some type. They are often well staffed and well financed. The organizations have dedicated members, often with considerable talent.

These organizations have characteristics that are typical of any enterprise. For example, they have a constituency—their customers—and they must perform well, which for most special interest groups means they must do something worthwhile for their constituents, usually every year or every month. In addition, like all organizations, special interest groups take on their own identity and evolve their own organizational goals and culture, which are independent of their constituents' needs, goals, and interests.

Because they have their own organizational identity, one of their goals tends to be to perpetuate their own organizations and their own jobs. For example, the Urban League will tend to perpetuate itself, and those who work there will want to keep their jobs regardless of the status of their constituency. And the organization can't switch to another constituency as did the March of Dimes.

Sometimes more than one organization seeks to represent the same constituency, causing competition among the special interest groups. Then you have a form of competition between special interest groups that can be very disruptive in the workplace.

Special interest groups are starting to form coalitions. One group will support another in return for something it wants very much.

Special interest groups represent their constituencies but are often not accountable to them. Special interest groups claim constituencies but are not usually elected by those they represent. Many special interest groups get financing from others who are not their constituents.

There are some important things we don't know about most special interest groups. For example, where do they get their money, what do they do in return for the money received, how are they accountable to their constituents, and do they make any disclosures about their organization or the principals in the organization?

By their nature, most special interest groups have a cause and are trying to bring about what they think are needed changes. Many who are associated with special interest groups believe in the work they are doing with great fervor. Many are almost evangelists and are often out to correct what they think are great injustices and make the world a better place. So emotion, perseverance, and great sentiment are often involved in dealing with special interest groups.

The issue of special interest groups will occupy time and attention throughout the next future strategic planning period. There are so many special interest groups and they are so visible that the planning item is obvious. Reasonable people disagree about the importance of any one group and what to do about them. But everyone should agree that special interest groups are a major factor to be reckoned with and that they are taking a lot of our time and attention.

Special interest groups are a product of our times. If you look for it, you can read something in the newspapers every day about some special interest group or some "study" that "proves" that some group should receive special attention. For one hundred and thirty-seven consecutive days before this manuscript was first drafted, at least one special interest group was featured in our local newspaper. Try it for yourself.

Studies have become a major tactic of special interest groups.

We can expect even more studies in the future. The study method has certain characteristics.

First, special interest groups undertake a study or commission someone to undertake a study to *prove something*. Like imaginative statistics, a study can be designed to prove what is known to be untrue or what is known to be unknown. For example, one study proved that minorities are disadvantaged in employment in companies that give preferential treatment to minorities to achieve quotas.

Another study proved that older workers had as much energy, adaptability, and enthusiasm for hard work as younger workers.

Another study proved statistically that unpaid leaves don't cost anything. Yet there isn't a company in the country that could supply the cost data for such a study.

Advocate groups of all types have joined the parade of new studies. The methods used in this work bring a new meaning to the word "study."

Special interest groups manage to get their studies on the front page. The material isn't news any more than the work is a study. Yet somehow they all make the front page.

Those who conduct these studies know what they're doing. Many have told me in one way or another that the end justifies the means.

These advocate studies are affecting human resources management. They are certainly serving the purpose of special interest groups, which is usually to get more support for some desired legislation or more favored treatment by the counts or by the administrators of laws.

One study by a large company showed clearly that employees believe these stories. They believe them partly because they are on the front pages of newspapers like *USA Today* and the *Miami Herald*. Then these employees know the study is true when it is discussed on network television.

Personnel generalists who work in facilities constantly report problems that are related to these same special interest groups in the workplace. The problems arise at work with respect to job assignments, pay, or conditions. A person wants something and claims status as a member of some group as the reason for entitlement. Some companies now report that about half of all formal grievances are demands from special interest groups for special treatment. Employees increasingly receive support in one way or another from special interest groups—or from the attorneys of special interest groups.

A great deal of time will be spent on matters relating to special interest groups of all types. The cost of that time and related expenses will also be great in the future. I estimate that the combined cost of all special interest groups *now* amounts to more money than business spends on private retirement plans.

In addition, special interest groups involve hidden costs that are difficult to calculate. Special interest groups almost always detract from productivity, and this may be the biggest cost of all. When you factor in the productivity cost, my calculations indicate that special interest groups cost more than health care.

One explanation for the productivity shortfall during the past dozen years, which was described in Chapter 5, is that in effect we have *spent* the productivity dividend in large part by financing the costs of the things sponsored by special interest groups.

Perhaps that's as it should have been. But it might also be nice if people knew what they were doing and were somehow given a choice.

If we spent the productivity dividend of only two percentage points for a dozen years, it was an enormous cost. One study claimed that lost productivity cost the average working family $30,000.

Special Interest Group Issues

Except for union representation, most employers don't deal directly with special interest groups very often. Rather, *all* employers must deal in some way with the issues created by special interest groups. Based on a survey of personnel professionals and the journals I scanned, eight issues were sponsored and supported by special interest groups in the past year that I think have special strategic significance. These eight items also illustrate the nature of future issues, although, of course, there will be a lot of new issues in the future and some old issues will be repackaged.

The eight issues that I think best illustrate the questions and problems of special interest groups at this time are:

1. Employment of handicapped workers
2. Day-care centers
3. Unpaid leaves
4. Plant closing notifications
5. Protection for problem employees
6. Use of multiple languages
7. Work opportunities for mentally handicapped persons
8. Protection for drug users

My purpose is not to support or criticize any of the groups but to use them to illustrate the issue. These eight items have been used as illustrations because they were reported by the media a lot during the past year and because they describe or illustrate the range of human resources issues presented by special interest groups.

Employment of the Handicapped

As far back as the 1940s, it was good business to hire the handicapped. I have worked as a consultant for over five hundred companies and would bet that every one of them hired handicapped workers. Studies show that handicapped workers are excellent workers and better in many ways than those who are not handicapped. For these reasons alone, employers thought it was in their self-interest to hire handicapped workers—and they did.

Now we have a law about handicapped workers. It says there is to be no discrimination against handicapped workers. But the law does much more than ban bias against the physically handicapped.

The law also says that every company must have special facilities for handicapped workers, whether it has handicapped workers or not. The law says that an employer cannot discriminate against handicapped workers in its hiring practices, and very much of the burden of proof will rest with the employers. It isn't certain yet, but from prior experience, it may well be that companies will have to have affirmative action to hire handicapped workers. There will likely be quotas of some sort for hiring handicapped workers.

It's not really clear what "handicapped" means. There is uncertainty about how the law will affect the relative importance of being handicapped and being the best-qualified. There are also questions about what happens if there are transfers—from jobs a handicapped person can do to ones the handicapped worker can't do. It is unclear how the law will affect layoffs or other treatment of handicapped workers.

Whether the costs involved are to provide equal opportunity or preferential treatment is a question that we should not deal with here because our job is to identify and describe human resources management planning items. Whether special provisions for handicapped workers are worthwhile is something each person will have to judge for himself. But this is an issue of special interest groups that will take a lot of time to resolve, and it will be a major issue in the years ahead.

Day-Care Centers

Working women with young children need day-care centers if there is no one else to take care of their youngsters during working hours. This has led to widespread demands by special interest groups for day-care centers. Now there are many employer-sponsored day-care centers. Sponsorship may mean minimum support or a complete company-paid and company-run day-care center.

This isn't a feminist issue. In fact, it's often an issue of women with children versus women without children, or women with young children versus women with older children. Some women see day-care centers as a matter of right. Other women object to favored treatment for working mothers. And, in fact, there are many women who think that women with young children should stay home and take care of their children.

Studies by some special interest groups claim that a company is able to recruit better workers if there are day-care centers and that top-level workers will go back to work sooner if day-care centers are available. Facts and experience do not support these assertions.

In fact, there is no evidence that women with young children are more effective than others, e.g., that they are more effective than women without young children. Actually, women with young children could be categorized as being problem employees because their first obligation should always be to their children, and this may show up in various ways at work in their behavior and in their effectiveness.

There are many problems with employer-financed day-care centers. Day-care centers cost money. In effect, when day-care centers are supported by the employer, then some employees are paid more than others for the same work.

Unpaid Leaves

If there was ever a special benefit that had everything going for it, it is the issue of unpaid leaves. It seems so reasonable to grant maternity leaves and leaves for family needs without pay. Unpaid leaves received a lot of media attention and were passed into law by Congress. But the law was vetoed.

Unpaid leaves were the result of pressure from a number of special interest groups. The issue is often put forth in terms of unpaid leaves for "important family reasons," but the overwhelming majority of cases are for childbearing.

Recognize that more than nine of ten companies in the country today already grant unpaid leaves for childbirth and other important family reasons. Unpaid leaves have been a standard personnel policy for as long as I have been in the field.

What is different now about the current demands of special interest groups is that they want a *guaranteed job* after their unpaid leave expires. And that's a problem to many employers and to many other workers.

When a person takes an unpaid leave, it is almost always necessary to hire a replacement worker—the work has to be done. If a job is guaranteed, then someone (usually the replacement worker) may have to be terminated at the end of the unpaid leave. Then a guaranteed job for someone who goes on unpaid leave is guaranteed termination of employment for someone else.

It takes weeks or months to learn many jobs today. Just about the time the replacement has been trained, the person with the guaranteed job comes back, and the replacement must be fired.

The issue of unpaid leaves will be on the agenda for many companies even if it is not enacted into law. In fact, there is now talk about *paid* leaves.

Plant Closings

Another bill that was sponsored by special interest groups (in this case, mostly unions) and later vetoed would have required notification of plant closings. Notification of plant closings does not always directly involve the issue of severance pay. Sometimes the main objective is to prevent the relocation of a facility.

With something like six months notification, the special interest groups would have an opportunity to "negotiate" a basis by which the company would not move at all. They would have an opportunity to bring pressure on the employer to stay at its present location. Pressure might include strong actions like boycotts, demonstrations, strikes, and disruptions of work.

Actions to prevent a relocation do not change the facts that led to the consideration for closing the plant in the first place. Plants are closed because they are inefficient or there is insufficient demand for products made in the plants. In fact, disruptive actions add to the cost of the plant and the reasons for closing it.

Stories about plant closings always play up the fact that some people will lose their jobs, and of course, losing a job for any reason is a serious problem. But net jobs are often not lost at all; lost jobs in one place are new jobs someplace else.

Recognize that a very small portion of the workforce is affected by plant closing notification proposals. Most of the workforce would not be protected at all by such a law. Increasingly today, jobs can be transferred one at a time, without moving equipment. Facilities can frequently be closed and relocated instantly; in fact, it would be difficult to notice that it even happened.

There is reason to ask whether this proposal for plant closing notifications is the first step toward legislation guaranteeing jobs. Advocates have said all along that money was not an issue; rather the issue was loss of jobs.

Expect more pressure from special interest groups to retard, discourage, or prevent the closing of facilities or the moving of work for any reason. In a period of increasing change, more old facilities will be closed and more new facilities will be opened, and therefore, this issue will likely become more important.

Problem Employees

There are different categories of problem employees. An employee with health problems is a problem employee, and all of us fit into that category at one time or another. As a strategic issue, problem employees are broad groups of workers who will disrupt work and/or cost more money. Problem employees are often represented by one or more special interest groups.

Increasingly, problem employees have special interest groups speak and act for them. Special interest groups can't directly represent their constituents in the workplace. However, they can and do call on employers, cause disruptions, and seek legal actions.

To illustrate the inclination of special interest groups to represent problem employees, note that homosexual groups now boycott some products because their manufacturers will not support "gay rights" and that there is pressure for local legislation in San Francisco that would require quota hiring of homosexuals.

Multilingual Workplaces

The issue of multilingual workplaces will likely be a special interest group issue in the future strategic planning period. Spanish-speaking groups are the most likely to be the special interest group that demands some form of a multilanguage workplace.

The more moderate demands will be for instruction material and signs in the workplaces to be posted in two languages. The demand for multilingual managers will be increasing.

A lack of skills in the English language is one of the facets of educational deficiency. Those who urge a multilingual workforce will want to have a form of institutionalized functional illiteracy.

"Multi" can mean any number. If it means English and Spanish, why not other languages as well?

The argument is that there is discrimination against the group, based on national origin, unless there is a multilingual workforce.

Some say that we are trying to deprive people of their heritage by forcing them to use the English language.

You can see the power of special interest groups in the fact that no one in the federal government will even say that English is the official language of the United States, which it clearly is. In a multicultural society, it is natural that many people speak two languages, but one of them must be English.

Mentally Handicapped Workers

If physically handicapped people receive special consideration at work, it seems reasonable to expect that mentally handicapped workers should also be given special treatment. Some special interest groups are now urging preferential treatment for mentally handicapped people. This will surely be a major issue in the 1990s, and legislation has been introduced in Congress.

There are many mentally handicapped people. There are many types and degrees of mental disadvantages between the extremes of derangement and serious problems, and there is almost no possible way to draw lines for the purposes of managing.

There has been little experience with this special interest issue, but the potential problems are scary. Just defining a mentally retarded worker and the enforcement of that definition by regulators could be a nightmare.

Yet those who push the needs of mentally handicapped workers can correctly point out that we are all limited in our intellect and that many who now work are functionally illiterate and/or mentally handicapped anyway. What the advocates of equal rights for mentally handicapped people will probably want is at least that all employers have their fair share of mentally handicapped workers through some form of quotas.

Drug Users

I once heard a speaker say in a joking manner that we might have quotas for drug users. But nobody laughed; everyone in the group thought it could happen.

Drug use by workers and drug use at work are important issues now. More and more companies have drug testing in their employment process, and there is more random drug testing of current workers. Using these methods, this country is winning the war on drugs, at least in the workplace.

Activists say that drug testing by employers will soon mean that drug users won't be able to get or keep a job and that drug users don't have an equal opportunity for promotions. Special interest groups want drug testing stopped. In fact, some defenders of drug users have proposed that drug users should be employed and promoted on a quota basis.

Commentary

Outlined were the eight special interest groups that I think will impact management significantly in the forthcoming strategic human resources management planning period and which also, in combination, illustrate some of the problems of dealing with special interest groups. Hopefully, each issue was treated with kindness and sensitivity. Yet there will probably be few readers who won't be upset by the description of at least one of these issues.

I avoided taking a position on any of the groups and tried to stick to work-related, factual comments. I made no recommendations with respect to any of the special interest groups' issues. Yet advocates of special interest groups often lash out at anyone who does not openly support their cause.

There is no way to treat the issues advocated by special interest groups without getting people upset. And that is one of the most important problems of this strategic planning issue. Special interest groups set out to get special treatment. They are open advocates. The inevitable result is confrontation. Then there is an adversarial relationship.

Matters relating to special interest groups are so sensitive that it is best to have as little commentary or opinion as possible. So here are a few thoughts, which are presented briefly and in a somewhat antiseptic manner.

To a large degree, special interest groups are a product of politics, and these groups get much of their power from the political system. Politicians increasingly cater to PACs and special interest groups (SIGs). We think we have a system of one person, one vote, but if you were a politician you would think one PAC or one SIG equals many votes.

The specific needs and demands of each special interest group vary, of course, but they are always the same in three ways. First, there is always some real need or perceived grievance on the part of the special interest group. Second, there are always spokespeople for the special interest group, often in politics, and they always get a lot of attention in the media. Finally, the demands of any one special interest group allegedly cost little, although there are many special interest groups and, in combination, the demands obviously cost a lot.

Almost all living persons are claimed as being part of the constituency of some special interest group. *Every* working person is in at least one special interest group. A study of one thousand workers showed that, on average, each worker is claimed by four special interest groups that are very active in the workplace.

The divisions of views and the intensity of feelings are what make the special interest group issues such a difficult problem. Special interest group activists see themselves as being crusaders for right, truth, and goodness. Adversaries often view special interest groups as pigs lined up at the trough.

One great concern about special interest groups should be their effect on productivity. One effect of concessions to special interest groups is almost always lower productivity. Some think that one of the reasons why productivity has improved less than 2 percent instead of the 4 to 6 percent that is possible is because of special interest groups—and their effect on productivity. I think this is partially true and noted that we may have spent the productivity dividend.

I personally think that what we are seeing in the emergence of special interest groups to power is the evolution of the new unions. There has been talk about the new unions for some time. As unions declined in number and influence, who was going to represent the needs and views of workers?

The new unions are the special interest groups. One thing that troubles me is that there is no special interest group for *workers*.

Recommendations

Giving advice to companies with respect to special interest groups (other than unions) is, in many ways, the most difficult area in my consulting experience. Presented here in brief form are my recommendations to clients for dealing with issues brought about by special interest groups.

First of all, we must always obey the law. Every company should obey the spirit as well as the letter of the law, regardless of its views about the law. Never play cute with legal matters, and don't take advantage of some legal loophole, even if you think you can get away with it.

Obeying the spirit as well as the letter of the law does not require "zero risk" management. Don't pass everything by the legal department or allow yourself to be paralyzed into inaction because of possible legal implications.

Be affirmative in conforming to the law. But your obligation is to the law, not some government administrator who might apply rules or guidelines that are administrative preferences and not legal requirements.

At the human level, be sensitive and caring about the genuine special needs and problems of any person or any group of people. We have all known people who have faced adversity and have had compassion for them in their trials; we have lent support to them in many ways, and when those with adversities achieved success in spite of their condition, we have had great admiration for them.

Always be willing to listen and consider openly and seriously the views of any legitimate special interest group. Never hesitate to admit errors or recognize that conditions require a change. Judge each case on its genuine merits, not because of persistence, evangelism, or threats.

A company should try to do what is right—what is right for its employees, owners, and customers; and in this case, mostly what is right for all employees. What is plainly legal is right by definition. You must also be guided about what is right by equal opportunity, equal treatment, and personal values.

Never yield to threats or blackmail. Many representatives of special interest groups are evangelists who believe that any method is justified for their goals. I have personally observed many latent threats from special interest groups, particularly in recent years. In the next strategic planning period, it is likely that special interest groups will become at least as violent in some cases as union relations were in the worst period of confrontation. It may be that some special interest groups will become domestic terrorists of some sort.

Don't yield even small points to big principles. Never yield or compromise on what is fair. If you find that you are compelled into conceding unfair advantages or preferences to any special interest group, be sure to report this to your employees.

The last and perhaps most difficult guideline of all is to treat all special interest groups the same: those you like and those you don't.

Most of all, recognize that managers are a special interest group, and most senior executives are a special interest group within a special interest group. The "company" can't oppose a special interest group's request for a plant closing notification if it establishes golden parachute contracts for executives. The "company" can't object to special facilities for the handicapped and then build an exercise room for executives—next to the executive dining room.

In my opinion, matters relating to special interest groups will mostly be resolved and determined at the political level. Employers must follow a policy of fairness to all employees, within the law, regardless of which special interest groups claim them as a constituency.

It is also my opinion that employers cannot really deal with special interest groups in good faith if the managers grant themselves preferential treatment. The end of grossly preferential treatment for executives is a central issue and is closely interrelated to the issues of special interest groups.

11

Fair Pay

With respect to pay, the 1970s has been described as the NOW decade, when many working people wanted instant wealth. Workers wanted to be paid before they earned it, and the motto of the 1970s could have been, "Pay me now; I'll earn it later." The 1980s was a generation of GREED, led by executives of large firms, people in Congress, Wall Street barbarians, and superstars of sports and entertainment. The 1990s will very likely be a decade of FAIR PAY. Fair pay will largely mean competitive pay and reward for performance.

Fair Pay in the 1990s

By my weighting system, "fair pay" is the seventh most important human resources management strategic planning item. My basis for forecasting fair pay as a high-priority human resources management planning item is based on the following considerations:

• This is the productivity age, and an increasing amount of work is controlled by the workers. Fair pay seems to be essential for work effectiveness.

• Because of more knowledge work and greater technology, there is an increasing performance spread, and this will mean that pay for performance will be a bigger issue than it was in the past.

• There will be pockets of labor scarcity, particularly in knowledge areas, so fair pay will be needed in more cases to help get needed workers.

• Quits by valued people who are hard to replace will become more costly. Under such circumstances, a company must have fair pay as one crucial step in retaining needed people.

• The greed of the 1980s will likely cause a reaction and will be replaced by a new focus; just as greed in the 1980s replaced the "pay me now" attitude of the 1970s. Fair pay seems to be a natural reaction to greed.

- Huge amounts paid to executives, lawyers, sports stars, and others are widely known, and an overwhelming majority of people have been disgusted. That disgust will likely lead to increasing public clamor for more fairness in pay through the tax system.

- In a political environment where more revenues are desperately needed, it seems inevitable that the politicians will discover an opportunity to tax the greedy.

There will likely be a great deal of disagreement about what fair pay is in the forthcoming strategic planning period. With a lot of effort and many battles, I think that companies generally will move a step at a time to five basics of fair pay:

1. *Competitive pay.* Sufficient pay for jobs to attract and retain the number and quality of people needed to run the company and achieve reasonable enterprise goals.
2. *Reward for performance.* Pay for individuals above or below competitive job pay, depending upon the excellence of their work.
3. *Success sharing.* Some system of sharing the success of the company overall with the employees who create the success.
4. *Equal treatment in pay.* No preferential treatment in pay for any person or group for any reason.
5. *Fair pay in benefits.* The same or equivalent benefits for all employees.

Competitive Pay

Fair pay and competitive pay don't mean exactly the same thing. Fair pay emphasizes unbiased decisions, justice, and free choice. Competitive pay emphasizes rivalry and, in business, sufficiency to attract and retain needed employees. However, where there are free choices and no abuses of power in labor markets or in pay decisions, so that both the employee and the employer decision makers are able to exercise judgments, then fairness and competitiveness are very close to the same thing, with rare exceptions.

All of this may seem to be somewhat philosophical, but it is an extremely important consideration. When there is not free choice by both the employer and the employee, pay is regulated. Regulated pay will cause some instances of unfair pay, because "fair" must be what an employee thinks is reasonable and acceptable.

Competitive pay means that the pay for a job is the same

amount that is paid for comparable jobs in the market. For the statistically minded, fair pay means that job pay is equal to market average.

From the employee's view, job pay that is less than market average is plainly unfair. Pay above market for some jobs is also unfair, because that necessarily means pay that is less than average for other jobs. From the employer's view, the company is able to attract and retain required people with market-average job pay, and paying above average would be unfair to its shareholders and customers.

Competitive levels of pay essentially involve two matters of compensation: salary levels paid for jobs and the completeness of the total compensation package. In the real-world sense of attract and retain, competitive salaries paid for jobs in relevant labor markets are what matter the most.

A company can pay competitively by having key jobs equal to market averages. This will always make it possible to recruit needed people as long as the company does vertical recruiting; filling the job with a person who is now in a lower-level job, as would be done if the job were filled by promotion from within.

With vertical recruiting and average job pay, it is easy to prove mathematically that companies are very competitive in the market. Yet many companies set salaries 10 to 20 percent above the market, although this is now usually done mostly for management jobs.

Paying higher than average salaries doesn't improve a company's ability to retain employees. The core reason why people voluntarily change jobs is often because of non-monetary considerations. When employees do voluntarily change jobs because of dissatisfaction with the pay, they get at least 20 percent more, on average.

My recommendations are always to gear job pay to the average paid for jobs in relevant markets unless there are compelling and provable reasons to do otherwise. An example of a reason to pay above market might be rapid company growth in a tight labor market. The compelling reasons for paying above average will always be temporary.

Because employers will have greater reasons for paying at market average and because that will accomplish the company's objectives, then it seems reasonable to conclude that fair pay will mean average job pay. Thus fair pay will mean that job pay will be average to the market for more people in the future than it has been in the past.

I recommend that employers GUARANTEE all employees that pay for jobs will be *maintained* at competitive levels. This policy guarantees that as pay for competitive jobs in relevant labor markets increases, the company will also increase the pay of its jobs automatically.

If it is important to pay competitively, it is equally important, and equally fair, to continue to pay competitively. I think that guaranteeing job pay is an important and essential part of maintaining fair pay in the future strategic planning period.

Here are some other specific recommendations about competitive job pay. In my opinion, each of them will be a consideration in the future because fair pay will be an important strategic human resources management planning item.

• Ensure competitiveness primarily with pricing by employment experience, which is the most correct and reliable way of assuring competitiveness and is much better than using surveys. Too often companies have become uncompetitive because of poor survey methods.

• Don't playact competitiveness, and always tell the truth about how pay for your jobs really compares to pay for others doing similar work in comparable firms.

• Talk openly and candidly with your employees about your policy on competitive pay and how your company assures that the policy is implemented.

• Demonstrate competitiveness at the top; set the right example by setting salaries at market average for highly paid people.

• Never try to gain cost competitiveness by shifting investors' risks to the payroll; for example, never pay below market to increase profits or reduce losses. It isn't fair—and it just doesn't work.

In personnel work during the 1990s, there will be many cases where companies must go back to the basics, and it is my opinion that the competitiveness of job salaries is one such issue. For the employer, the basic requirement is to have job pay that is sufficient to attract and retain the number and quality of people needed to run the business and achieve enterprise goals. That means average market pay for jobs and a reasonably complete compensation package.

In addition to the level of job salaries, the completeness of the compensation package is important to assure fairness. The need is to have each of the major forms of compensation granted by most employers in the labor market that are expected by employees. Your company doesn't necessarily have to have the same or equivalent amount of each major compensation element, but each important compensation element must exist.

Pay for Performance

Whenever talent can affect work output and quality, it seems compelling to pay more to those employees who do better work. Therefore, while companies should pay market average for jobs, there should always be a variation in pay for each individual on each job based upon how well the work is performed. In the 1990s, pay for performance will be a major part of the fair pay issue.

A business and those who work in the business gain from pay for performance. It is both fair to employees and good business for an employer to have a pay spread that matches performance spread.

In addition to the fact that pay for performance is good business and fair to employees, there are some specific advantages of fair pay for performance, and I think these will be more important than ever in future years.

- Pay for performance provides financial motivation for employees to strive for work excellence.
- The company will have lower payroll costs and get an "investment yield" from a truly effective pay-for-performance program.
- There will probably be fewer employees on the payroll if a company pays for performance.
- While job pay will only be average to the market, individual pay may be higher than market average, and payroll costs can be below those of competitors when there is effective pay for performance.
- Pay for performance creates a preferred employer position in the labor market with respect to candidates with a high level of talent.

There are reasons why many pay-for-performance systems have failed and why some people dislike pay for performance. Here are some reasons why pay-for-performance systems have often been opposed in the past:

- Some subordinates receive larger increases than their supervisors.
- A large portion of employees will think that they do less well under pay for performance than under some other system.
- There is a concern that pay for performance may cause divisiveness.
- If performance is the system for paying salary increases, then the supervisor loses discretion, which means that the supervisor may lose some of his power.
- The manager must deal with low performers, and this is often unpleasant.
- If many employees are rated high for purposes of salary increases, then the unit will be expected to perform well or someone may draw negative conclusions about the ability of the supervisor.

- Pay for performance might cause problems in government compliance cases.
- Pay for performance is contrary to some widely held views, such as seniority and entitlement.
- For many reasons, some managers think they need "flexibility" in pay increase decisions. Too often flexibility means pay increases based on favoritism and bias.

These are all issues that will have to be dealt with, but all of them are manageable issues.

More than anything else, pay for performance failed in the past because top management really didn't have a commitment to reward for performance. The result was pay programs that were not designed to reward for performance and an executive group that usually lacked the will to apply such a pay system. I think that without a doubt there will be compelling business reasons in the future for executives to insist on pay for performance and have a commitment to the success of such systems.

Strategic trends are almost always cross currents, and that will be true of fair pay. There will be those who argue for actions that do not pay at market average for jobs and that do not involve pay for performance.

For example, some special interest groups want to impose some types of quotas on pay decisions. Others want the same salary result for some groups or classes; for example, those who favor comparable worth want the same average pay for women as for men, regardless of jobs held or performance.

It would be both fair to employees and good business for the employer to have the pay spread fully match the performance spread. There will likely be more emphasis in the future to achieve that objective.

Expressed mathematically, the percentage of output (amount and quality) actually produced as a percentage of the standard output should be matched by the ratio of the pay received by outstanding performer to the average pay for the job. The performance spread can range from as little as 20 percent in lower-skilled jobs where there is little latitude of action to perhaps 500 percent in some jobs filled by managers and senior professionals.

Pay spread should match performance spread. Data suggest that the potential pay spread matches the performance spread in lower-paid jobs, is insufficient in middle-level jobs, and is more than sufficient in executive jobs.

Extra pay for performance above standard that matches performance spread involves zero cost. If a company pays job market averages and has greater output than other companies, then its pay costs necessarily are lower. If the performance spread represented by greater productivity is as great or greater than the pay spread, then the company gets an investment return.

In work on salary reward for performance, it is important to recognize that three methods are used in business to reward performance and that salary reward is only one. The three basic methods of financial reward for performance are:

1. Salary increases
2. Bonus payments
3. Promotions

Each aspect of pay for performance should be integrated with the other. Salary pay for performance has proven to be the most difficult and will be the area requiring the most work in the forthcoming strategic planning period.

There has obviously been a great deal of experience with salary reward for performance, yet most companies don't do it very well. I have ten guidelines for effective salary reward for performance plans, including such simple rules as having effective performance appraisal information and being able to identify the amount of the increase that is for performance.

In a survey I conducted in 1990 covering more than one hundred companies, not one met all ten of the requirements for effective salary reward for performance and only half met five of the ten requirements. Almost one-fourth of the companies in this survey met only one or two of the requirements.

To have salary reward for performance, you must meet *all* of these requirements. More and more companies will do this in the 1990s; they will be driven largely by executive managers who are determined to increase productivity and achieve greater fairness.

I think that if that same survey were conducted in the year 2000, more than half of the companies would have pay-for-performance plans that met all of the ten guidelines that were listed. Under tomorrow's conditions, pay for performance will be too important, and there *must* be salary reward for performance if there is to be high productivity.

There are many types of incentive pay or performance bonus plans. It would take a great deal of space just to catalogue and describe them, and that wouldn't serve our purpose. The fact is that incentive bonus systems should be applied wherever they are applicable. The know-how and experience exist to do this work well.

There will be pressure for more companies to have effective performance bonus pay plans, and for those who already have such plans to improve them. More and better organizational unit management and available computer technology suggest the possibility of achieving a high level of excellence in performance bonus plans in the future strategic human resources management planning period.

Don't underestimate the importance of promotional pay increases. For most upwardly mobile people, promotional pay increases exceed performance salary increases for a period in their careers. In fact, a promotion pay increase *is* a performance pay increase.

Success Sharing

It seems fair to many that those who create the success of an enterprise should share in that success in some way. This is the logic of success-sharing plans.

There are reasons to think that there will be a great interest in success-sharing plans in the future strategic planning period. Some of these reasons are as follows:

• In a more competitive environment, plans that link the welfare of employees to company success will be favored even more in the future than they were in the past.

• The high pay of executives is allegedly based on company success, and many employees also want a share of the success when they see what this means to executive pay.

• Companies that cut salary levels back from the 75th percentile to average levels may see success sharing as a way to soften such a reduction in pay.

• Some people think that success sharing is a form of pay for performance. To the extent that this is true, all the reasons for pay for performance also apply to success-sharing plans to some degree.

• Success sharing is sometimes thought to be a way to gain a competitive pay advantage without high fixed levels of cost. This is much more true in small companies and in highly people-intensive companies than in most other companies.

• Success-sharing money represents savings, and there will be more support than ever for compensation plans that encourage savings.

• Working people *like* success sharing as long as it does not reduce current cash pay.

• In an era of delegative management and more knowledge workers, success sharing will seem to be more appropriate for the knowledge workers who contribute so much to the company's success. In fact, it may seem unjust not to have these workers share in the success of the company. Therefore, success sharing may be a fairness issue.

These are a lot of reasons for thinking that success-sharing plans will become much more widespread in the future strategic human resources management planning period. Here are some of my thoughts about success-sharing plans that I hope you will find helpful.

Success-sharing plans should always be structured so they represent extra compensation for business results above what is standard or expected. Companies must pay fairly for the job and reward fairly for performance, and there should be no payments from success-sharing plans until reasonable business target levels are achieved. Thus success-sharing payments represent *extra pay* for all employees when, as a group, they are *exceeding reasonable enterprise goals.*

In commercial businesses, success sharing means extra compensation based upon a part of the profits. In not-for-profit enterprises, measures of success will have to be developed. In a hospital, success sharing might be based upon measures of patient care and hospital cost containment. In a school district, success-sharing payments might be partially geared to students' SAT scores, drop-out rates, and grade point averages. Expect success-sharing plans to become widely used in not-for-profit sectors during the next strategic planning period.

The dollar value of profit-sharing and other success-sharing plans doesn't have to be very much in a single year, and it should be expected that there will be some years in which there will be no payments at all because enterprise goals have not been exceeded. Even under these circumstances, however, payments from success-sharing plans can accrue into substantial funds over a number of years.

For example, if payments from success-sharing plans were accumulated from entry into the workforce until retirement, such plans could typically provide more retirement income than either Social Security or most private pension plans. In successful enterprises, values accrued in success-sharing plans could also pay the room and board expenses at college for three children.

Payments from success-sharing plans are important to employees well beyond their dollar values, even though the dollar values can accumulate to substantial amounts. Funds accumulated from success-sharing plans can make practical for workers the achievement of financial goals that would otherwise be impossible dreams.

The effect of success sharing on the attitudes of employee-stakeholders can be impressive if the plans are structured correctly and administered well. There is a consciousness about the company's welfare; about effectiveness, quality, and cost. In many small ways, when there is success sharing, work is done better or different enough to cause better results.

Equal Pay Treatment

As a strategic human resources management issue, equal treatment* has become a major strategic issue, partly because of questions relating to equal pay treatment. Fair pay involves the fairness of the payment as well as the amount of the payment, and there appears to be a lot of unfairness in pay that must be corrected.

About one hundred and twenty million working people in this country do their daily chores very well and usually with difficulty. There are few easy jobs, and the one hundred and twenty million or so who are lucky enough to work full-time all year spend a lot of their working lives doing difficult things. They work an average of almost twenty-one hundred hours doing these things each year. For this, these one hundred and twenty million or so workers get an average annual pay of about $25,000.

This seems to be fair enough until people read the newspapers. Then they read about so many cases that seem to be very unfair. The unfairness is often gross—sometimes grotesque, and it goes on and on.

While there are many cases of unfair pay, they have tended to fall into three categories:

1. Executive pay
2. Electronic pay
3. Regulated pay

The fair pay problems related to executive pay involve substantive issues and perceptions. Working people are among those who overwhelmingly think that executives are grossly overpaid.

---

*Chapter 8, the fourth ranked strategic human resources management planning issue.

For example, there are companies where the chief executive office earns more in one day before his morning coffee break than the average employee in the same company earns in a year. On average, chief executive officers of commercial companies earn almost one hundred times as much as the lowest-paid employee. I know of many cases where the chief executive officer of companies with more than a hundred employees earns more than all the other employees combined.

In fact, executive pay is now running out of control in this country, and the employees know it. Directors in most companies aren't doing their job of controlling executive pay.

I have made recommendations many times about what is needed in executive pay. To have fair pay for executives, either the board of directors or the government must direct and control executive pay decisions. Executives can't be allowed to set their own pay without independent review or control, as most are doing now.

If board members are to manage executive pay, they must at least do all of the following:

• At least one member of the compensation committee must be well informed and experienced in human resources management. Alternately, the board, or at least the compensation committee, must be well briefed on the essentials of executive pay.

• The board must have access to *independent* sources of information and advice, and not be in a position where they get information and advice only from employees and from consultants who are paid by the executive whose pay is being considered.

• Directors must independently set basic policies and guidelines with respect to executive pay, and these policies should be communicated to stockholders.

• Directors must visibly be in control of executive pay, and at their own initiative, directors must make a few specific decisions.

There are few public corporations in this country where the board does any of these four things. There will be major efforts in this area in the next ten years.

Executive pay will be a big issue in the forthcoming strategic planning period. Unless most boards do all of the things outlined above, we will inevitably have more and more government control of executive pay.

The term "electronic pay" may not be familiar to you, but you see cases of it all the time. The technical label for this form of pay is "leveraged pay." Entertainers and sports professionals, for example, are beneficiaries of electronic pay.

The first-round draft choice by the NFL gets a multimillion-dollar contract, not just because of talent or even what people are willing to pay to watch him play in a game. Those megabuck salaries aren't financed just by the purchase price of the tickets. Those payments are mostly financed by television advertising.

You may or may not choose to watch the game on television. But whether or not you do, you pay for it. The price of those big contracts goes into the price of products through advertising, and you pay. By my shorthand math, I figure that each family in this country pays $500 a year for sports stars and entertainers on television, even if they never watch them. It's like a tax.

It's a tax paid mostly by those one hundred and twenty million or so full-time working people who earn about $25,000 a year. The contrast in the pay of working people and the pay of the stars is becoming obscene, and we are all reminded of it every time those megabuck stars go on strike for more millions—to be paid by the working people.

Those working people are increasingly becoming aware of all of this. The feelings run deep. Who knows how it will work out, but it is part of the strategic issue of fair pay.

Employers can't do anything about this. Electronic pay can only be dealt with by Congress through taxation.

Some companies may find some variations of electronic pay in some jobs in their own firm or in fees from service organizations, like legal firms or consultants. If, for example, I prepare material that gets into a computer expert system, should I get a royalty each time it is used—like entertainers get royalties or residuals?

Regulated pay is also unfair pay. That working person earns an average of $25,000 a year because that's what free choice in the market determined, what an employer was willing to pay and what the worker was willing to accept—the best deal he could get. That's all very fair.

But there are others who are now exempt from the free-choice setting of fair pay. As noted, executives set their own pay, with their rubber stamp boards. Unions set pay that is higher than the fair market by sheer power every chance they get—even though there are fewer and fewer unions, partly because many union jobs have been exported. Reports of airline baggage handlers and unskilled auto workers being paid $60,000 a year must seem unfair to people in other companies doing essentially the same work for one-third as much pay.

The public saw clearly just how regulated pay works when the members of Congress voted themselves a huge pay increase in 1989. Regulated pay is, by nature, unfair to working people, and now working people know it.

Who knows what will happen with regulated pay. Only Congress can deal with this problem, but they are part of the problem. Some politicians may discover that it is a hot vote-getting issue. What you know is that those who work in your company know about regulated pay and executive pay and electronic pay. And they think they are very unfair. That's what makes these matters part of the strategic human resources management planning issue of fair pay.

Fair Pay in Benefits

Health-care and retirement plans are themselves strategic personnel planning issues (Chapters 12 and 13). As a strategic issue of its own, health care relates mostly to matters of cost. Retirement issues mostly involve the changing role of private pension plans. However, both involve fair pay issues as do all employee benefits and conditions of work.

The issues of fair pay in benefits that are evolving include:

- Equivalency of coverage
- Equal treatment in benefits
- Employee choices
- Employer obligations

Every class and group of employees should have the same coverage or benefits of proportional value to salary. Differences in benefits should only be based on competitive necessity or the needs of the job. However, some are often favored in the benefits they receive.

Differences in benefits between hourly and salaried workers almost disappeared in the 1970s and 1980s. Differences in benefits for executives will be a big issue in the 1990s, and sometime in the future there may no longer be preferential benefits for executives.

Equal treatment in benefits will also be an issue of fair pay. Employees with children often receive preferential treatment in benefits, but that advantage has been narrowing. The cost of benefits will always be higher for some employees than for others for various reasons, such as age. But the cost equivalency of benefits will be more of a consideration in the 1990s. A dramatic case of this is the increasing popularity of cost-based health-care plans.

An equal treatment issue with regard to benefits will be that some workers get better benefits than others. Some employees don't get some types of benefits like health care, or they can only get the benefit at such a high cost that coverage is not practical. These illustrate a major issue of fair pay in the 1990s.

Flexible benefit plans may popularize employees' choices in benefits, even though the purpose of flexible benefits is to reduce health-care benefit coverage and/or pass more of the cost of health-care plans to employees. These plans will popularize the notion of a choice in benefits, and then employees' preferences in benefits of all types will be factored into benefit decisions more and more.

There is also talk about flexplace and flextime. So the idea of employee choices of conditions is also part of the employee's choice in benefits. The interest in customizing benefits and conditions to the choices of employees and the values of employees will be very high, and communications technology will likely make the input of such choices into decision making very practical.

There has also been talk about an employer's obligation to provide benefits. This is being discussed mostly in terms of health care, as an argument in favor of national health insurance. There will likely be a list of items where there will be serious consideration of an employer's obligation to provide some types of benefits and minimum amounts of benefits that must be provided by any employer.

The Importance of Fair Pay

I think that fair pay is an important strategic human resources management issue. But it is at the head, or near the head, of the *second tier* of strategic personnel issues. Productivity, educational deficiency, delegative management, fairness, managing differences, and special interest groups are in a class of their own in importance as strategic personnel issues. In fact, I would think that these six items in combination are more important than all of the other strategic personnel items described in this book.

However, fair pay is at the top of a group of very important strategic personnel issues. This group of important but not top in importance items includes benefit cost containment and retirement plan issues.

Of course, pay has always been of great importance to employees; the number one satisfier at work by far. As a strategic issue, fair pay is now more important than ever because it is such an integral part of productivity management (Chapter 5) and fairness (Chapter 8).

Fair pay, rather than greed or "pay me now," will be the focus of compensation in the 1990s. It will be the focus of a lot of work and some controversy.

Two items especially will be dramatically changed in the next decade. Effective pay for performance will be widespread, and compensation methods in this area will reach a new level of excellence. I think that salary reward for performance will be a particular subject of attention—and successful work.

The other area of special attention will be the three areas of gross unfairness in pay in society today: executive pay, electronic pay, and regulated pay. These matters will largely be resolved at the political level. Business must factor whatever changes occur into their management practices.

It seems inevitable that two other changes relating to fair pay may occur, and most businesspeople won't like either of them. There will be increasing control of executive pay in publicly owned corporations, and there will be changes in the tax system that put a preference tax on high levels of cash income.

12

Health-Care Cost Containment

Health-care cost containment was a strategic human resources management issue throughout the 1980s and will continue to be a strategic issue through the 1990s. It has been a major cost issue for employers. Now it is also an issue of cost containment for employees as well as a question of health-care coverage.

A lot of work has been done on health-care cost containment in the past. In the years ahead, more hard work will have to be done and even harder decisions will have to be made. By the end of this decade, I think that health-care cost containment issues will be resolved in some manner, and after more than twenty years, the subject will no longer be a strategic human resources management planning item.

A Brief History of Work Done in the Past

It became clear in the mid-1970s that there was a problem with health-care costs. Many analysts use 1974 as a base year and the last full year before aggressive health-care cost initiatives were undertaken.

One early warning indication of trouble in this area (e.g., a current human resources management planning indicator of that time) was that benefit costs were increasing at a rate that was greater than the rate of the increase in payroll costs. The identification of the reasons for this suggested that health-care costs would continue to increase significantly more than payroll costs. In fact, one forecast in 1974 indicated that if health-care costs continued to increase at the then current rate and if payroll trends continued as they were, health-care costs would be greater than payroll costs by the year 2001.

By the late 1970s, company human resources management staffs, consultants, actuaries, accountants, lawyers, and others began to work hard on the problem of health-care cost containment. There was a frenzy of activity during the next five years—and an avalanche of words. In the 1980s, the rate of payroll increases slowed down, but the increase in the rate of health-care costs became even greater—and the problem got worse in spite of all the activity and costly efforts to contain health-care costs.

By the middle of the 1980s, health-care costs were increasing at more than twice the rate of payroll, and efforts to contain health-care costs intensified.

During the mid-1980s, it seemed that employers would try anything. We heard a lot about programs like HMOs, preferred providers, cost-sharing plans, wellness programs, and cost data bases.

Some of the programs seemed to be intriguing, and some were just trivial. But the cost of health care was escalating so rapidly that there was a sense of great urgency and a willingness to consider almost anything.

By the late 1980s, it was possible to look back and learn some things from all those many programs and millions of words. Those lessons are the basis for future strategic thinking.

The fact is that almost all the cost containment in health care in the fifteen year period from 1974 through 1989 was due to higher deductibles and more employee contributions. In essence, the cost containment success of the period from 1974 through 1989 was almost entirely due to shifting benefit costs to employees.

During this period (1974 through 1989), health-care costs increased about tenfold—from roughly $50 a month per employee for family coverage in 1974 to about $500 a month in 1990. Employees absorbed about half of that cost increase, and the employer's payments increased from about $50 a month for family coverage to about $300 a month.

Through higher deductibles and higher employee-paid premiums, the employee's costs on a payroll basis went from an average of less than $10 a month to an average of more than $200 a month. That represented a twentyfold increase in health-care costs paid by employees.

If you added all the programs related to cost-effectiveness, wellness, preferred providers, etc., during this period, they absorbed *at most* $25 of the monthly cost. The managed part of health-care cost containment was about 5 percent of the total cost-containment success over this fifteen-year period.

That is a generous judgment of managed programs for health-care costs, partly because it does not account for management costs.

Nor have we seen yet if there are fallout problems caused by employer-payees who undertook to manage health-care matters.

Those who undertake health-care cost containment activities for the next strategic planning period have a lot of work to do. One clear lesson from the past is that in the future companies should never assign work relating to health-care cost containment to those who sell or service the health-care plans. I also think we should have a better understanding of the factors that caused the rapid escalation of health-care costs in the first place.

Reasons for the Increase in Health-Care Costs

To manage health-care costs properly, we should understand the causes of the increases in costs that have been occurring in the recent past. Most of all, health-care costs have increased because health care has improved greatly over the past twenty years. We are paying more for better health care.

Furthermore, health care is a key part of the third basic element of our economy: personal welfare products and services. In other words, there is much more demand for a variety of health-care services. This greater demand has strained available resources and predictably increased costs rapidly.

In addition to much better health care and the rapid growth of the health-care field, here are some of the other reasons why health-care costs have been increasing at a more rapid rate than payroll costs:

• The pay for some jobs in health care was greatly depressed in the 1970s. That was mostly corrected in the years from 1974 to 1984, but it accounts for a significant amount of the health-care cost increase in that period.

• Large companies went on a frenzy of buying improved health-care benefits in the 1940s, 1950s, and 1960s. This was part of an effort by big companies to have an advantaged position in the labor market by providing higher pay, great security, and superb benefits.

• Malpractice insurance rates have escalated incredibly, and these costs wind up in health-care costs.

• With rapid growth, there have been inefficiencies and duplication of health-care equipment and facilities on many occasions. This is normal in a rapidly growing industry, and there should be less of this in the future.

• As is typical in a rapidly growing business, management in the health-care field has been stretched thin. The deficiencies in management have added to the rise in health-care costs. There has been a great improvement in management in the health-care field, but they still have some way to go.

• There are many "participants" in the health-care field other than those who provide the services—namely, the hospitals and the doctors. These other participants include the payers and the corporate buyers. The interference of third parties has not always been helpful and has itself been part of the increase in the cost of health care.

• Even when health-care costs began to escalate rapidly, a "fringe-benefit" mentality was associated with health care. In the automobile industry, for example, health care costs more than the steel in a car. Yet the UAW continues to demand and management continues to concede further improvements in health care.

• The enormous increase in indigent care has also caused a great amount of the increase in health-care costs for those who do pay. This element of cost could triple in the next twenty years.

These are plenty of reasons for the escalation of health-care costs. Some of these factors will run their course by the year 2000, and that's mostly why I think that health-care costs will be increasing at about the same rate as payroll increases sometime after the turn of the century.

Some factors that cause health-care costs to escalate cannot be controlled by anyone, and they shouldn't be. Patients really want a better quality of health care. Other factors, like adding benefits to health-care plans, should be managed by the employer who provides the health-care benefits, and such matters should be the focus of health-care cost containment during the 1990s.

Strategies for Health-Care Cost Containment in the 1990s

The experience of the past fifteen years with health-care cost containment and an understanding of the basic causes of the escalation in health-care costs should position companies to manage health-care costs more effectively in the future strategic planning period. Each company needs to develop its own action plan, but there are some strategic matters relating to health-care costs that apply to most companies.

First of all, companies can do very little about health-care costs. Looking back, one of the problems was that managers of companies that provided benefits somehow became caught up in the notion that they could contain health-care costs and that they could even manage health care. The employer is just one payer and can't manage health care. Company actions designed to manage health care, however well intentioned, involve meddling in medicine. Cost management mostly involves which medical services are provided and how they are provided. That is a matter of managing medicine, and managing health care is a job for physicians and those who manage the health-care businesses.

Employers are buyers of the benefits provided and clearly have a lot to say about what benefits are covered in health-care plans and what payments will be made from such plans. Some important strategic issues are involved with respect to the scope and nature of health-care benefits provided under employer-supported health-care plans.

During the past fifteen-year period of health-care cost containment, more than nine of ten companies significantly *improved* their health-care coverage. The studies I have seen suggest that while we were struggling to contain the costs of health care, *new* benefits *added* by employers amounted to about one-fourth of the increase in the cost of health-care. It seems like a contradiction to add costs to benefits while trying to contain the cost of benefits.

If you factor out better health care and more coverage in company health-care plans adopted by companies, then health-care costs have, in fact, not increased much more than payroll costs since 1974.

In the strategic period ahead, employers who are serious about health-care cost containment must be very careful not to *add* health-care benefits. In fact, in the next strategic human resources management planning period, it would seem logical that employers will be purging some "frill" items now covered.

It's hard to take out any benefit or think that any health-care coverage is a frill. Clearly, though, things like eyeglasses are affordable, and most cosmetic surgery is not really necessary. No one really wants to say no to any health-care coverage, but if there is to be health-care cost containment in the future, *coverage* must also be contained.

The era of "every benefit" is over, at least for the time being. If we are successful in increasing productivity at the rate of 4 to 6 percent a year, then by the year 2020 we *can* afford to have every health-care benefit known to man covered by an employer-supported plan. For the immediate future, we will have to contain our appetites for more benefits.

In your strategic thinking, don't compare your benefits with "the Joneses" of benefit coverage: banks, the insurance carriers who sell benefits, the government, or companies like IBM. Look at your company's real labor market and your own company's situation.

Your company's real labor market for benefits, including health-care benefits, encompasses private businesses, excluding the 5 percent of those who, for whatever reason, provide super benefits. Get information that is readily available about health-care benefits provided by most employers, not the "Joneses," preferably from local companies or from companies in your own industry.

Remember that you can't compare different companies' benefit costs with any degree of accuracy. I limit all such comparisons to five groupings: average, somewhat better, much better, somewhat worse, and much worse.

As a matter of policy, I recommend "average" or "somewhat below average" general benefit coverage—based mostly on the demographics of the company's workforce. Be sure you consider all benefits, not just health-care benefits. Your company must provide some types of benefits, including health-care benefits, to be fair and competitive, and they can't be "much worse" than benefits paid by other relevant companies. Otherwise the level and specific type of benefits have little effect on your company's ability to attract, retain, and motivate employees.

A sensitive strategic health-care issue that you should also consider is the question of payment for dependent coverage. When health-care benefits were fringe benefits and fringe costs, employers not only added every benefit but every family member as well.

Now there is a question about equal treatment as well as health-care cost containment. Why should employers provide more dollars for some employees than for others, based on the number of dependents they have?

The issue of the equivalency of treatment is another equal treatment aspect of health-care cost containment that must be considered as a strategic issue. The fact is that executives get much better company-paid health-care treatment than other employees. In fact, many companies have supplemental health-care benefit plans just for executives. Many companies have various other benefit programs that are only for executives, and somehow the company pays great amounts for health-care costs, in special ways, for executives, their families, and their friends. This issue is not likely to get much attention from employers in the near future, but it is an issue with employees, and I think there could be a major media expose within a few years.

I think that one other strategic question relating to health-care cost containment involves employee determination.* Each dollar of health-care cost is fungible as far as the employer is concerned. Why not then let employees determine how the health-care dollar is spent—what health-care benefits are provided for whom and what the levels of employee contribution should be. This can be done simply in this age of electronic equipment.

Health-Care Cost Reduction

Increasing numbers of companies will undertake health-care cost *reduction* in the near future, and this issue will be a strategic consideration. Some companies will cut health-care costs by at least one-third in the next ten years.

If your company is going to REDUCE health-care costs, there are only three ways of doing this:

1. Shift costs to the employees.
2. Reduce benefits.
3. Have multiple benefit plans.

All of these involve hard choices, but any significant health-care cost reduction at the company's initiative must come from these sources.

In the past fifteen years, most of the cost containment has been accomplished by shifting costs from the employers to the employees. Looking back, this was done to an astonishing degree. If you had talked about increasing the employees' share of the cost of health care by twentyfold before 1974, no one would have listened, and just about everyone would have believed that such a thing was unthinkable. But it was done because effective actions had to be taken to contain the escalation in health-care costs, and everyone, including the employees, knew this.

Because of all the past increases in the share of health-care costs paid by employees, there isn't much more that most companies can do in this respect in the future. Companies must find other EFFECTIVE methods of controlling health-care costs rather than just shifting still more costs to employees.

One possibility is to shift most or all of the cost of dependent health-care coverage to the employees, if your company hasn't done

---

*This is not the same as flexible benefits.

that already. This would be consistent with the trend toward equal treatment.

If your company hasn't eliminated health-care for retirees, you should consider it. At least, don't extend health-care coverage to future retirees.

Don't overlook the possibility of cutting back on health-care coverage. If nothing else, consider scaling back health-care coverage to the level that existed in 1974.

Some companies have used flexible benefits as a method of reducing health-care costs. Under these plans, you structure the choices so that the combination involves a lower cost. If employees don't use some benefit, like health care, they have that cost charged to them anyway, so the cost is reduced even more. This is a rather indirect way of reducing actual health-care costs; and, in fact, that is usually the intent of flexible benefits as they are structured today.

Those who urge this approach argue that giving employees choices in benefit coverage is the correct thing to do and that employees get more of the coverage they want with flexible benefit plans, even though the overall coverage is less. I don't favor this approach because it seems devious and is based partly on the fact that employees will make the wrong choices. But you must consider flexible benefits as one of the alternatives for reducing health-care costs.

Another approach to health-care cost reduction that I do recommend is to have a two-tier health-care system. One plan (plan A) might be the health-care plan that is now in effect in your company. The alternate plan (plan B) would have lower benefits or would require much higher employee contributions—or some combination of the two.

Those eligible for plan A must also meet all of the following requirements in order to be participants in the preferred coverage:

- They must be in a reasonable weight range.
- They must be nonsmokers.
- They must be drug-free and agree to random drug testing to ensure that they remain drug-free.
- They must be moderate users of alcohol.
- They must have no dangerous hobbies or activities, such as skydiving.

People who do any of the things listed above are poor health risks, and their health-care costs are higher. Plan B is for such people and provides lower benefits at a cost equivalent to the cost of plan A.

By applying this new generation of cost-based health-care systems, a company will reduce health-care costs significantly. Then continue reasonable actions to contain health-care costs—from a lower base.

National Health Insurance

In the future strategic planning period, it is likely that the question of national health insurance will be given serious legislative consideration. As of June 16, 1991, our cut-off date, a bill had already been submitted to the House. By the time you read this there will probably be new legislation on health care. Don't think that this will be the last legislation on health care.

One inequity in the current health-care system is that many working people get unequal treatment with respect to health-care coverage. A minority get full and comprehensive health-care coverage, mostly paid for by their employer. Many working people have no benefit coverage at all. About half of all employees have rather modest health-care coverage, with many types of plans in effect. This disparity in coverage means that there are clear inequities in health-care coverage, and many people think that these inequities can only be corrected by legislation.

An increasing number of employers who have spiraling health-care costs now actually favor or don't oppose the idea of national health-care coverage. National health-care plans will likely never have more support than they will in the next five to seven years.

Because of the possibility of national health insurance, some companies are inclined to do nothing about health-care costs on the grounds that some national health plan will replace all plans anyway. That thinking overlooks three factors. Clearly, the company pays the high cost until there is a national plan. Second, there may never be national health insurance. Finally, if there ever is a national health-care plan, the coverage may not substitute for the employer's plan but might complement the employer's plan.

I don't think there will be national health insurance in this country like there is in Canada. If there is national health coverage in this country, it will most likely complement and not replace private plans.

There is also a possibility that voluntary national health insurance plans will be enacted to provide some type of coverage for individuals or small groups of employees. Such coverage is greatly needed. These changes would probably not necessarily affect company plans, and they would not affect the employer's efforts at health-care cost containment or reducing the cost of the employer's health-care plan.

I recommend that you proceed with health-care cost management actions as if there won't be any national legislation, or that legislation in the next strategic period won't affect your company's health-care plan. This seems to be the most likely event, and it is really the only sensible course to be followed, unless you want to predict specifically what the national legislation will be and when it will be enacted.

Looking beyond the next strategic human resources management period, it is very likely that there will be legislation again and again—and perhaps again. I think that in the longest strategic period (ten to thirty years) there will be no tax-sheltered employer health-care plans. I don't think there will be national health-care plans as they are talked about now. Based on current trends, what I think will ultimately happen is that there will be a nationally financed core plan and then private plans will be available for purchase directly by the person and that some of these will be at least partially tax-sheltered. This type of a national plan will evolve a step at a time; perhaps four steps at a time.

Basic Thinking About Employee Benefits

In the future strategic planning period, those who work in human resources management will have to allocate time to some basic thinking about benefits in general. It's not just the cost of health care or even health-care plans. The basic issue is *employee benefits.*

Employee benefits have grown and grown and now they are a real problem. There were many reasons why benefits were added until they ran out of control. Many people contributed to the benefit mess. However, most of the blame, in my opinion, must be placed on the managers of large companies and those who did benefit consulting.

We must all learn from the past and do some basic rethinking about benefits for the future. Briefly stated, here are seventeen basic matters that I think should be considered in all areas of benefits, including health-care benefits.

1. Managers must change their mind-set about a number of things relating to benefits. Benefits can no longer be thought of as something extra that employees would like and that won't cost the company very much. Benefits must now be viewed as an alternate form of compensation.

2. You should have a total benefit cost control approach rather than dealing with the cost of each benefit item. Don't undertake health-care cost containment by itself; do it in the context of benefit cost control. If basic health-care costs are increasing because health-care benefits are better, improved medical practices might be worthwhile and other types of benefits might be trimmed back or contained to manage overall benefit costs.

3. With respect to benefits of all types, make sure that coverage involves matters of real need and reflects employee preferences. Look carefully at frill benefit items.

4. All employee benefits with a dollar cost expenditure should require employee contributions, with few exceptions.

5. Consider a much higher employee contribution rate for dependent coverage or have employees pay the full cost of dependent coverage. This will be an important equal treatment issue.

6. Never design a benefit or any provision of a benefit just to take advantage of a legal provision or accounting rule. Tax laws change regularly, and accounting rules are just a way of counting.

7. There should be absolute equivalency in benefits at all levels and in all jobs. No benefit or perquisite of any kind should be extended to one group of employees unless it is necessary because of clear and compelling competitive needs or because it demonstrably contributes to more effective work by people in that group.

8. Get employees' inputs on benefits and consider their preferences carefully. However, never give employees choices about benefit packages unless the employees themselves are qualified to make the choices and they have information available to help them make informed judgments.

9. Keep all benefit plans as simple as possible. If the average employee cannot understand the plan, then it is too complicated.

10. Make sure that your company is able to respond to employee questions about benefits quickly and accurately.

11. Never extend any type of benefit coverage to retirees. Once people retire, they are not your company's employees. Actually, many retirees worked for your company for a very short time, and all of your retirees are eligible for Medicare.

12. Always remember that all benefits are part of employee compensation. Each dollar of benefit cost is a dollar of compensation cost just as surely as is a dollar of pay. You can't add benefit costs without diminishing salary costs if total costs are to be the same.

13. A company can measure its own benefits but it cannot really measure the value of the benefits provided by other companies. Comparisons of benefits must necessarily be very rough.

14. Recognize that benefits have little effect on your company's ability to attract and retain. It may be necessary to have a certain type of

benefit to be competitive, but the details of the plan don't affect a company's competitiveness in labor markets very much at all.

15. Develop good information with respect to alternate benefit systems. With computer technology it should be practical to develop models that show the value and cost of alternate insured benefit systems and different benefit provisions.

16. Never treat a proposal for any benefit as an isolated event. One reason why benefits have become so costly is that companies tended to add them like they were decorations on a Christmas tree.

17. Cut back to a minimum the communication about benefits, and rely mostly on your response capability.

Value Payments

Perhaps we must stop using the word "benefits" for things like health-care *benefits*. In spite of what the dictionary says, too often the thinking is that benefits are entitlements or extra payments that don't cost very much. Actually, benefits are an alternate method of compensation. Salaries and bonus payments of all types are cash compensation. All other payments are non-cash payments of value: they are "value payments."

Value payments and cash payments are different methods of paying earned compensation. Many of the problems with benefits generally and health-care costs specifically are due at least in part to our failure to view them as value payments to employees for work performed.

When you think of health-care costs as value payments, for example, dependent coverage would be unthinkable. We don't pay some employees more in salary because they have more dependents, and we shouldn't pay more in value payments based on family size.

When you think of health-care costs as value payments, the escalation in health-care costs necessarily means relatively lower cash pay increases, or a corresponding reduction or curtailment of other benefits, such as retirement benefits.

It wouldn't be useful to carry the philosophy of value payments too far or be too detailed, but we must never forget that benefits are payments—they are part of the total compensation package for work performed.

Value payments exist mostly for two reasons: a benefit is only available (or affordable) on a group basis and/or the benefit is tax-sheltered, which means the employer gets a tax deduction and the employee has no equivalent taxable income. These conditions favor value payments over cash payments; but value payments are still compensation for the employee and a payroll cost for the employer.

It is that view of health-care benefits as value payments rather than entitlement payments that led me to recommend the following:

- No increase in health-care benefit coverage—and perhaps scaling back as required the health-care benefits adopted since 1974.
- Coverage of health-care only for employees, not dependents and not retirees.
- Cost-based multiple health-care plans, with far fewer benefits for those who choose life-styles that provably cause higher health-care costs.
- Inputs of employees in determining value payments (but not flexible benefits).
- A total benefit view.

Addendum

The elapsed time between the first draft of this chapter and the submission of the entire manuscript to the publisher was about six months. During that six-month period it was necessary to revise this chapter twice because of new events that impacted health care.

I mention this because it illustrates a basic aspect of strategic planning. This is a continuous process, and there are continuous changes.

This manuscript was finished on June 16, 1991. It won't take long to get it on the market, but during that time there will be more changes, and some of these might be important. Then there will be a period between the publication date and the time you bought this book. In this time there might be more changes. And finally, there will be a period between the time you purchase the book and the time you read it, and there could be more changes.

All of this is the nature of change, and it is part of strategic planning. I have presented a snapshot of health care at a point in time— June 16, 1991. Actual events, of course, are really like a motion picture.

I could have added this addendum to a number of the strategic human resources management planning items. I chose to do so in this chapter because legislation will probably be passed between the time I finished the manuscript and the time you read it.

13

Retirement Issues

Retirement income for workers is a major strategic human resources management planning issue. Retirement planning involves many strategic questions and problems, and these will likely be resolved in one way or another in the next ten-year planning period.

Not every company will be affected by the pension issue in the future strategic human resources management planning period. This would include many companies that don't have pensions and some that don't have problems with pension plans. However, most companies that have pension plans will have to do some work in this area, and much of that work will require great thoughtfulness.

Retirement Plan Issues for the Employer

The private retirement income system for many workers is crumbling. About one-fourth of all pension plans that existed in 1970 have been terminated; there are about three thousand cases of reversion before the Internal Revenue Service; and about half of the private pension plans now in effect have been changed in some way in the past ten years, almost always resulting in diminished pension coverage.

There are many different cases, but here is a brief description of the issues relating to private retirement plans.

• On the average, employees work for one employer for a little over five years. This means that many of the people who draw pensions from a company will have been with the company only a few years, and the time with the company might have been long before retirement.

• The potential impact of inflation on fixed-benefit plans could be very great. A private fixed-benefit pension plan geared to final pay represents a particularly imprudent risk for a private company.

Double-digit inflation for even a few years could cause severe financial problems for a company with a final-pay fixed-benefit pension plan.

• There is an aging workforce, and for most companies this will add dramatically to the cost and the risks of pensions. By the twenty-first century, an increasing number of companies will find that retirement payments will be increasing at a much faster rate than payroll increases. There will be many cases where the payment of retirement benefits under a company pension plan exceeds the payroll of that company.

• When pensions were being adopted by many companies starting in the 1930s and through the 1960s, it was a way of building "golden handcuffs" into the compensation package and retaining valued employees. But that was in the era of career employees, company loyalty, and twenty-five-year vesting. Those conditions no longer exist, and private pension plans have very little holding power now.

• The regulation of pension plans is burdensome, particularly for the smaller company. The cost of compliance is high, and regardless of efforts to comply, there is a risk of prosecution and litigation. There have been too many cases when an employer made an innocent error and was prosecuted harshly for making a mistake.

• There are pressures for indexing retirement benefits, and this represents a potentially great increase in pension costs.

• In many companies, pensions cost a lot. Some see pension cost reduction as a way to offset increases in health-care costs.

• There are many potential problems in the financing of pension plans. Most plans have been considered adequately financed; and, in fact, many have had surplus funds, which is a basis for reversion. But much of the adequacy of financing is based on the stock market. Perhaps the market will never go down very much, but if it does, large numbers of plans will require more money from the employer—perhaps at the very time when the employer can least afford the additional funds.

• Voluntary retirement is the law of the land. While that hasn't yet affected the financing of pensions, it makes manpower planning more difficult.

• There is a generation of younger workers who have inherited wealth. It is estimated that one-third of all workers have inherited (or will inherit) significant amounts of money and that the amount will average about $100,000. That affects workers' attitudes toward private pensions.

• Congress has made savings much more attractive, and that also affects employees' views about private pension plans.

These eleven problems give employers plenty of reasons to cancel or scale back pension benefits. Such issues make at least a review of pensions a high-priority issue for every company that has a private pension plan. Many companies will be reviewing pension issues in the coming years, and there will certainly be many changes.

Too Old to Work

The pension issue is still the same for employees. The employees' problem is still what should they do for income when they are too old to work.

If we live long enough, there will be a time when our energy declines, our strength diminishes, and our ability to work productively declines. Then the employer must accept less output, reassign the employee to other work (either at the same or reduced pay), terminate him, or provide retirement pay. Pensions have always seemed to be the correct thing to do.

Most workers are covered by Social Security or other federal retirement income plans. In addition, about one in four workers is covered by generous pension programs from his employer. This includes most people who work for the government at any level, executives of most corporations, employees of a few large and mostly smokestack-industry companies, and members of some of the long-time traditional unions. These people, on average, can draw retirement pay from Social Security and from their private pension plan, so their total retirement income is sufficient to maintain about the same standard of life after retirement that they enjoyed during their working years.

At the other extreme, about half of those who work in this country don't get any private pension payment at all. During their retirement years, they are dependent upon Social Security, if they are eligible for it, and their personal savings, if they have any.

Then there is the in-between group, which has a private pension from one or more companies plus Social Security. When Social Security and private pension plan payments are combined with their savings, this group has a retirement income of between one-third and one-half of the amount earned at retirement. Almost one-half of all people of retirement age are in this category.

The in-between group includes many who were once among the privileged group and thought at one time that they would enjoy high levels of retirement benefits. But their companies cut back on benefits or they lost jobs in companies that had generous retirement income plans.

There is thus a great polarization of retirement income in this country. The trend is for even greater differences in retirement benefits. Polarization of retirement income is itself a problem of perceived fairness. For example, it seems fair to ask why government workers, including those in Congress, should have such generous pensions when many others, who fund these pensions with the taxes they pay, have a modest pension or no private retirement income at all.

These considerations suggest a number of things, each of which is important in your strategic thinking about pensions. First, there must be retirement income for people who are too old to work. Social Security payments are, by design, the minimum for sustenance; they are at the threshold of the poverty level for retired persons.

Second, every employer should probably provide at least a modest pension. This should be viewed as part of compensation. This would supplement Social Security and provide a level of income sufficient for decency and comfort.

Finally, it seems likely that the disparity of retirement income will be an issue in the future strategic planning period. This would parallel current concern about differences in health-care coverage.

Pension Plan Cost Containment

In addition to questions about the need for more pension coverage and greater equality of coverage, there are also concerns about future pension costs. The basic issues regarding pensions suggest that a lot of activity will be directed at pension cost containment during this strategic planning period. The potential cost containment and cost-saving dollars from retirement plans are substantial. Pension plan cost containment must include consideration of financial risk management.

There are seven important pension cost containment areas:

1. Plan design
2. Benefit levels
3. Retirement age
4. Investment management
5. Retiree benefits
6. Indexing of pension benefits
7. Employee contributions

Plan design involves policy matters and technical issues. When you work on plan design, a company often needs professional advice and inputs from actuaries.

As far as pension cost containment is concerned, plan design most importantly involves the pension benefit formula. There has been a distinct tendency for more plans to use defined contribution formulas rather than defined benefit formulas, mostly to confine the cost of pensions. That trend will likely continue, and defined benefit plans will mostly exist in the future only in government operations, a few union contracts, and where such pension plan benefit formulas are adopted for high-paid employees.

Defined retirement benefits geared to final pay are extreme risks. They represent imprudent risks and will become very rare in the private sector.

Defined contribution plans can accrue a flat amount each year for all employees or a fixed percentage of pay. It isn't clear that there will be any particular trend in favor of either one of these retirement benefit formulas, and neither one has a cost management advantage.

The question of levels of pension benefits is simply one of amount. For example, if the pension is a percentage contribution plan, then the question is whether 4 percent or 5 percent of pay should be put into the pension plan. In an era of pension cost containment, questions about amounts and therefore costs will be of extreme importance.

A plan that accrued 5 percent of payroll over a thirty-year period would yield a monthly pension for the average paid employee that is approximately equal to payments from Social Security. Alternately, if the money was kept in a fund for the employee, it would accumulate and be sufficient to educate his children and buy an annuity to supplement Social Security payments.

Sixty-five has been the normal retirement age in most plans since the 1930s because that was the average life expectancy of men when Social Security laws were enacted. The average life expectancy today is over seventy-two, so seventy-two might be considered as the normal retirement age. Starting retirement benefits at age seventy-two would be a major cost containment measure and will very likely be seriously considered in the near future.

It's likely that suggestions will be to continue to accrue benefits for workers as prescribed in the retirement formula up to actual retirement, whatever age that might be in each employee's case. The thinking recognizes pension accrual as *compensation* and also places a heavy burden on management for voluntary retirement action.

Such a provision will represent another pension plan cost containment issue.

Early retirement dates and adjusted benefits for early retirement might also be a pension cost containment issue. Employees usually get reduced benefits for early retirement, and these should be at a reduced rate so there is equivalency in total benefits paid per years of work. As part of pension cost containment, companies must consider curtailing early retirement and eliminating preferential payments for early retirement cases that are designed to achieve a reduction in manpower.

Some now think that investment management is the primary method of containing pension costs. In fact, many companies have contributed very little in new cash to their pension plans in recent years and have financed growing benefits and larger retirement groups by better yields on pension investment funds. This was done when the stock market was rising steadily. In the next strategic planning period there will likely be periods of down markets, and then investment management and proper funding will be a major problem of pension cost containment.

Expect that there will be a lot of interest in fund management in the future and there will be keen competition among fund managers. As a cost issue, fund management is very important. My concern is that some pension fund managers have been much too aggressive and that many funds will be in trouble in the 1990s. Then employers will have to contribute large additional funds in the future, the government will have to bail out another fiasco, or pensions promised will not be paid.

It seems inevitable that there will be cutbacks in health-care benefits for retirees. This will probably be necessary when there are more and more retirees whose average time with a company was only a few years. Cutbacks or the elimination of benefits of all types for retirees can amount to substantial cost savings for some companies.

Another opportunity for cost containment will be with respect to increases in pension income for retirees. Upward adjustments of pensions for retirees will be less common, and increases that are made will be more modest.

Indexing of retirement benefits will likely be proposed, partly because Social Security benefits are indexed. Increases in living expenses are a major problem for retirees. The need for indexing private retirement income plans will obviously be very intense in times when living costs are increasing rapidly, and some predict periods of double-digit inflation in the 1990s.

Some companies should also consider shifting more of the cost of retirement benefits to employees. Based on experiences with health-care cost containment, higher employee contributions to pensions may be a major pension plan cost containment action.

We should expect a ten-year period of pension cost containment that will have many similarities to the era of health-care cost containment. The biggest difference in pension cost containment work is there is an opportunity to cancel plans altogether or substantially modify the type of retirement plan in effect.

Rethinking Private Pension Plans

There needs to be a significant amount of rethinking of pension plans and basic pension questions. Every company must rethink its pension situation. In general, however, circumstances have changed a great deal since most private retirement plans were implemented, and these private company pension plans must be viewed in the light of these changes.

The retirement income issue is postponable, and many companies *will* postpone it as long as possible. In fact, for most companies, there is no reason why the issue must be addressed this year instead of next. Postponing pension reviews may result in manageable matters becoming major problems.

There are some good reasons to postpone work on retirement income issues. For one thing, these are complex issues. Pension reviews take a lot of time and cost a lot of money. It is very easy to make a mistake or follow poor advice, and the cost of mistakes can be very high.

A company can't postpone reviewing pensions forever. I think a better course is to review pensions in manageable steps. Start with a strategy review of pensions.

A strategy review identifies items of major vulnerability that need attention. A strategy review can also sketch out an ideal planned retirement approach for your company so your company can work toward that ideal a step at a time over a number of years. This type of a review can be done in a few days by well-qualified people.

In your work you must recognize that pensions are not the factor in employee compensation that they were in the past. Not many years ago, the conventional wisdom was that a company had to have a pension plan to attract and retain the number and quality of persons required to run the business and achieve business goals. That is much less true or untrue today.

Also keep in mind that for almost seventy years pensions in this country were based largely on a particular three-tiered concept of retirement planning. The three tiers first evolved as government-mandated pensions (Social Security), supplemented by private pension plans, and personal savings. Private pensions are thus conceived to be an integral part of employee retirement planning. A great deal has changed since this thinking first evolved in the 1930s and shaped retirement thinking for the next three decades.

Social Security was considered to be the base, and coverage was very broad. Social Security was to provide the minimum income necessary for sustenance, a level of income that would support a retired couple somewhere around the poverty threshold.

Private retirement plans were supposed to supplement Social Security. Combined benefits from Social Security and private pension plans generally were supposed to bring retirement income to levels of decency and comfort. It was thought that an overwhelming portion of workers would be covered by private pension plans.

Personal savings from all sources were the third tier of retirement income. In the original three-tiered concept of pensions, retirement income from savings was thought to be for the fortunate few and was not really an integral part of pension planning.

The three-tiered thinking still exists and probably will for a long time. But circumstances have changed, and the role of the three components of employee retirement income has also changed. Social Security will not likely be changed in the next strategic planning period. But the cost of Social Security will be a major problem. The contribution rate will be increased substantially sometime in the 1990s and again in the first decade of the twenty-first century.

Private pension plans are going through the many changes that have been described. Most workers won't have retirement income from private pension plans at all, or they will receive small amounts from private pensions.

Savings have become the dominant part of retirement income. The enhanced role of private savings in retirement income has been largely due to the government through the establishment of 401(k)s, Keogh plans, and IRAs. The result is that personal savings from tax-sheltered plans alone cover more employees and account for more retirement income than private pension plans.

Workers also have more savings in the form of investments and property ownership. As noted earlier, we are now a generation of workers who at some time receive inheritances. The inheritances mostly come from home equity and workers' parents' pension plans. Personal savings and inheritances often provide more retirement income to more workers than private pension plans do.

Today Social Security mostly continues to perform its role as a broad base of retirement income. But savings replace private pension plans as the most basic supplement to Social Security. Fewer workers have the advantage of retirement income from private pensions, and private pensions, on average, pay relatively less than they did not many years ago.

In your pension review, you must consider the likelihood of future government action. In the 1990s, there are a number of possible legislative changes with respect to retirement plans, and directly or indirectly, these will affect pension planning in every company. Here are some of the most likely government actions in the area of pensions:

• Social Security contributions by employers and employees will be increased. Some funding for Social Security may also come from general tax revenues.

• The government will be under great pressure to lighten up on the regulations and the reporting of private pension plans. The present rules and regulations are much too burdensome and almost force small employers to cancel their pension plans.

• There will be a lot of "tax the rich" considerations in terms of Social Security payments and perhaps preferred taxes on pension premiums above certain amounts.

• The government cannot be in the business of guaranteeing pensions for workers. There will be talk about cutting the amount that is guaranteed. As things stand now, we are inviting another savings and loan situation and are almost encouraging irresponsibility in pension decisions of various types.

• There may be substantial penalties for cancelling plans unless there is a substitute plan of equivalent value.

• The practice of permitting reversions may be made more difficult.

Recommendations for Company Action

In spite of the problems and issues relating to pension plans, there seem to be compelling reasons why every company should have a pension plan. It is a fact that employees still become too old to work, and when they stop working they must have income.

Of course, many people have savings when they retire and some have inherited wealth. But many workers retire with nothing but Social Security unless they are part of a company pension plan.

Most of those who are among the working poor (Chapter 19) will retire with no pension other than Social Security and private retirement plan income.

I urge companies to have modest pension plans that are company paid and that will supplement Social Security. I suggest that about 3 or 4 percent of employees' earnings should be paid into funds by the employer in years of reasonable company success with no employee matching. I don't think companies have strong reasons to do much more than this, but there are compelling reasons why every company should contribute a modest amount each year toward employees' retirement income as part of the compensation of those employees.

Companies will likely continue to encourage employee savings in the future, and this can be viewed as part of retirement income planning. The business purpose of thrift plans of all types is not provably great. The cost of supporting IRAs or 401(k)s is not great either. I always urge companies to consider some employee savings plan, and any contribution from the company to any of these savings plans should be modest and a form of success sharing.

The last piece of pension planning that I recommend is what I call the omega pension. It is the last of the pension pieces—the icing on the cake.

Omega plans would always be financed by the success of the employer. There would be no employee contributions, other than the employee contribution to the success of the company. The omega plan should be structured to provide retirement funds only in the event of substantial company success. With extraordinary success, very large retirement funds would be accumulated for employees.

In a company with a stock price growth that is significantly higher than inflation, an omega fund that is a phantom stock plan would yield substantial retirement benefits, even if the company contributed modest amounts.

Based mostly on known needs, current situations, and demonstrable trends, it seems that a new generation of pension plans is emerging and that they are in three parts: basic plan, savings, and the omega plans. Here is a specific plan that was recently adopted that serves as an example of the new generation of pensions.

- The base plan was a fixed contribution pension plan, and the company contributed from nothing to 4 percent of compensation, depending upon profits.
- The company had a 401(k) plan and a thrift plan, and the company's contributions to both plans were based on profits.

- The third plan involved phantom stock grants to individual accounts, financed by purchase of the stock by the company on the open market.

The omega pension in this case involves no cost to the company whatsoever, except for the cost of the use of the capital. Phantom stock retirement benefits would potentially have very high values. Note that this plan is a non-qualified plan with serial vesting. This can result in substantial holding power.

The Future of Pensions

It seems almost certain that pension problems will be a future issue for many companies. In the strategic planning period that is ahead, you can be reasonably certain about the following:

- There will be Social Security, and it will continue to be indexed.
- There will be continued turmoil with respect to private pension plan features.
- There will be further legislation relating to provisions in private pension plans, most likely resulting in full portability and possibly some form of indexing of private pension benefits.
- By the year 2000, there will be about half the number of private pension plans that there were in 1970. Two-thirds of those who work will have no private retirement plan coverage where they work.
- Some form of a national retirement income plan in addition to Social Security will be considered. This will be an individual account, true pension system available to all workers whether or not they are covered by any private pension plan.
- The disparity of pension coverage will be a big issue. Some employees receive lifetime income after twenty years of work. Others receive only Social Security after a lifetime of work.
- There will be major efforts at retirement plan cost containment.

Pensions are part of our society and our economy. There is no possibility of turning back in any respect. The only issue is how retirement income plans will be provided, not whether they will be provided. All of this will be even more true in the future because of an aging population and, therefore, an increasingly higher average age of voters.

14

Chronic Labor Scarcity

Pockets of chronic labor scarcity will exist for at least the next ten years, and some of these areas of scarcity could still exist thirty years from now. We are confronted with the problem of *chronic* labor scarcity, not the shortages of workers normally associated with periods of prosperity and full employment. These *chronic* labor shortages are due to a basic ongoing imbalance between the demand for workers and the supply of qualified workers.

In strategic planning work it is necessary to remember that the importance of a planning item for business generally may not be the same as it is for your organization. For many companies, labor scarcity may turn out to be the number one issue in the future. Other companies will experience no chronic labor shortage at all.

Notes About Labor Scarcity

When you consider the issue of labor scarcity, remember that there are chronic shortages of talent in the economy overall and in some labor markets generally. Any one employer, however, would need only a small portion of those who are available. In fact, some individual employers may have a surplus of talent that is generally in short supply.

Some companies have learned to manage chronic labor scarcity well. Their ability to meet their labor needs gives them a competitive edge over other companies that do not manage chronic labor scarcity well.

There have been many cases of labor scarcity in the past. In addition to the shortages of workers in periods of high levels of business activity and low unemployment, there have been many instances of shortages related to new industries (e.g., nursing homes) and new technologies (e.g., computer programs). These work shortages were temporary and were resolved with time when more people were recruited into jobs where there were openings, often from other fields of work.

The forthcoming strategic human resources management planning period will be different from anything experienced in the past because there will be basic and chronic shortages in whole classes of workers, not just those who fill a particular job or a family of jobs. This scarcity of whole classes of workers will be related to basic shortages in supply, and the shortages can only be resolved over a considerable period of time.

We have never dealt with chronic labor scarcity in a broad class of workers. A growing population and waves of immigrants always supplied our manpower needs in a quantitative sense. The infrastructure, such as education, was always sufficient to assure the proper quality as well as number of workers. The supply and the infrastructure are now both inadequate to meet the needs.

We count unemployment (the scarcity of jobs) but not unfilled jobs (the scarcity of people to fill jobs). This is because we experienced unemployment and thus labor surpluses but not labor shortages, at least not chronic labor scarcity.

In the future period of chronic labor scarcity, there will be a need to measure labor scarcity by counting in some way unfilled jobs. Individual employers could begin to count labor scarcity now, and I recommend that we do this.

It is sometimes difficult to measure labor scarcity. In some cases, jobs do not remain unfilled but rather are filled by those without proper qualifications or talent. Filling needed positions with underqualified people only partly meets the issue of labor scarcity.

Normal or acceptable unemployment in the economy or in labor markets is generally 5 to 6 percent. Anything less than this standard is labor scarcity associated with business cycles. Anything more than 6 percent is socially undesirable and is an economic loss as well as a human cost.

Normal or acceptable underemployment (labor scarcity) is *zero*—or not more than 1 percent. Underemployment of more than 2 percent seriously erodes productivity and competitiveness. Underemployment of as much as 5 percent could cause economic turmoil and some business failures. At the present time in this country, my guess is that chronic underemployment is almost 3 percent.

Unemployment should never be a problem for an individual employer. Unemployment is a terrible problem for employees as well as a social and community issue, but it is not necessarily an issue for any one employer. Employers don't keep count of unemployment for business or operating reasons, although I think this should be done for human relations reasons and as part of a broader measure of business success.

Underemployment or chronic labor scarcity *is* an individual company problem; and underemployment is not directly a social issue. Basic data about underemployment must be kept by organizations. These broad measures could be determined for the economy by sampling data from employers.

Two broad types of chronic labor scarcity will be important. One is a general shortage of knowledge workers. This is basically caused by a combination of exploding technology that requires more and more knowledge workers and, at the same time, a deficiency in the educational system.

The other general area of chronic labor scarcity exists at the lowest skill levels. This area of labor scarcity involves in part the growth of the third leg of our economy, which mostly involves health care, recreation, personal conveniences, and services. Shortages of unskilled workers also involve some basic social and political issues.

In both types of labor scarcity—knowledge workers and unskilled workers—long lead times are required to solve the shortages. The scarcity of knowledge workers, for example, requires a massive improvement in the quality of public education. Even if that happened quickly (and it hasn't happened at all after a dozen years of talking about it), it would still take a dozen years to get the better educated people from kindergarten through the twelfth grade.

Chronic Scarcity of Knowledge Workers

The chronic shortage of knowledge workers is a classic case of a supply and demand imbalance. In an increasingly technological work environment, the demand for knowledge workers has increased enormously. The supply of knowledge workers has not nearly kept pace with the demand, largely because of the deficiencies in education (Chapter 6).

The Problem of Scarcity of Knowledge Workers

There is a shortage of well-educated talent in the physical sciences and in other recognized academic disciplines. There are also shortages of well-educated people with know-how in business disciplines.

In fact, we have been in a period of talent scarcity for knowledge jobs for a long time. Cases of a chronic scarcity of knowledge workers in a number of work areas go back to the 1970s. Companies were then experiencing longer lead times in filling certain knowledge positions. These jobs were often ultimately filled with people who were underqualified.

There isn't a generalized shortage of knowledge workers. What is happening now and which will continue in the future strategic human resources management planning period is that there are *pockets* of labor scarcity in some categories of knowledge work. In the future there will be more pockets and the shortages will be deeper.

While the chronic scarcity of knowledge workers is mostly due to educational deficiency, there are other contributing circumstances. Most of all, some companies don't use talent well, and that has seriously aggravated the problem of scarcity. For example, some companies have used scarce knowledge workers in areas of work that could be performed by others with backgrounds that are not in scarce supply. An example would be engineers assigned to administrative work or mathematicians assigned to personnel work.

Remember that for any one employer, there isn't necessarily a scarcity of knowledge workers in any category. Even the largest employer uses only a portion of knowledge workers in any category. The basic issue of chronic scarcity of knowledge workers for any single company is, therefore, to get what is needed from a generally short labor supply—leaving other employers with an even greater shortage.

Also keep in mind that there is a great deal of transference among knowledge jobs. For example, if there is a chronic shortage of chemists in a specialized field, then those who work in related fields of chemistry might be recruited. There are also many opportunities for dealing with pockets of labor scarcity in knowledge categories by transferring people from related fields and giving them special education and training. Skill in discipline transference or "career crossovers" will be important in the next strategic planning period.

Chronic labor scarcity among jobs requiring education in recognized academic disciplines is mostly quantitative; for example, there are not enough engineers. In the business disciplines, scarcity is mostly qualitative; for example, they don't know enough or they don't know the right things.

The competitive advantage used to be with the company that had facilities that were as good or better than its competitors and utilized these facilities better. Excellence of management often meant better management of facilities. Today and tomorrow, the competitive advantage will more likely go to the company that has more human talent and is as good or better than its competitors in getting the best talent and using that talent the best. The competitive advantage in the future may be with the company that has the least shortage of talent in areas where there is chronic scarcity and manages in the best way possible the talent it has.

In every respect, the scarcity of knowledge workers is a major issue for many companies that requires serious attention now. Superficial actions or complaining won't accomplish anything. The successful company will often be the one that recognizes that human talent is the unique asset of the firm, identifies where there are talent shortages, and then takes aggressive and innovative actions to deal with this issue.

Recommended Answers to the Scarcity of Knowledge Workers

Chronic scarcity of knowledge workers is a manageable problem. Here are specific recommendations for dealing with this issue, action steps that have been used successfully in many cases.

Start by identifying specifically where there are talent shortages in your own company. Be specific about your company's needs. Don't just look at unfilled jobs; consider the quality of the people who are holding the jobs now. Only when there is a concrete and clear understanding of a company's specific problems can you take corrective actions that are likely to be effective.

You should count underemployment and keep an index for your own company. In addition, once you identify knowledge jobs that are subject to chronic scarcity, monitor underemployment, turnover, and performance levels separately for these jobs with intensity and great care.

Before you start affirmative actions to deal with chronic labor scarcity, get a sense of how well your company is now doing in attracting and retaining scarce knowledge workers. If you can, find out how well other companies are doing and what actions they are taking to deal with scarcity.

If you know a qualified consultant, consider using him for advice and problem-solving work in dealing with chronic labor scarcity. This type of assignment should involve modest fees and might only cost a few thousand dollars. If the work is really contributive, your company will get a return on that expenditure within a few months. This is very high-value consulting, but only a few are qualified to do this work.

Most of the specific affirmative activities that successfully dealt with the problems of labor scarcity of knowledge-level workers used one of nine methods. The techniques are listed in Exhibit 14–1. A few comments about each of these actions follow.

Exhibit 14-1. Methods of dealing with chronic labor scarcity.

Technique	Usefulness Rank	Usefulness Index*	How Often Used	Ease of Approach	Cost
Better Recruiting	1	100	Almost always	Easy	Moderate cost
Leveraging Knowledge	2	67	Often	Fairly difficult	Low cost
Increasing Productivity	3	60	Seldom	Difficult	May be costly
Manpower Management	4	55	Often	Fairly difficult	Moderate cost
Compensation	5	50	Often	Easy	Very costly
Crossovers	6	40	Sometimes	Modest	Costly
Reducing Turnover	7	30	Sometimes	Difficult	Low cost
Redesigning Products	8	20	Seldom	Very difficult	Very costly
Redesigning Jobs	9	10	Seldom	Easy	Low cost

*This index is provided only to present my judgment of relative importance in general.

The technique most often used to deal effectively with chronic labor scarcity was simply to *improve the effectiveness of recruiting*. Most companies have allowed their recruiting effectiveness to deteriorate a great deal over the years. Perhaps that was inevitable in a period in which there was generally a labor surplus or adequate supplies of workers in all important categories. In an era of pockets of chronic labor scarcity, recruiting, at least for jobs in short supply, must achieve a high level of excellence.

Make sure your recruiting is as good as it reasonably can be and that it gets a sufficient amount of high-level attention. Check to make sure that you use the technologies of recruiting that are available at this time, including computer-aided personnel and expert systems designed to help in the selection of candidates.

In recruiting scarce knowledge workers, the most important single activity is the search. Your recruiters must find and interest qualified people. Second in importance is setting realistic specifications. Recruiting for scarce jobs is difficult enough without adding to the problem with unnecessarily high specifications or unneeded requirements.

Be sure you also evaluate the effectiveness of the selection process. Effective recruiting is not just a matter of getting qualified people to apply for a job. Effective recruiting also means doing an effective job of selling candidates and then selecting the most appropriate people. In your recruiting evaluation, also include performance evaluations of new hires versus people replaced.

The second most useful method of dealing with the scarcity of knowledge workers is by *leveraging knowledge*. This involves organization, systems, and practices that are designed to make optimum use of scarce knowledge workers, so it is a practice that is likely to be used a great deal in the future.

A company can leverage knowledge in many ways. This can involve simple networking, a project organization, or making high-level knowledge people internal consultants. Leveraging knowledge may also be done with complex expert systems.

It is mathematically provable that *greater productivity* reduces the number of workers needed in an operation for a given volume of activity. If a company has fewer jobs, it will have fewer job openings to fill. Then recruiting costs will be less and recruiting effectiveness can be greater—even if somewhat more effort and cost are expended to fill jobs that are scarce in the labor market. Thus productivity improvement is another way of dealing with labor scarcity.

Productivity management methods are often very difficult to apply in the knowledge areas where there is a chronic scarcity of qualified people. That first means that a company should put its best talent and best efforts at managing productivity. In jobs where there is chronic labor scarcity, be particularly sure that you follow the proper methods of productivity management (Chapter 5).

Next in importance in dealing with labor scarcity among knowledge jobs is *manpower management*. Excessive manning levels are a waste of talent, and that is a tragic error in job areas where there is a scarcity.

Some large companies have a tradition of hoarding talent. They have traditionally recruited more talent than they needed, created work for them, overpaid them, and then applied retention pay plans to retain them. The idea was to have an inventory of talent and keep it tranquilized until it was needed.

At the very least, keep basic manpower management information. For example, make sure your company produces relevant data about the effectiveness of the managers of personnel in recruiting, selection, and retention; and give that information to every manager. Accountability data like this makes the managers of personnel more effective in manpower management.

Another essential manpower management activity involves the determination of proper staffing levels. Companies will be developing reference information from experience, analysis, and modeling about the correct number of people required when there is a chronic shortage.

Compensation management is another method of dealing effectively with chronic labor scarcity. When a company uses higher pay to make a difference in recruiting and dealing with labor scarcity, it must raise pay 20 or 30 percent. Few companies can afford to do this for all jobs.

However, companies can adopt a selective pay premium strategy in a few job categories. Even a company that suffers the most from chronic labor scarcity among knowledge workers shouldn't have more than 5 percent of its jobs in the category of labor scarcity. If the company paid 30 percent more for 5 percent of its jobs, it could pay a percentage or so less for the rest of its jobs and have no incrementally higher compensation costs.

Applying pay premiums successfully is difficult and companies often have problems doing this. Because of chronic labor scarcity, multiple pay strategies will be worth considering.

Another compensation action for dealing with labor scarcity involves pay retention devices. When there are only pockets of chronic labor scarcity, specific pay retention actions for those jobs and those individuals are appropriate. This may even include retention bonuses.

Crossover transfers have already been noted. Constantly look for areas where transfers can be made into labor-scarce jobs from jobs with an adequate supply of workers and jobs that are relatively easy to fill from the outside. Crossovers are worth considering, even if there are substantial training costs, if they effectively fill jobs characterized by chronic labor scarcity.

Basic human resources management practices can help you deal with issues of chronic labor scarcity in knowledge jobs. If your company *reduces turnover* among jobs where there is labor scarcity, that can be a very effective measure. In labor-scarce jobs, a lot of preventive work is justified. Pay progress and quality of supervision are two particularly important areas to monitor. Your field personnel people should know well all the employees in labor-scarce jobs, to the point where they have a good idea about which of them is likely to leave the company.

Another action for dealing with chronic labor scarcity among knowledge workers is to *redesign products or services* to eliminate the need for such scarce jobs or to require fewer people in labor-scarce jobs. This has been extremely effective in many cases.

Having replacement modules rather than providing service is an example of redesigning products and services to reduce man-

power needs. Expect major efforts in this area with respect to knowledge jobs throughout the 1990s.

There are also cases where *redesigning jobs* is an effective method
of dealing with labor scarcity. For example, this is a method that has
often been used in engineering work. Jobs were redesigned so that
technicians and draftsmen could do work that was formerly done by
the engineers.

Management has many tools for dealing with chronic scarcity in
some knowledge jobs. For whatever it's worth, in every case that I
have known or been involved in over the past ten years, the company was successful in dealing with chronic labor scarcity among
knowledge jobs.

Labor Scarcity in Unskilled Jobs

There is also chronic labor scarcity in unskilled jobs. The labor scarcity problem here is concentrated mostly in service industry jobs,
such as those in motels, fast food restaurants, contract cleaning, and
recreational parks.

Estimates of labor scarcity are difficult to make in unskilled jobs
as well as in knowledge jobs but for different reasons. In the case of
unskilled jobs, part of the equation of the shortage involves the fact
that some facilities are never opened because of labor scarcity; jobs
aren't created because they can't be filled.

Labor scarcity in unskilled jobs also has the problem of quality
measures. Companies report that many of the lowest jobs are filled
with marginally performing employees.

The Problem

No one really has good data on labor scarcity in unskilled jobs,
but it numbers in the millions. Forecasts of further shortages vary,
but all forecasters agree that there will be a greater chronic labor
scarcity in unskilled jobs in the future.

Like the shortage of knowledge workers, the shortage of unskilled workers is due to a basic imbalance between supply and demand. In the case of unskilled workers, the greater demand is
mostly from the growth of service businesses. The limited supply is
due to entitlement payments, various personal handicaps, upward
mobility, social values, and the problems of the inner cities.

There are differences of view about whether entitlement benefits are too high and whether entitlement payments should be
geared more to a willingness to work. But the fact is that the pay for

working in unskilled jobs, after deducting taxes and the cost of working, is very little more than what is paid under entitlement programs. At the unskilled level, the increment of pay for working is little more than $1 an hour. Whatever your views, the level of entitlement payments compared to the pay for unskilled jobs is an important factor in labor scarcity.

Many who might want unskilled jobs can't be used because of handicaps. This may be a physical handicap or illiteracy. Either way, there are thousands of unskilled people who are unemployable unless they get special education or special treatment.

Upward mobility causes shortages in the lowest levels of jobs. It is good business and socially desirable to train and promote high performers among the ranks of the unskilled even if it involves a lot of training costs. But that creates shortages of qualified people to fill unskilled jobs. Data I have seen suggests that upward mobility may, in fact, be the largest single cause of shortages of unskilled workers.

If a person doesn't move up, then it is easy for him to become discouraged and frustrated. A career of working as a housekeeper or dishwasher is not very rewarding. Many people do it, but sooner or later they may chose entitlement payments or another activity. That is one of the social values contributing to the scarcity of unskilled workers.

There is also a whole underclass of people in this country who have never worked and who probably never will. There are, in fact, third-generation welfare families. Their choice of life without work adds significantly to shortages among unskilled workers.

The chronic shortage of unskilled workers is also due to the fact that the unskilled jobs are not located where many potential candidates live—namely, in the inner cities. The conditions are terrible for locating new businesses in the inner cities. The costs are very high, public education is inadequate, crime is rampant, and there is potential destruction of property at any time. These conditions have brought to a halt the movement of new businesses into the inner cities in this country, but that is where there are so many people who could fill the unskilled jobs that are in short supply.

Recommended Actions

Four methods will be widely used in trying to deal with labor scarcity in unskilled positions. I think these are the only likely alternate methods companies will be able to use in the future. These are:

1. Redesigning products or services
2. Compensation actions

3. Recruiting among the unemployed
4. Immigration

The principal method of dealing with the scarcity of unskilled labor in the past has been the redesign of the product or service to eliminate the job. Examples are self-service gas stations and the elimination of ticket handlers at some theme parks. With respect to labor scarcity of unskilled workers, redesigning products or services is the first action for a company to consider.

An important variation of redesign is modeling. Modeling uses computers and the techniques of expert systems to determine the various forms of organization and manpower configurations for an operation. These models may indicate a way to eliminate unskilled jobs, or they may show a way to redesign jobs to justify higher pay for some or all of the lower skilled jobs.

Compensation actions can be a big help in dealing with labor scarcity in unskilled jobs. If a company pays $7 an hour instead of the minimum wage, it may find that all unskilled jobs can be filled. If many companies paid $7 an hour, then it is very likely that many workers would come into the labor market from among the chronically unemployed.

Benefits may have a special value in recruiting and retaining low-paid employees. A company can offer benefits that are not otherwise available to these workers.

The third method of dealing with chronic labor scarcity among unskilled jobs is to recruit from the ranks of the underclasses and the chronically unemployed. To do this, a company must pay an amount significantly more than entitlement payments. A company must also develop special skills in recruiting and screening the chronically unemployed.

I have been in meetings with personnel persons from large, well-regarded companies in the hotel and recreation businesses who concluded that it was not possible to recruit from among the chronically unemployed. I argued then as I do now that it can be done. But only a few companies had been successful, so it appeared that my optimism was unfounded—until two years ago, when free enterprise took over.

There are companies in the business of recruiting people who are on welfare. They have been successful in making placements, and 80 percent of the people recruited are still working. Free enterprise does it again!

If your company is having difficulty filling unskilled jobs, hire one of these recruiting firms. If you are a big enough company, perhaps they can teach you how to recruit from the underclasses.

If you can't eliminate the job, pay more, or find new labor pools, and you must have the work done, then one of the other possible answers is immigration. There are those who predict massive immigration, primarily to deal with the problem of chronic labor scarcity in unskilled jobs. If immigration doesn't work, then export the job or go out of business.

A Manageable Problem

Pockets of chronic labor scarcity will be an issue for a very long time. For example, there will be pockets of scarcity as long as there are major deficiencies in public education and as long as the inner cities are economic wastelands.

However, the issue of labor scarcity is very manageable. Nationally, or even regionally, the problems of the chronic scarcity of knowledge workers and unskilled workers are very difficult. An individual employer, however, can solve these problems within months—and usually at a very low cost.

Chronic labor scarcity is a very manageable strategic human resources management planning item. Therefore, scarcity is a business opportunity for the employers who learn how to deal with pockets of chronic labor scarcity.

Clearly, some strategic human resources management planning items are more manageable than others. Issues like productivity management, delegative management, fair pay, and retirement are very manageable. At the other extreme, issues like educational deficiency, equal treatment, and the demands of special interest groups are very difficult to manage. Chronic labor scarcity is probably more manageable than any of the other human resources management planning issues.

15

The Impact of Technology on the Work Experience

Technology is plainly changing conditions of work. These changes can be observed and are experienced in the workplace.

The changes caused by technology impact the work experience in a number of ways. In my opinion, such changes, in combination, are a strategic human resources management planning issue of some importance.

There are a dozen ways in which increasing technology is affecting the work experience. Before identifying technology's effect on work, a few general comments about its impact are relevant.

At this time, it may be sufficient to be aware of the fact that technology is significantly impacting the work experience and to identify the specifics of how technology at work affects the work experience.

It may be that the capacity of people to change fully matches the rate of change. Then the effect of technology on the work experience might be interesting but it would not prove to be a relevant strategic human resources management planning item.

Keep in mind that technological changes don't happen with one great leap forward. In most cases, technology changes the work experience in many ways over a period of time. Most changes would not be noticeable in the short run and would certainly not be major events in a single year. Computers, for example, were first used in business after World War II, so that's almost twenty-three hundred steps to today, if you count each week as a step.

Also recognize that the overall time period between the introduction of some major technology and its broad use is generally very long; sometimes there is a thirty-year strategic planning cycle. That means that changes in the work experience because of technology may cover a number of generations. What first generation workers see as great and disruptive changes may be perceived by third generation workers as the normal conditions of work. I am still uncomfortable with PCs, but my grandchildren use them like I used pencils.

In my work I have identified about a dozen ways in which technology is affecting the work experience. Each of these items is summarized in this chapter in a random order.

High Tech–High Touch

One of the fashions of the day is to say that technology requires high touch. The saying is "high tech–high touch."

But there has always been a need for high touch at work. So a better phrase might be "higher tech–higher touch." In fact, however, higher technology automatically brings higher touch in most instances.

Higher touch means personal contacts and personal relationships as contrasted with lonely work or interacting only with machines. However, I don't know any higher technology jobs that are devoid of personal contact. Knowledge work inherently means some interpersonal relationships.

Technology has brought delegative management, and that is higher touch than the programmatic methods it generally replaces. Technology has brought smaller units and smaller scale operations, and this also means higher touch. Technology includes communication technology, and that also means higher touch by far.

There are high-tech jobs that involve little contact with others. But at the same time there are also many jobs in automated factories, offices, and warehouses where there is little personal contact.

It isn't really certain how much personal touch is desirable at work. There are no studies and no experiences to determine the optimum amount of personal contact required at work, either for personal satisfaction at work or to assure excellence of work. So we don't really know how much "touch" is appropriate. We do know that technology automatically brings higher touch, which is one way in which technology impacts the work experience.

Job Enrichment

More technology at work means the use of more knowledge. The use of more knowledge generally means more diversity of work. More diversity also means job enrichment. In a number of ways, higher technology results in job enrichment.

Not many years ago, job enrichment was considered to be an important subject in human resources management. Some large companies even had job enrichment specialists and separate departments to do this work.

In the industrial age of machine-controlled work, more machines meant more routine and repetitive work. Work became methodized beyond the endurance of the human nervous system, and that required job enrichment. Personnel experts worked to restructure jobs, modify conditions, and added work elements to enrich jobs.

As a field of work, job enrichment never amounted to much, partly because the most routine jobs were eliminated by computers and robots, and technology automatically enriched many other jobs.

Coping With Choices and Stress

In twenty short years, we have come from a period of boredom and a need for job enrichment to a world of higher technology where the problems involve coping with choices as well as changes. Too many choices rather than the boredom of mindless repetitive, routine work will be a problem of personnel in the future planning period.

Some companies are now focusing their attention on stress that are due partly to the tensions and pressures from choices relating to work.

I think that the management of choices by workers is a key new part of the job of managing personnel. But this is an evolving area, and there is much to be learned and much to be done.

As we learn to make choices better, stress should decline. New generations of workers will likely be able to deal with stress about as well as previous generations, even though the conditions of stress will be different.

Better Conditions of Work

Another way in which technology impacts the work experience in a significant manner is with respect to working conditions. Generally, higher technology automatically results in improved working conditions in many ways.

In very general terms, higher technology turns skilled hourly jobs into salaried technician jobs and unskilled jobs into more skilled jobs. Higher technology often turns repetitive clerical work into worker-controlled machine operation jobs. Sometimes higher technology turns unskilled jobs, like clerical positions, into administrative jobs.

In most cases where there is greater technology, the conditions of work become less routine, cleaner, less noisy, less physically demanding, less dangerous, or some combination of these. Almost always, distinctly higher technology of work results in noticeably improved conditions of work.

Better working conditions go with distinctly higher technology, partly because of the nature of the work involved in high-technology work and partly because such work is typically higher in value, justifying a higher cost for better conditions. In higher-technology work, the cost of things like facilities and equipment becomes relatively less expensive when compared to the payroll for professionals.

Some argue, in fact, that the cost of better conditions is modest and that the effect of better conditions on the productivity of professional workers in technology operations is very great. That seems plausible, but it has yet to be proven beyond a reasonable doubt.

As you consider the impact of technology on the work experience, keep in mind that the essential point is that high technology automatically results in better working conditions. This happens because of the nature of the work and it doesn't have to be created artificially.

Less Travel

For some people, new work resulting from higher technology has meant more travel, but for others, more technology has meant less travel. On balance, it would seem that over a long period of time there is net less travel with higher technology.

In the future strategic planning period, the trend toward less travel will likely start to accelerate, and there will be a further net decline in travel because of greater technology. For example, people will increasingly be communicating through computers. There will be teleconferencing and closed-circuit television. Even basic communications devices such as VCRs will reduce the need for travel.

Technology makes it more practical in more cases to move information rather than to move people. Instead of bringing sales representatives from all over a region into the sales office, they can get information electronically at their different locations.

In the future, we will be transferring more jobs to where people are located rather than just transferring people to where jobs are located. Less travel also includes less relocation of personnel.

Less travel will mean less commuting for many people. One futurist predicted a cottage workforce where vast numbers of employees would work at home. That never happened and very likely never will happen on the grand scale that has been predicted. But there will be a significant growth in the amount of subcontract work, and some of this will be done by people working at home or in a facility that is closer to their homes.

You can't always say that less travel is an advantage. For some employees, more travel is desirable; for most, travel is a disadvantage; and for some, it is a terrible disadvantage. On balance, there will be less travel in the future because of technology, and more workers will see this as having a positive effect on their work experience.

More Pay

Technology affects pay. More technology always means that more knowledge is required, and in unregulated labor markets, this usually means more pay. Higher pay is another result of greater technology.

The impact of technology on pay is statistically obscured because pay is the result of cross currents in the marketplace. For example, many jobs in the smokestack industries have been lost because of new technology or uncompetitiveness with foreign operations, and many of these lost jobs were high-paid jobs. In addition, as the "service" industry has grown dramatically, more low-paid jobs have been created. These are the changes that are most visible and most reported in the media.

Greater technology is happening every day just about everywhere, and the media can't report such undramatic events. However, when you look at the experience of business overall, higher technology almost always means higher pay, and average net pay has increased constantly in this country for many years.

Because of chronic labor scarcity in technology work and the resulting shortages of qualified people, pay for knowledge work is being leveraged up, and this is indirectly due to technology. Labor scarcity also makes it cost effective to upgrade and train candidates for technology jobs, extend career ladders downward, and redesign jobs to leverage technology that exists in a company. All of these factors result in more pay for more people.

Work Security

In the world of the factory environment, which has dominated our thinking in the past, work security meant freedom from being laid off. Job security meant having enough seniority so that a cutback in production would not affect a person. Work security meant freedom from worrying about plant shutdowns—which meant layoffs for everyone regardless of seniority. And if all else failed, work security meant severance pay and unemployment payments.

In technology jobs today and in the future planning period, work security will increasingly mean that the overwhelming majority of knowledge workers can get another job. In most areas of knowledge work (not just in areas of chronic labor scarcity), even the average worker in technology work always seems to be able to get another job, usually in the same geographic area. Better than average workers will find many opportunities.

Technology has been blamed for a loss of jobs. In fact, technology means many more new jobs and benefits and greater security. Technology means new areas of work in the new technology fields.

For knowledge workers, technology has meant many job opportunities. Technology has increasingly enhanced the ability to get another job. On balance, technology improves work security.

Safety

Technology is affecting safety at work. This is another way in which technology has impacted the work experience.

Technology has helped to improve safety engineering. Technology has automated many of the routine mechanical jobs that had safety problems. This also enhanced safety. In many ways, advanced technology has made more jobs safer.

Some express concern about the unknown effects of a lot of the new technologies. In terms of what we do know, technology has greatly increased safety at work in a number of ways.

Multiple Careers

Increasingly, employees will have multiple careers. This will involve more than a job change or a change of employers. A career change isn't just a change of work in a field, such as engineering to engineering sales or accounting to financial analysis. A career change means from accountant to dentist or from underwriter to salesman.

In a career change, there is a distinct change in knowledge disciplines. That usually requires some formal education and training. Normally, it would take years of work to become qualified in a new field after a career change.

In the past, a change in careers has been a rare occurrence. Very often, a change in careers was voluntary, e.g., it happened after a person had succeeded in one career and had saved a sufficient amount of money to pursue some other area of interest. Career changes will be common in the future.

For many, a change in careers will be imposed by technology. In the twenty-first century, as many as a fourth of all knowledge workers may change careers at least once, and the principal cause will be new technology obsoleting other technology.

Many people will have no choice about a change in careers. They will have to do it. The alternative would be permanent technological unemployment.

The consequences of a career change for the employee are profound. Career changes are traumatic and usually involve long periods when income is lost or severely reduced. Those forced to change careers because of technology will experience major difficulties and may experience a substantial loss in income.

For some people, a career change may mean a fresh start. A career change may mean moving to the career of choice.

For employers, multiple careers in business will mostly mean a cost. The cost will be related to outplacing some workers, reassigning others, recruiting some workers, and considerable amounts of education and training.

Dealing With Change

Technology means change and often extremely rapid change. Part of the impact of technology on the work experience will, therefore, involve coping with change.

Change at work involves far more than new products, methods, and practices. Change also means doing work differently.

Technology will mean that work changes. Work changes may be frequent and dramatic. Changes will increasingly be the only constant in work life.

There will be many new uncertainties because of change. People will have to learn to deal with change. In a sense, individuals as well as companies will have to "manage change," or more accurately, manage their lives at work in an environment of change.

Changes resulting from technology will thus have a mixed effect on the work experience. More workers will have to learn new ways and new things during their entire careers. There will be fewer cases where the worker will know what to do because he has done it before. But the work will be less boring and more challenging.

Mystery

Greater technology generally means that we know less and less about the work environment. Workers use a lot of machines and equipment in this technology era, but they often have little if any understanding about how many of them work. Therefore, technology has brought a lot of mystery into work, and that changes the work experience.

Not many years ago, education provided sufficient knowledge in all disciplines so that a knowledge worker understood the technologies at work. Well-educated people understood how things worked. They understood about machines and leveraging and mechanical things and physics and electricity. Today a lot of work is a mystery. For example, most people who work on computers don't understand how a computer works.

Understanding the technology at work was a positive factor in work conditions. It was also helpful because such knowledge usually meant that the worker understood enough to ask the correct questions and he could understand the answers.

Now education is a sampling of the existing disciplines and knowledge areas. You can't learn enough in college or in postcollege educational experiences to have a basic understanding of all discipline knowledge. For some people, this unfamiliarity detracts from the work experience and at times affects productivity management.

Working With Strangers

Relationships with other workers are different in a world of technology. Not many years ago, most people knew everyone at the office or the shop and had known them for many years. Now we spend a lot of our time working with strangers. That changes the work experience.

Working with strangers means privacy. For those who value privacy, technology will generally mean more satisfaction at work. For many people, however, the fact that you know casually those at work may detract from work.

The casualness of working relationships is part of the shallow roots at work that is matched with loose ties with family and community. We are increasingly becoming strangers everywhere we go.

Technology tends to bring more small-scale operations into being. This means fewer people at work. And that can mean fewer working relationships, although smaller groups tend to grow close in a short period of time.

There are those who think that the shallow relationships at home and in the community make workers seek closer ties at work. In a social environment of shallow roots, some workers may seek these closer ties even though there are fewer people or less frequent contacts with work associates. It may be part of the future challenge for human resources management professionals to nurture closeness among workers who do not work with each other for long periods of time or on a continuous basis.

Identification

Workers used to know what their work unit did and had at least some idea about how that fit into the overall operation of the company. Today that is much less true or untrue. Technology tends to isolate workers and work groups and erode identification of one person's work with the ultimate product or service.

Today there are many specialized fields of work and many specialized jobs in each. That's part of the inevitable result of higher technology.

Working people often want an identity—an identity for themselves and for their group. There is an interest if not a need to know where we fit into the whole picture—and what difference we made. Technology may often diminish identity and create isolation.

Recommendations for Company Actions

A substantial amount of material was published in the last decade about the impact of technology on the work experience. Some of that material was helpful, some was entertaining, and some was misleading. But technology is clearly affecting the work experience.

Exhibit 15–1 identifies the thirteen ways in which I think technology is affecting the work experience. You may think of other ways in which technology has impacted the work experience in your own company.

Look first at the impact of technology in terms of whether it improves or diminishes the work experience. Exhibit 15–1 indicates

Exhibit 15-1. The effect of technology on the work experience.

	Impact on Work Experience		Impact on Work Effectiveness	Manageability
	Positive	Negative		
More pay	+6		No Impact	High
Job enrichment	+5		No Impact	High
Better work conditions	+4		Unclear	High
Higher touch	+3		Moderate Plus	High
Less travel	+2		Plus	Moderate
Work security	+1		Unclear	Moderate
Safety	0		Unclear	Moderate
Working with strangers		−1	None	Low
Mystery		−1	Negative	Low
Identification		−1	Negative	Moderate
Multiple careers		−2	Negative	Low
Choice and stress		−2	Unclear	Moderate
Dealing with change		−3	Little	Moderate
	+21	−10		

my judgments of these issues. You can make your own decisions. On balance, I think technology has substantially enhanced the work experience.

Also consider the impact of technology on work effectiveness. Clearly, technology makes possible the improvement of productivity. In this instance, the question is whether each item of change in the work experience affects productivity and how much. Generally, the change in the *work experience* from technology has little provable effect on productivity; and more often than not, when there is an effect it is negative.

Finally, consider the manageability of the impact of technology on the work experience. Every item is manageable, and a few are highly manageable.

I think that there is a need for more understanding about the impact of technology on the work experience. But special studies or projects may not be needed. We will learn from experience. If we have good networking and communication, then the evolving changes in conditions resulting from technology can be managed well, a step at a time, as the changes occur.

Be careful that you don't overmanage the relationship between technology and the work experience. People don't change much, but they adapt and adjust with amazing ability. Don't try to *change* people when people will *adapt* to a working environment of change and technology. People also adjust to technology in different ways, and the company's way of adapting is not likely to accommodate many workers.

It is natural for social scientists and psychologists to place heavy emphasis on work attitudes, work satisfaction, and causes of dissatisfaction—often with little regard for issues relating to the effectiveness of work. These people often have support for their "research" and have the time and the inclination to publish. In the past, their views may have been too influential on personnel thinking and personnel practices relating to the impact of technology on the work experience.

The 1980s also saw the emergence of popular books on business and personnel, some of which were best-sellers. These were usually entertaining, written by those who were mostly novelists. They focused on attention-getting items, including the impact of technology on the work experience. The entertainers were usually wrong, but they were widely read.

Those in human resources management will need all of the *correct* and *usable* information and support they can get about the impact of technology on the work experience. But don't confuse the volume of the material or its entertaining nature with value. I think that companies should be alert to the problems of technology and listen carefully to their employees.

Essentially, you are not going to hold back technology, and you don't want to. You are not going to change people's attitudes and feelings. A company can help people adapt to changes, but evidence from the workplace suggests that employees are adapting well without help or interference from their employers.

16

Employee Owners

Employee stock ownership plans have been around for many years, and at one time or another, most companies with publicly traded stock have had employee stock ownership plans of some type. Today, two-thirds of all companies that can have employee stock ownership plans have them for a broad class of employees. Ninety-eight percent of all companies with traded stock have at least some employee stockholders.

Current trends and developments suggest that there may be much more stock ownership in the future and that before very long employees might be the largest block of shareholders in many companies. In fact, in many companies, the employees as a group could own enough stock to have effective control.

This is twelfth on the list of planning items, so it isn't a megatrend. In fact, some in the field of personnel don't think that this item should be a planning item because, in their view, the evidence is not convincing. While there are clearly questions about the likelihood of employees becoming the largest block of stockholders, employee stock ownership was included in my human resources management planning list because of the profound consequences of such an event.

There is a possibility that workers will be the owners of American business. The result of such ownership would be mind-boggling—it would virtually be a revolution. Even if there is only a one-in-four chance that employees could become the majority owners of company stock in even one of four companies, it would be such a profound change that it should be a human resources management strategic planning item. I think the probabilities are realistic that this is what will happen.

Advantages of Stock Ownership

Because there has been a lot of experience with employee stock ownership, the place to start to evaluate this planning item is to review that experience. The values of employee stock ownership have been substantial.

Experience with stock ownership plans provides compelling evidence that when employees own company stock they will take more of an interest in the company and feel more like participants in the business. Greater employee identification with the employer has proven to have a positive effect on company operations. It also makes sense that if employees have their money invested in the company, they will care more about the company.

Don't expect stock ownership or any stock ownership plan to motivate employees directly. Stock ownership plans are *not* incentive compensation. Ownership creates an interest in the welfare of the company and more concern for work excellence but is not a direct motivation. Ownership plans don't create a direct incentive, but they do create more of an "our company" attitude.

The sale of stock to employees has other advantages. Stock ownership plans represent a source of equity capital. Employee ownership can be a low-cost method of equity financing, and employees tend to be stable and supportive investors. Employee stockholders can also be a force in resisting unwanted takeovers.

As owners, employee stockholders are more likely to favor legislation or other proposals or actions that support the company (their investment) and oppose anything that would disadvantage the company.

Stock ownership by employees has a communications value. For example, when employees own stock, they are much more likely to read company publications like the annual report.

Stock ownership has values to employees. In any stock ownership plan, there are some advantageous features. Then the employees acquire stock on some favorable basis.

Ownership of stock in the company you work for may enrich somewhat the work experience. Employees like to have ownership, although, of course, they like ownership best if the stock does well.

Stock ownership can have a great value in meeting the personal estate needs of employees. From a stock ownership plan in a growing and successful company, an employee can accumulate sufficient capital to take care of his children's education and supplement his pension to create a style of life in retirement that is equivalent to the one enjoyed during his working years.

Renewed Interest in Employee Stock Ownership

A substantial resurgence of interest in employee stock ownership is now underway. During the next strategic human resources management planning period, many companies will consider adopting some form of employee stock ownership.

Here are the reasons why I think there will be great interest in employee stock ownership in the forthcoming strategic human resources management planning period, presented in a random order.

• New employee stock ownership plans have been developed, and new features for existing plans have been introduced. These new plans and new features will make widespread stock ownership more practical.

• The increasing number of higher-paid knowledge workers indicate the likelihood of broader stock ownership. Knowledge workers are higher paid and have a greater ability to save.

• There is a strong interest in a higher rate of savings in this country. The low levels of savings that have existed are due partly to the absence of good investment opportunities for working people. Employee stock acquisition plans can be designed to be an excellent employee investment. This fact suggests that there might even be legislation to facilitate the use of new employee stock ownership plans to encourage savings via stock ownership.

• With greater delegative management, workers will have more opportunities to impact the company's welfare, and that argues for those workers owning significant amounts of company stock.

• Employee stock ownership can be an important source of equity capital. This is particularly important to small companies with more narrowly traded stock and less access to capital markets. These are the companies where most of the employment growth is likely to occur in the 1990s.

• Employee stock owners can be a powerful force in preventing unfriendly takeovers. Such features will be much desired in the future.

The widespread interest in employee stock ownership will generate more work on developing new and better employee stock ownership plans. New types of stock ownership plans will be explored, and that work will probably be successful. I think that there will even be ownership plans in privately owned companies and not-for-profit organizations.

As you think about employee stock ownership, evaluate the plans in the light of decreasing company loyalty, the absence of strong golden handcuffs in compensation plans (such as pension plans), and the era of shallow roots. Under these conditions, other methods of bonding employees to the company would seem to be more important, and stock ownership would seem to be more valuable than ever.

This seems to me to be a compelling collection of reasons to think that there will be a substantial increase in employee stock ownership plans of all types. If that conclusion is even partially correct and there is a significant trend toward more ownership of stock, then companies will have more experience with such plans. That experience plus the normal "stampeding crowd" effect is what makes me think that the movement to stock ownership plans will be very great, and that by the turn of the century, American workers will be the largest single class of stockholders in American businesses.

Stock Ownership Plans

Employees may become owners of company stock by having part of their compensation paid in stock, by stock award plans, by the use of stock to fund compensation plans, or by purchasing the stock. Companies often have more than one type of compensation plan that results in employee stock ownership.

Compensation Paid in Stock

An example of earned compensation paid in stock would be bonus plans that involve payments of some of the amounts under the plan earned in the form of stock. That stock is often restricted for a time, so an employee must retain ownership until the stock vests. Equity stock ownership plans that involve the acquisition of stock from earned compensation are only practical in higher-paid positions, and that is usually less than 5 percent of all employees.

Awards made under contingent compensation plans are usually paid in stock. These involve awards only for achievement in excess of budget and personal objectives. These plans generally apply to all levels of managers and knowledge workers. Future deferments can be for many years. The compensation paid in stock under contingent compensation plans can involve more than 5 percent of the outstanding stock.

Stock Award Plans

Stock options are an example of stock award plans. One basic purpose of options, in fact, has always been said to be that such plans result in stock ownership by manager-employees. Restricted stock plans are also stock plans that result in stock ownership throughout the period of restriction.

Stock award plans, such as stock options, are really appropriate for high-level managers (usually 1 or 2 percent of all employees). However, large amounts of stock are reserved for these plans. Under options plans, 1 percent of the outstanding stock is typically used *each year* for granting options.

Whether options result in substantial stock ownership depends upon the period of time before the options are vested and whether executives retain the stock after exercise. Vesting in many companies is very short, and many executives liquidate the stock after exercising, often helped by stock appreciation rights. Nevertheless, executives own an average of almost 5 percent of all outstanding stock, and more than half of that resulted from stock award plans of some type.

The Use of Stock to Fund Compensation Plans

There are a number of stock award plans that apply to all employees or an entire class of employees. Usually, the payments are in the form of the employer's contribution to thrift, success-sharing, or retirement income plans.

In some cases, stock contributions to thrift, success-sharing, or retirement plans are made to individual accounts. In this case, the employees own the stock directly. In other cases, the amounts contributed by the employer go into a fund, and each employee has a beneficial interest in the trust.

All such payments represent extra compensation to the employee, often on a tax-sheltered basis. Therefore, there is never a loss of after-tax income as can be the case with the purchase of stock.

The stock used to finance compensation plans can result in substantial stock ownership by employees. All contributions from an employer that could legally and prudently be made in the form of stock can result over a period of time in an amount of employee-owned stock that is one-third of payroll. This would mean employee ownership of more than 10 percent of all company stock. That would make employees the largest block of stockholders in most companies. Ten percent ownership is usually considered to be effective control.

If you add up the number of shares owned by employees from all of these sources, then it is very practical for employees to have a controlling interest in a company, even without the stock owned from stock purchase plans. In fact, some companies have financed going private with the stock owned by their employees that was acquired because of compensation paid in stock, stock award plans, or stock used to fund compensation plans.

Stock Purchase Plans

Finally, there are stock purchase plans where employees actually buy stock with after-tax earnings. The stock is usually purchased directly from the company.

The problem with most existing stock purchase plans has always been the potential decline in the value of the stock after it was purchased by employees. When employees use after-tax income to buy stock and the stock declines in value, employees lose money and hold the company accountable. This creates employee relations problems.

It may not seem logical that employees hold their employers accountable when the price of their company's stock declines, but the employees often reason that the company would not offer them stock purchase arrangements unless the company thought they should buy it; they think their employer encourages them to purchase stock by adopting the purchase plan.

Many lower-paid employees cannot afford losses in their after-tax savings. The stock acquired under company purchase plans often represents most of the savings of lower-paid employees.

Because of the risk of loss under stock purchase plans, employers have developed many new types of stock ownership plans. Many of these new purchase plans provide a safety net—a maximum amount the company stock could decline before the company would offer to repurchase it from employees. Other plans provide a discount in the purchase price or company matching stock to minimize or immunize employee losses. Most recently, a few companies have granted options to all employees or most employees, which is another form of a discounted sale.

The problems with all of these discount purchase arrangements, regardless of how they are done, are twofold: there is a great cost exposure, and the discount doesn't really solve the problem of employees' loss of savings. The more the safety provision adopted for employees, the greater the potential cost. Before you consider any safety provisions, calculate the cost. Whether by discount, floor price, or options, the cost of the purchase safety practices can be enormous.

Employee stock ownership plans (ESOPs) have encouraged employee stock ownership on a tax-favored basis. ESOPs are subject to various regulations by the government, and a limited amount of stock can be used for stock ownership by employees under an ESOP.

The single advantage of an ESOP is a tax advantage. This has the same effect as a sales discount. But the essential problem—the risk of loss to employees—with the purchase of regular common stock still exists.

Many companies are also exploring new methods of encouraging employees to own more company stock. The most promising plans by far are the new employee class stock plans.

Under an employee class stock plan, a company issues a class B stock that is sold only to employees. This stock would only be traded between the employees and the company. The company would sell the stock to its employees for cash. Employee class stock can also be granted to employees in any type of a plan where common stock is used, including estate-building programs and pension plans.

Employees could sell the stock back to the company for cash at any time using the same valuing system. In fact, employees are *required* to sell employee class stock back to the company if for any reason the employee leaves the company.

This stock would not be traded on any market. It would be transacted between the employees and the company on some formula basis. For example, the employer might sell and buy the stock at current book value.

Many variations of employee class stock are possible. These variations would involve such questions as voting rights, dividend payments, and the right to convert to common stock.

New types of employee class securities are being developed. One is a convertible bond. Another is a convertible stock. I also expect that different types of basic securities might be developed and that there will be more legislation to encourage more employee stock ownership.

Employee Stock Ownership

Employee ownership is one of only a few of the twenty-four human resources management planning items in this book based on more than observable current trends reasonably extrapolated into the future. With respect to this item, there were other factors that seemed to justify special treatment. One of these was that employee stock ownership may be a defense against unfriendly takeovers. Second was the fact that plans have been developed that deal effectively with the major problems experienced with stock purchase plans in the past. Finally, I think these plans may become major items even though they are not a clear current observable trend because they will serve the national purpose by substantially increasing the amount of savings in this country.

The idea that workers would be the principal owners of business in this country is very significant. Even the possibility that this could happen would reasonably make "employee owners" an important strategic human resources management planning item.

When employees own a controlling portion of shares, what does that mean in terms of the management of the business? If the directors shape policies for the benefit of shareholders, they will necessarily then focus more on employee performance and capability.

In my opinion, employee ownership and the effect it would have would be highly favorable. In an era of rapidly increasing technology, the workers—particularly knowledge workers—largely "own" the business anyway.

In high-technology work, knowledge is the only real unique asset. But knowledge does not belong to the company; you can't patent know-how—only the results of know-how. People possess knowledge. People can use the knowledge they have or refrain from using that knowledge in any way they choose. Employees own knowledge. In a high-technology world with delegative management, people really own the business. So if they also own the stock, that seems to be natural.

There are many reasons to consider employee class stock plans, and they have been outlined. At least take a day to understand and consider this possibility. Listen to ideas for implementing employee class stock.

A very compelling case can be made for using employee class stock as at least part of the company's contributions to success sharing plans in particular. It is hard to think of reasons why any company would not use company stock in matching grants. It is difficult to explain why many companies do so little matching with company stock.

If there is any reason why some matching cannot or should not be in common stock, then use company bonds or company notes. Not-for-profit organizations can use company debt certificates as their method of company matching in extra pay plans for employees.

If you combined the stock acquired in appropriate management compensation plans with stock acquired under the plans for employees generally, then it would be very practical to have employees with a controlling interest in their company. If there is such a thing as a typical or average company, then through stock plans of all types and some employee stock purchase plans, the employees could own a clear controlling interest. If there were also an employee class stock, then the employees in combination would own more than half of the company's stock.

Today and during the immediate future, I recommend that every employer consider doing three things:

1. Use company stock to fund thrift, success-sharing, and retirement plans to the extent permitted by law.
2. Use stock in management compensation plans as an *incentive*.
3. Explore employee class stock.

I think that much greater employee stock ownership is a very exciting opportunity. If many companies supported employee stock ownership, then this item could easily turn out to be one of the top strategic planning items.

17

Restructuring the Organization

The thirteenth strategic human resources management planning item involves organizational change. In my opinion, restructuring the organization is vital to the success or survival of many companies. Restructuring will impact many organizations. Most working men and women will be affected in some way by organizational restructuring. There are reasons to think that just about all privately owned companies with more than a hundred employees will go through a convulsion of reorganization in the future strategic human resources management planning period.

Notes About Organizational Change

I am very specific in my predictions about the restructuring of organizations. The hierarchal organizations that generally exist now will be dismantled. The span of management will at least triple. In many companies, from one to four organizational levels will be eliminated entirely. The number of organizational units will at least double.

Furthermore, there will be multiple organizations. In the future, companies will have a number of interrelated organizations, not just one.

Some well-known business authors have characterized the new organization as informal and chaotic, and that is wrong. In every necessary way, organizations of the future will be as real, as specific, and as orderly as the organizations of today. The organizations will just be different, and they may seem to be complex to some people.

Restructuring the organization will often take place a step at a time, so the changes won't always be dramatic. As we become experienced and skilled in working with the new organizations, they will seem to be very natural and not really difficult to deal with. The total elapsed time between the first organizational changes and the new organizational structure may take as little as three months in some companies and as long as ten years in others.

The reasons for thinking that there will be massive restructuring of organizations are based on observable trends, but the link between observed conditions and restructuring is not inevitable. There are many current observations to rely on, and in combination they seem to me to be very pervasive.

For example, as noted in Chapter 7, a changed organization and greater span of management are essential for effective delegative management. Delegative management is in the process of happening, and so greater span of management seems inevitable.

In fact, hierarchical organizations were part of the apparatus of programmatic management. As business moves to a more delegative style of management, that apparatus would logically be dismantled.

Furthermore, technology will make the new organizations more practical. For example, with computers and communications technology, it will be very practical to establish, understand, administer, and communicate with multiple organizations. Whether that means we can have two organizations or two hundred organizations is yet to be demonstrated.

Another observable reason why there will be great restructuring of the organization relates to productivity. This is the productivity era, and executives will be preoccupied with greater productivity and lower costs. You can get far greater productivity and much lower costs by restructuring the organization.

There are, in fact, observable events which indicate that restructuring is already underway. Some large companies have already eliminated one level of their organizations. Consultants are once again involved in large projects in the area of organizational structuring. There has been a surplus of middle-managers, which is mostly due to increasing the span of management that has already occurred.

Don't expect to see all operations go through organizational restructuring in the same way or at the same time. Some innovative and leadership companies are into restructuring now. Others will only restructure if it is absolutely necessary. And some organizations, such as the various branches of government, may not restructure at all.

Organizational structuring work has always been a way to describe one facet of the process of management. Specifically, organizational structures identify the work done by units and people and how units normally work together. These reasons for doing organizational structuring will be just as important in the future as they were in the past.

Work on restructuring the organization will require some rethinking of the basics. Organizational structuring has always involved identifying the parts of the business and how they fit together. The ability to do this in the future will be much greater, and the organizational descriptions will always be up to date because of electronic methods of keeping organizational information.

These organizational pictures provide a basis for organizational analysis. It will be possible to do all types of analyses on computers. In fact, software programs and models will be of great help in this work. Such capabilities will greatly enhance the usefulness of organizational structuring.

In the past, organizations were changed from time to time, and each change involved a major disruption of work. In the future, organizational changes will be more frequent—almost continuous. But each change will be targeted and generally affect few people. Organizational changes will then be less disruptive.

In the past, organization also took on a personal and social purpose in many companies. Like pay grades and titles, the published organizational structures showed who was most important and which jobs were more valued than others. Organization became a public display of ego. There is a danger that such tendencies will be even greater in the future because of the communication capability.

Organizational work also became a handmaiden of compensation work. Organizational levels became an important determinant of salary levels in many of the most widely used job evaluation plans. As more companies price jobs directly by market systems, this should be less of a factor in organizational work.

It was popular to do planning that related to how the organization would have to evolve with a changing business. This was often called organizational planning. This organizational planning work, in turn, was part of manpower planning and some career pathing activities. With computers, this type of manpower planning should be extended greatly.

These few notes won't make anyone an organizational structuring expert. However, it seems clear that there is a need for a substantial rethinking about organization and that there are many new capabilities for restructuring the organization. This is what is significant for strategic human resources management planning.

We are very early in the learning curve of this rethinking about organizations: the analysis, structure, and planning of the organization. However, the new thinking has already resulted in a basic change, and there will continue to be major changes in organizational structuring ideas and concepts during the 1990s.

So far, the basic rethinking of organization has mostly resulted in the following:

- Focusing on increasing the span of management
- Creating less hierarchical organizational structures
- Creating more organizational operating units
- Using guidelines for organizational work

The Span of Management

The span of management refers to the number of people *managed* (not overviewed) by one supervisor. It involves the number of workers the manager makes decisions about: hires, fires, pay increases, performance appraisals, etc.

You can measure your span of management simply enough by examining the organization and looking specifically at those who approve or effectively recommend personnel actions.

Among salaried jobs today, the average span of management is three. That is, each manager of personnel manages an average of three people.

The span of management *should* be at least *ten*. Ideally, the span of management should be twenty. This is a basic issue, an issue that affects the excellence of management. The span of management significantly affects the productivity of the workforce.

A large company with ten thousand salaried employees that has a span management of three would have ten levels of organization, and companies of this size now almost always have ten levels of organization. If the span of management were seven, then there would be six levels of organization. If the span of management were twenty, there would be four levels of organization. Therefore, one consequence of a low span of management is a very hierarchical organizational structure. A high span of management creates a flat organizational structure.

With a low span of management, there are inevitably many managers of people. In a company with ten thousand employees and a span of management of three, there would be more than three thousand managers of people. This is an enormous number of people to select for management and then train and monitor.

Most importantly, however, a narrow or small span of management means that each person is managing very few people. To be a good manager, a person requires a body of knowledge about human resources management, plus specific knowledge about the company's human resources management practices. It is inherently cost-ineffective to spread that required knowledge over the management of three people. Just to keep up to date on necessary knowledge in the field of personnel takes many hours each year. Clearly, that is cost-ineffective if the know-how is then utilized to manage only three people.

Recognize that the time cost of know-how in managing personnel is fixed. A manager needs to know about as much to manage three subordinates as he does to manage ten or twenty. Part of the overstaffing of American businesses—and the need for rightsizing—is a failure to recognize this basic fact.

The span of management is a very important issue. Broadening the span of management can have an immediate and substantial impact on improved business results. A broader span of management will eliminate *levels* of management. A broader span of management means fewer managers, and a much lower cost of management. A broader span of management should contribute to increased work effectiveness, better organizational communication, and a capability for quicker reactions.

But there are problems in broadening the span of management. The current span of management has been determined in part by separate functions or activities, e.g., quality control and industrial engineering. Broadening the span of management requires grouping or linking operations. Broadening the span of management also necessarily means the elimination of many managers' jobs.

In spite of the problems and the opposition, the need for a broader span of management is overwhelming. There will be work on increasing the span of management, particularly at the third through the sixth levels of organizations. It is reasonable to think that the span of management will average at least ten by the year 2000 in many organizations.

Organizational Levels

The only way to increase the span of management is to reduce the number of organizational levels. Similarly, reducing the number of organizational levels automatically increases the span of management. Exhibit 17–1 shows the relationship between the span of management and organizational levels.

Organizations have become much too hierarchical during the past twenty years. Whatever the reason for the past tendency to add

Exhibit 17-1. Organizational levels and span of management.

Number of Employees	Number of Organizational Levels with Span of Management of:				
	3	*5*	*10*	*15*	*20*
200	6	4	4	3	3
2,000	8	6	5	4	4
20,000	10	8	6	5	5
200,000	12	8	6	5	5

more and more layers to the organization, there are now truly compelling reasons to flatten the organization. Here are some advantages of flatter organizations for you to consider.

- Flatter organizations, as noted, make it possible to have a much broader span of management, and that contributes to the more effective management of people. In my opinion, it is the most compelling reason to create flatter organizations.
- Flatter organizations contribute to better communications simply because the lines of communications from the top to the bottom and from the bottom to the top are much shorter.
- There are no problems with pay compression in companies with flat organizational structures.
- When the span of management is increased, a lot of supervisory jobs are eliminated, particularly middle-management jobs where the span of management has been the lowest. In fact, it is mostly the elimination of organizational levels that has caused the much publicized—and grossly overpublicized—decline in the number of middle-management jobs.

In combination, these are compelling reasons for eliminating organizational levels. Better management, lower costs, better communications, and improved compensation improve the operation of the company. The egos, bureaucratic procedures, and the status of hierarchical organizations will have to go.

The trend in the next decade will be toward much flatter organizations. In fact, that trend is well underway, and many companies have streamlined their organizations somewhat. Even those that have taken action will find that they can do a lot more streamlining.

There have been some dramatic cases of organizational streamlining in the past few years. One company, for example, eliminated three organizational levels in one year. In the process the payroll costs for middle management were cut by two-thirds. A large company saved thirty million dollars in payroll a year by eliminating one organizational level. In most cases I know, companies have saved much more with organizational streamlining than they ever did from downsizing.

Some business leaders have claimed that there should be a maximum of six organizational levels. I have not always been able to accomplish that target in my organizational structuring work. Here are my guidelines, which are based on what I have been able to do:

- Very large companies; more than 100,000 employees—eight organizational levels
- Large companies; usually multiple business areas and more than 70,000 employees—seven organizational levels
- Intermediate companies; frequently multiple locations and multiple business; less than 20,000 employees but more than 1,000—five to six organizational levels
- Moderate-size companies; usually one business area and 250 to 1,000 employees—four organizational levels
- Small companies; fewer than 200 employees—three organizational levels

In counting organizational levels, the chief executive officer is one organizational level and all nonsupervisory employees are one organizational level. Thus in a small company, there is only one intermediate manager level.

Try my guidelines for your own company's organization. They may be the guidelines for the future, and they have been achieved in the past.

Organizational Unit Management Centers

Another significant aspect of organizational restructuring will involve the establishment of more organizational units. The organizational focus is increasingly on the following:

- First, the company
- Second, complete businesses within the company
- Next, profit and loss centers within businesses
- Then another level of profit and loss centers
- Finally, organizational units with partial profit and loss measures or statistical measures of unit performance

The identification of businesses requires intelligence, a deep knowledge of the business, and a lot of common sense. The goal is to organize by business areas to facilitate focusing on the unique operating needs and critical success areas of each business. Very different businesses often require different management styles and marketing methods.

Every business is a profit and loss center. There are opportunities to set up profit and loss centers within each business, even though sometimes there are shared facilities, common customers, or allocated expenses.

The trend is to increase the number of profit and loss centers to the maximum extent practical. Some companies have been successful in establishing profit and loss centers at the next lower level of the organization, so there are often two levels of profit and loss centers.

When it is not possible to establish profit and loss measures, companies are setting performance measures for units within a profit and loss center based on partial accounting measures of the performance of the unit and/or statistical measures. The establishment of this type of organizational unit isn't new. For example, there have been cost measures for factories. What is new is that organizational units are being established in many new areas and the number of organizational units is increasing.

I worked for a company in the smokestack industry that has 40,000 employees and sixty-two business units. A company in the health-care field I worked for had more than two hundred units: twenty-two businesses, one hundred and six profit and loss centers below the business level, and eighty-three organizational units within profit and loss centers with statistical measures. For a short period of time I was the chief executive officer of a consulting firm that had about four hundred employees. It was one business and one profit and loss center, but there were thirty-two organizational units, each with statistical measures of performance.

Work will continue on establishing more and more organizational units, and this work will be facilitated by computers. The basic reason for the evolution of organizational management is that corporate executives manage best when they manage by organizational results. Also recognize that organizational unit management facilitates a more delegative management style, and that also accounts for some of the great interest in the subject.

There will be problems with organizational unit management. The biggest problem of all will be one of measures. Whenever profit and loss measures involve derived data, pooled resources, or joint activities, there must be some type of accounting allocation, and this is always judgmental. Organizational performance unit measures are always partial, and this is not only an issue of the correctness of the measures but the danger that partial measures will cause inattention to crucial matters.

Personnel professionals must be attentive to the danger that a "bottom-line management" mentality at the profit and loss and unit organizational levels is not too short term and that it does not involve a violation of the company's personnel policies.

Organizational Guidelines

In organizational structuring work, there used to be rules that were rigorously applied. I studied the rules in graduate business school and applied them in the 1960s and 1970s. They involved rules like basic functional subdivision, one person–one boss, and chain of command.

With some variations, the rules were rigorously applied and seemed to work well, as long as the style of management was programmatic and there was (or seemed to be) one model of how a business worked. Organizational rules also worked the best when the rate of economic change was comfortably slow. By the middle of the 1970s, none of these conditions existed, and the rules crumbled and fell into disuse.

Organizational guidelines have evolved in place of the organizational rules. These guidelines are simply ideas to consider and are not requirements. In the 1980s I used about three dozen of these guidelines and listed them in my book, *The Management of Personnel.**
I have never listed these guidelines since then because, regardless of my intent and statements that they were only guidelines, they were sometimes used as rules and were regarded as requirements.

However, you might guess that some of my guidelines relate to the span of management, the number of organizational levels, and organizational unit management that is appropriate for various types and sizes of businesses. There are three other guidelines which, in my opinion, will be so important in the future that they must be mentioned. These are:

1. Design organizations for the effective management of people.
2. Consider networking in your organizational work.
3. Concentrate organizations on critical success areas.

As you design an organizational structure, consider the effectiveness of the management of people as well as the facilities, func-

---

*Robert E. Sibson, *The Management of Personnel*, R. B. Keck & Co., Inc., Vero Beach, Florida, 1985.

tional subjects, and financial resources. Have work groupings that assure the proper span of management, consider knowledge needs, and support job movement through career pathing.

Also recognize that organization for the effective management of people should organize jobs that fit people as well as assign people to prescribed jobs. Traditionally, organizational structuring identified work to be done, organized that work into what seemed to be the most logical functions, and then hired people to do that work, bending and shaping people to the extent necessary to fit the jobs. More frequently in the future, it will be necessary to consider jobs designed to use people's talent to the greatest extent possible.

Consider networking in your organizational work. Networking refers to communication exchanges and informal working relationships that evolve in a company. In the course of their work, people establish these communications and work links simply to get things done in the most efficient manner possible. With management information systems there can be an enormous amount of networking in a company.

Because networking does involve communications and work relationships, however informal they may be, they represent an integral part of the organization of the company. In its most positive form, networking involves people contacting and interacting with others both inside and outside the company who are the most informed or the best qualified. In a negative sense, networking can become uncontrolled and represent a form of organizational Nintendo.

Networking is part of organizational structuring today and will become more and more a part of the organization as the information and communications revolution continues to evolve. Effective networking must be nurtured and controlled.

All businesses have activities that are critical to the survival or success of the company. For example, in some packaged-food businesses, quality control is critical; in pharmaceuticals, it's research. Organization of the company should reflect these critical success areas. Oversimplistically, quality control should report directly to the chief executive officer in a packaged-food business.

The organizational guidelines are ideas for organizational structuring work and will be helpful in organizational thinking and judgments. Most of them are really general references. But the three that will be most important during the next strategic human resources management planning period are very specific, namely, increasing the span of management, creating less hierarchical organizations, and creating performance unit organizations with statistical measures of performance.

18

Job Security

Job security has always been a basic issue for workers. The most traditional views of protection from losing a job will persist and, in addition, there will be new issues with respect to job security. Job security now means downsizing as well as layoffs. Job security also means a change in jobs, a change in careers, and technological unemployment.

Layoffs

People who work in agriculture, seasonal tourist businesses, or for toy manufacturers are subject to rather regular annual layoffs. People who work in cyclical industries, like construction and automobiles, are used to layoffs when there is a recession. Seasonal and cyclical layoffs are part of the work experience for millions of people.

Layoffs also happen in mature businesses. There is a natural and inevitable shifting of jobs as different industries start up, grow, mature, and decline.

There are also layoffs because of management errors or changes in business plans. This type of layoff can happen in any competitive business.

The economy is now facing a massive dose of changes in jobs because of the emergence of a new third economic area and maturing smokestack industries. The third leg of the economy has not yet been labeled, but it mostly has to do with personal welfare, entertainment, and leisure—personal services. This personal service segment has more employees than either manufacturing or agriculture and is by far the most rapidly growing part of the economy.

Job security may also be affected by the potentially high increase in productivity in the near future. A 6 percent increase in productivity would cause a lot of layoffs.

There is also a great deal of business restructuring. Mergers, acquisitions, leveraged buyouts, and all types of corporate restructuring will continue to be commonplace. This restructuring often causes many layoffs.

There is increasing diversity in the reasons for layoffs. There are also new issues relating to layoffs.

Much of the capital substitution now taking place is general purpose equipment and even general purpose facilities. This makes changes easier and reduces the certainty of work. That means less job security and more likelihood of layoffs.

Furthermore, much of the new equipment can easily be moved, e.g., copiers and PCs. Much of new computer and communication technology is relatively inexpensive and can be left idle. Thus work can be eliminated or transferred, and facilities can be relocated or closed more easily than ever before.

Shifting work from one facility to another can be accomplished in minutes. The type of work done in a facility can often be terminated and transferred to other facilities in a day or even an hour. Work in a facility can be transferred one department at a time or even one activity at a time. There are now more ways to close facilities than just a plant shutdown.

Layoffs are still a big part of job security. There are new elements of layoffs, and these should cause at least some rethinking of layoff policies and practices in the 1990s. Then security from layoffs may be as big an issue in the 1990s as it was in the 1930s.

Downsizing

There is also a variation of a layoff, which is called downsizing. Generally, a layoff means a loss of a job because of reduced business activity. Downsizing means a reduction in the number of jobs for the same volume of business, although downsizing has always happened during periods of depressed business conditions.

Layoffs generally affect lower-paid people and are supposed to be temporary. Downsizing mostly affects highly paid staff people and is intended to be permanent. In either case, a person loses his job and is out of work for an indefinite period of time.

It's hard to believe the number of jobs being eliminated from some of the largest and best-known companies. Many thousands of jobs are going to be eliminated in the 1990s. Many people wonder why these jobs were put on the payroll in the first place.

One strategic human resources issue in many companies involves the question of the correct size for a company. This involves manpower planning. Until there is an answer to this question, uncertainty will surround future possible downsizing, and that will be an issue of job security.

Job Changes and Changes in Jobs

Job security involves more than being laid off from work. The issue involves changing jobs with the same employer or substantial changes in the job that is being performed to the extent that the work done results in a different job. To some degree then, job security today and in the near term involves four things: layoffs because of reduced levels of operations, downsizing, job changes, and changes in a job.

In an era of technology and change, people are changing jobs much more often, and that is a new job security issue. A person still works for the same company at the same location but in a different job. There isn't any layoff in this case. However, such a change in jobs would be an important job consideration and might be a matter of job security to many employees.

A change in jobs may be from what a person does well to what he does less well. That may effect his status, his future pay increases, and his future promotional opportunities. Work performance in a new job may affect future assignments or even lead to dismissal. In all of these ways, a change in jobs is a job security issue; *every* change in jobs is a job security issue.

People change jobs and their jobs also change. With greater technology and changing styles of management, the content and the requirements of jobs change frequently in more and more work situations. There are often a series of changes in a job, none of which makes a great difference. However, in combination, these changes in jobs make a different job.

Changes in jobs as well as job changes involve issues of job security because such changes affect the ability of people to do their jobs satisfactorily. For example, a great deal of educational deficiency in jobs is because of changes in jobs, changes that required knowledge not possessed by the incumbents.

In all of these ways, changes in jobs and job changes are an important new job security issue. It is an issue in many types of jobs. These changes in jobs or job changes can be frequent events, and so the issue of job security is always present, in all seasons and under all business conditions.

Technological Unemployment

In the next future strategic human resources management planning period, there will be a new breed of unemployed, and in a practical sense, many of these people will be functionally unemployable. They will be forced to retire or pursue an entirely new career, often at a much lower pay level. Some of these people will be knowledge workers who are replaced by machines. Their knowledge will become obsolete, usually because the machine can do the work much better.

These people will be technology workers who are unemployed because of technology. Technological unemployment will be an important element of job security in the forthcoming strategic human resources management planning period because a great deal of machine knowledge will be substituted for human knowledge.

Traditionally, workers with no skills or few skills were replaced by machines. There was a great transference of low-skilled workers from one low-skill job to another, regardless of the type of work or the type of business. At the most, there were short training periods. These workers were laid off from one company, and if jobs were available, they were relocated within days or weeks, usually in the same geographic area.

The problems of the low-skilled unemployed were intense, but the issues and the answers were simple. One issue was that these workers had little if any savings and could not survive economically without income. The answers were termination pay and unemployment compensation. There also had to be a job somewhere. The answer in this case was to let the worker find a job and help him do that through such services as those provided by the United States Employment Service. For the unskilled or low-skilled person, the main issue was the continuation of income.

Knowledge workers also receive termination pay and unemployment insurance. In addition, knowledge workers usually have some savings. For these workers, the critical issue is finding another job.

A rocket scientist has a job only if a company is making rockets. An insurance underwriter has no place to go if all of the insurance companies do their underwriting with computers. The choice in these cases may be reeducation or driving a taxi.

Reeducating and training people like rocket scientists and underwriters take a very long time and a lot of money. Many of these workers will have family expenses and can't be without income long enough for many forms of reeducation.

Hopefully, rocket scientists will find work in some related activity such as jet engine production, and underwriters will be able to find related work such as a mathematician or as a statistician. Hopefully, there will be a job in a related field of work so that only some reeducation and training will be necessary and much of that can be done while working.

Some planners predict that by the early twenty-first century there will be millions of technologically unemployed persons. I don't think this is correct because I think there is a great transference of skills between jobs in closely related knowledge fields. I also think that reeducation will be very effective in dealing with retreading unemployable knowledge workers to new careers and equivalent-level jobs in many cases. Whichever view is correct, technological unemployment will be a major issue in the near future.

Recommendations

Restricting productivity improvement, adopting make-work practices, or actions to prevent changing facilities or operations *are not* appropriate measures for dealing with the problem of security but rather guarantee massive future losses of jobs. Four affirmative methods that *are* appropriate for dealing with the job security issue involve:

1. Job manning levels
2. Expanded worker capability
3. Job placement services
4. Income protection

Employers must be involved in each of these activities and they must frequently take the initiative. In some ways, the government can help.

Manning Levels

One way of dealing with job security is to take steps to avoid layoffs of any type because too many people were hired in the first place. This involves proper job manning levels, and there are a variety of ways to manage complement size.

Employers cannot guarantee jobs. There will likely be pressure in the next strategic human resources management planning period for some types of job guarantees, including higher severance payments and penalties associated with terminations and facility closings. There will be many such proposals in the future, and legislation on the subject will likely be brought before Congress probably more than once.

Employers will likely oppose all costs related to guaranteeing jobs. However, the pressure to lighten the burden of those who lose jobs will be intense. In the future, employers should be more careful about adding jobs that are not essential.

Correct manning is the first step to consider in the management of job security. There wouldn't be much downsizing if there hadn't been so much upsizing in large companies for so many years. Complement management will be a critical management skill in the future.

Another method of managing job levels is by job sharing. There may be a great deal of job sharing in the near future. It is going to be an important subject in the area of human resources management.

Job sharing wasn't practical in production line jobs or where work stations were definite and fixed. In the future, however, there will be more fluidity and flexibility in the workplace. Groups of people will be able to handle more work or less work by varying their hours rather than their numbers. I think there are compelling reasons for employees and employers to do this. For the employees, the reasons for sharing jobs relate mostly to job security. For the employer, the compelling reasons relate mostly to productivity management and the cost of hiring.

You will find that employees will overwhelmingly support job sharing versus layoffs up to the point where all overtime is eliminated. A distinct majority of employees will favor job sharing over layoffs up to a reduction of one-third of their hours and their pay; and this is also true of those who would not likely be terminated.

For the employer, there is a need for new management skills when job sharing is practiced widely. Issues of compensation reduction, work quality, and reassignments, for example, are associated with job sharing.

The greater cost and the complications of job sharing can be managed, and they are moderate. The costs can be recaptured many times over when business improves and there are no recruiting and training expenses for new employees.

Expanded Worker Capability

People with a high capability in one or a number of areas in which qualified people are coveted by many employers do not have a problem with job security. If they are terminated by one company, they can get work in another very quickly. Thus greater capability generally means greater job security.

An employer's interests are served by having capable employees. The employer's interest is to broaden and heighten the capability of employees as a method of productivity management.

Capability management has to do with creating the talent that is needed now and might be needed in the future. Capability management aims for a workforce with flexibility so the organization can work with effectiveness as the mix of work and operational require-ments change. This tends to mean *broadened talent* for those in the workforce. When a company builds more capability into its work-force, its competitive strength is greater as is the ability of its em-ployees to get alternate employment if needed. Thus in many ways, a more capable workforce serves the interests of both the employer and the employees.

Greater capability is often a matter of education. Generally speaking, the better and broader the education, the greater the abil-ity of a worker to get another job and, therefore, the greater the job security.

Job Placement Facilities

Job security and the ability to get another job are also dependent upon on the excellence of placement facilities. With the increasing complexities in the job security issue, it would seem logical to expect the emergence of better job placement facilities in the near future. That hasn't happened yet, but the need exists and is becoming greater. Better placement facilities in the next strategic human re-sources management planning period are greatly needed and are very likely to emerge.

The U.S. Employment Service, private employment agencies, and newspaper advertising are mostly what's available to help people who are laid off or terminated. In my opinion, these available job placement services are now inadequate.

We do a better job of listing houses for sale and matching them with interested buyers than we do matching jobs and job seekers. For example, there is no multiple listing service for jobs, and in the electronic era this should be corrected.

A better placement service is needed for those who are unem-ployed. I am vigorously pushing the establishment of a national job market network. I think something like this proposal will emerge in the next five years.

Under my job market system, every employer would register open jobs with the national job network. The system could be man-aged by a private company or by a network of corroborating private companies.

If an employer advertised an open job or listed it with an agency, then that employer would be required to register the job with the national job market network. Registration would be simple, and the employer would be required to supply only the type of information that would be used in an ad or given to an agency

Unemployed people would register with an established unemployment office of the government, whether or not they are drawing unemployment benefits. Once certified as unemployed for any reason, they would receive an authorization number. Using that number, they could call, say, 5627 in any area code, just like you use a telephone credit card, except that there would be no charge to the user.

The individual would then be given information over the telephone about jobs of interest that were reasonably within his qualifications. Follow-up information would be sent by mail. Registered clients could call for information as often as they wished and they could call any area code.

The unemployed person would then apply for positions, following normal employment procedures. All this system does is get unemployed persons quickly in touch with open jobs.

The national job market network would have substantial worth in assisting the unemployed get a job. The cost would be paid by the employers. It would be based on successful placements and be equivalent to the cost of recruiting methods now in effect.

Income Protection

Whether you are unemployed a long time or a short time, it seems like eternity. Savings go fast. Therefore, a critical component of job security has to be income protection.

Income protection is in three parts. Unemployment compensation benefits are provided by the government. In addition, most employers provide for some type of termination payments. Finally, employees may fall back on their savings or work part-time while they are unemployed.

Unemployment compensation is part of our economic system. I may be biased because of my work in personnel but I think it ranks with the best legislation ever passed. I think the regulations must be tightened to eliminate those who quit, are fired for cause, or are otherwise not eligible. I could also make a case for higher benefits, paid over a longer period of time. I argue that unemployment benefits should continue until a person gets another job. However, after a time, benefits should be reduced and then perhaps reduced again in order to continue the incentive to get another job.

Termination payments by employers are intended to supplement unemployment insurance and provide additional income protection, mostly for those with long service with one company. I have always found fault with most termination payment plans. For example, it is incorrect to gear amounts to length of service; payments should be geared to needs. Also I think that payments should not be grants but should be designed to provide an income stream until a person gets another job.

Thought should also be given to some type of pay equalization plan because of the substantial number of terminated people who must take a job with less pay. Such plans are being considered and may be implemented in some way during the next strategic human resources management planning period.

I have also been suggesting company job insurance for employees. Such plans are badly needed, and I hope for legislation on this subject by 1995.

A company job insurance plan would provide income supplements to unemployment insurance payments. Participation would be initiated by each employee when he elects payroll deductions into an individual account under the plan.

The company would make a matching contribution. At least some of the company's contribution would likely be based on company profits. All funds would be trusteed.

When he is unemployed, a person could prescribe the amount of payments he receives from the fund each week or each month. However, the total amount from the fund and from unemployment compensation could not exceed 80 percent of his salary at the time of termination. Payments would be made until the fund was exhausted.

When the employee reaches the retirement age requirement set by Social Security, any unused amount in the job insurance fund could be used to buy an annuity that would supplement retirement benefits under Social Security, whether or not Social Security benefits were drawn. In the event of the employee's death, the unpaid funds would go to his designated beneficiary.

Job Security in the 1990s

Job security will become a high-priority issue with working people in the near future. Therefore, it will become an important item on union agenda and will probably become a political issue. It will be important for company leadership to be responsive to what working people at many levels of the organization perceive as a real need.

This issue is not well understood or easily accepted by executive management. Those at the top often don't think that this is a problem. Furthermore, executives think that there are enough company plans for dealing with job security, including unemployment insurance, severance pay plans, early retirement payments, outplacement services, and, of course, golden parachutes.

Employees and executives seem to be at odds on this issue. This is one reason why I weight job security as the fourteenth most important strategic item.

As a consultant, I have often been asked to work on job security matters. My views are:

- Companies in general are spending enough now on job security.
- This money is not being well spent. Consider taking money *from* severance pay plans, outplacement services, early retirement programs, and golden parachutes and putting that money *into* job protection insurance and more effective job placement activities.

I think there is a need for human resources management professionals and consultants in the field to take the initiate and work out practical new answers to the issues of job security. There is much work to be done and there are many opportunities for good work.

19

The Working Poor

The issue of the working poor is related to both fair pay and the fairness issue. The issues relating to the working poor also have political implications and, therefore, this subject might also relate to special interest group matters. In addition, the problems of the working poor are closely related to chronic labor scarcity in some unskilled job categories. For these reasons, I include the working poor as a strategic human resources management planning issue.

The Problems of the Working Poor

The government publishes poverty data that is the basis for various government entitlement benefits. At the beginning of 1991, the poverty threshold averaged about $11,000 a year for a family of four.

About one-fourth of all working men and women who work full-time earn less each year than the amount set as the poverty threshold. That means that about one-fourth of all full-time workers live in poverty unless more than one member of the family is working.

The government's data are based upon a definition of payments that relates to food for minimum nutrition, required housing, and necessary clothing. The basis for calculating the poverty threshold, which was developed in the 1930s, was technically sound and reasonable. There have been some statistical errors in updating the poverty threshold, and these errors inflate the poverty threshold by about 20 percent. On the other hand, the poverty threshold does not include the expenses related to working because it was calculated for non-workers. For example, the poverty threshold does not take into account the cost of working. Today, the costs just of getting to and from work can amount to 10 percent or more of the worker's income.

Overall, the poverty threshold for those who work in 1991, considering technical defects in the calculations and also the cost of work, is between $8,000 and $10,000 for a typical family, depending upon geographic location.

This strategic planning issue deals with the working poor, not just workers whose income is below the poverty level. Obviously, many who earn something above the poverty threshold are still poor.

There is no official data about what constitutes the working poor. But you can describe poverty and you can describe poor.

Poverty is insufficient income to provide *essential* food, medicine, housing, clothing, and transportation. You are poor when there is no money for even small amounts of recreation, education, and savings.

By my calculations, a family of four, on average, was poor in 1991 unless they earned more than $15,000. Based on those figures, more than one-third of the workers in this country today who work full-time all year could be counted among the working poor or are very close to being among the working poor.

A Strategic Human Resources Management Planning Issue

From surveys on personnel priorities conducted every year by *The Sibson Report* and from discussion with colleagues in the field, it is safe to say that less than half of all human resources management professionals would regard this as a strategic personnel issue. A substantial majority of executive management would think that the working poor are not even a subject for business to consider.

These views are partially based on the fact that the employer is conducting the business legally, by paying at least the minimum wage. It is true that the same government that publishes poverty data sets the minimum wage well below that poverty threshold.

Those who think that the working poor are not a matter for business consideration can also correctly say that they are obeying the laws of supply and demand. In fact, for many jobs in most parts of the country, there is an abundance of workers who are able and willing to do the job at rates below the poverty level.

There is logic in the view that the working poor are a national political problem, not a business problem. Not even the largest company could make a significant difference in the income of the working poor.

Nevertheless, I argue that while all of these points are correct and reasonable, the working poor are a big issue for each company. I have been recommending actions for dealing with the working poor for more than five years. Here are my reasons for considering this a strategic human resources management planning issue for every company with workers earning much less than $15,000 a year:

- The contrast between the very rich and the very poor makes the working poor a major fairness issue. When you are earning barely enough to provide the necessities for your family and there is constant media exposure to the rich and the superrich, there is an obvious reason to think that the working poor could become a major, contentious issue.
- Executive pay excesses cause a deep resentment among the working poor. Ninety-nine percent of the top executives in companies with more than a hundred employees earn much more in one year than the working poor earn in a lifetime.
- Where there is chronic labor scarcity in unskilled jobs, employers will have to take actions to raise the income of some of the working poor in order to fill some of these jobs.
- Studies have shown that the line between the working poor and the next higher-paid group is also a demarcation of substantial differences in productivity and work excellence.
- The issue of the working poor is a prized political issue, and many legislators will see it as a political opportunity as well as a matter requiring attention.

You must decide this for yourself. At least consider the problem of the working poor as a strategic personnel issue. Then you might decide to do nothing, but it is important enough for you to reflect on it.

There is a group of people in the personnel field and in politics who think that the issue of the working poor will become a very major problem—a megatrend. Their view is that pressures are building and that problems of the working poor might soon become what employment problems for minorities were not many years ago. They think fairness will be the driving force and that political as well as economic factors will project the issue of the working poor to center stage.

It is also possible that the working poor could be a powerful special interest group in a very few years. The working poor could become a large voting block. As a group, they are the largest single group of working men and women in this country.

Recommended Company Actions

There are many things a company *might* do about the working poor. There are other actions that a company might consider in special circumstances.

During this strategic human resources management planning period, I think that each company should take some time to consider the issues related to the working poor and plan affirmative action steps. There is a range of possible action steps that could be taken. Briefly described, here are some actions that a company might consider with respect to the working poor.

A Company Minimum Wage

Consider paying a minimum wage that is somewhat higher than the legal minimum wage. Your minimum wage should be at least 10 percent higher than the current minimum wage.

Also consider setting a minimum wage near the threshold of income for the working poor. I recommend a company minimum wage of $7.00 an hour in 1991.

For most companies, even those in service industries, the cost of having a minimum wage that is 10 percent above the legal minimum is moderate. In every case I have seen, the extra cost added less than 2 percent to the price of a product.

Paying a minimum wage of $7.00 an hour would be a substantial cost issue, and it is only practical in some cases. It takes just a few minutes or an hour to calculate a minimum wage of $7.00 an hour. Don't factor into these calculations the cost of maintaining pay differentials; workers affected will accept the same pay for all jobs at or below the level of the working poor.

Special Benefit Contributions

This action involves higher contributions by the employer to some employee benefit plans. As one example, consider higher company contributions to health benefits for the working poor.

Employers have been shifting the costs of health care to employees by having higher deductibles and greater employee contributions. Higher employee contributions plus escalating benefit costs have meant that employee costs for health care have been increasing rapidly. Those among the working poor can't really handle the rapidly escalating costs. Consider, therefore, a different contribution schedule for health-care coverage for those earning less than $7.00 an hour.

Another example would be with respect to 401(k) plans. Some companies have problems with qualifying plans because low-paid employees cannot afford to save for the future. Plus up the pay of the working poor if necessary. Structure your 401(k) to *favor* lower-paid employees.

Job Salaries at the 75th Percentile

For many years I spoke out against using the 75th percentile as a basis for setting pay for jobs. Few companies do that anymore.

Now I am urging companies to consider paying at the 75th percentile for jobs held by the working poor. Actually, at the legal minimum wage level, I recommend approximately the 84th percentile; then there is a gradual reduction of the differential until entry rate exceeds the threshold for the working poor. That system is illustrated in Exhibit 19–1.

Even in the lowest pay grades, employees can reach an income level that will keep them from being part of the working poor. At levels five and six, people are hired at or near the threshold of the pay level for the working poor.

A Wage Commitment

Consider a policy that guarantees employees that the pay for jobs will be continuously competitive, regardless of business or financial circumstances. Whatever your decision with respect to posturing your pay relative to the market, this policy would mean that you guarantee that the company will maintain that position, at least for jobs in the levels of the working poor. This specifically means that as market rates (not the cost of living) increase, you assure your employees that you will raises their wages proportionately, regardless of economic consequences or what this might do to profits.

Communicate this commitment to all employees. Let them know it's a commitment.

Exhibit 19-1. Higher competitive pay for the working poor.

Salary Grade	Salary at Market Average			Suggested Salary Level		
	Minimum	Midpoint	Maximum	Minimum	Midpoint	Maximum
6	$6.85	$7.87	$9.05	$7.00	$8.04	$9.29
5	6.23	7.16	8.23	6.67	7.66	8.81
4	5.67	6.52	7.50	6.29	7.24	8.32
3	5.15	5.92	6.81	5.92	6.81	7.83
2	4.68	5.38	6.19	5.62	6.46	7.75
1	4.25	4.89	5.62	5.29	6.08	7.00

Obviously, this involves major considerations, and you first need to be assured that your pay is correctly postured against the market. Such a commitment is very valuable to all employees, but it is particularly important to and valued by the working poor.

Special Pay Increases

The traditional wisdom in wage administration is that if there is any difference in performance in lower-level jobs, it is minimal. Data I have seen in many different companies suggest that this theory is untrue.

Too often, productivity in lower-paid jobs has been based only on factors of performance that can be counted. For example, the number of rooms cleaned is a measure of performance for house-keepers, but how well the rooms are cleaned above a pass-fail standard is also a measure of performance.

The quality of work done is not always considered in performance in low-level jobs as much as it should be. At least reconsider the question of performance pay at lower levels.

Regular Work and Overtime

The problems of the working poor are exasperated greatly if they work part-time or are laid off. A rate of $6.00 an hour is about the poverty threshold and close to the borderline of the working poor only if the individual works full-time all year long. If an employee is laid off for a couple of months a year, then his annual income is below the poverty threshold.

Moderate amounts of overtime will keep a worker above the poverty threshold. When it is practical, cut back the number of low-skilled people and provide overtime on a regular planned basis. This practice is particularly helpful when it is applied to low-skilled jobs where there is chronic labor scarcity.

Upward Mobility

The way to be propelled from the ranks of the working poor is by promotion. To do this requires upward mobility. Upward mobility means an opportunity to get ahead regardless of race, sex, religion, or national origin.

Getting ahead is a national tradition. Every minority group started mostly in lower-level jobs and was part of the working poor. They got ahead through their talent and effort, which meant that they were promoted to better jobs because they earned it. In this way they escaped form the ranks of the working poor. Upward mobility and promotions are and always have been the primary method of getting out of the category of the working poor.

If I were ever tempted to be an activist for any special interest group, it would be for those who work hard to get ahead. Increasingly, the American dream is being frustrated, partly by technology, partly by the preferential treatment of some vocal special interest groups, and partly by lack of support for upward mobility of the working poor by top management.

Strategy for Dealing with the Working Poor

Many companies have no strategy for dealing with the problems of the working poor, which may be one of the biggest problems of all. Their view is that they obey the law, pay the best they can, do what must be done, and manage the operation in the best interests of the organization. They don't see the problem as an issue, so naturally there is no company strategy.

The proof that there is a problem is that this strategic issue relates to the *working* poor. These poor people are the company's employees. They *are* poor, and they know it. The contrasts between the poor and the rich (including the executives in their own company) are very clear and very painful.

Business executives and consultants must be practical. There are social problems that should not be dealt with by business. But first scan the pages of this chapter again; the issues relating to the working poor *are* a business problem, and specific ways have been identified where the problems of the working poor are detracting from business results.

When you consider the action steps that have been outlined, you may conclude as I have that the problems of the working poor are manageable. When you think about the issues, you may also conclude that we face the fundamental issue of fairness and that practical business actions can be helpful.

There have been an encouraging number of companies that have successfully managed the issue of the working poor. In these cases, the opposition always raised the issue of cost. The main reason for not doing something about the working poor was almost always that the company could not afford it.

Whenever possible, get a serious analysis of costs if that becomes an issue, and everyone may be surprised. How much more would a cheeseburger in a fast-food restaurant cost or how much more would a motel room cost if a company followed these recommendations and raised pay to above the level of the working poor? I was told once that if the companies involved paid 10 percent above the minimum wage, the price of a cheeseburger would go from $1.80 to $1.83 and a motel room would go from $49.00 a night to $49.45. We would all pay the difference, and the companies wouldn't lose much business if all the fast-food firms raised the price of cheeseburgers three cents or motels raised the cost of their rooms by forty-five cents a night.

If it is correct that the working poor are a major strategic human resources management planning issue, you should be considering this issue. Look first at the recommended action steps and consider their appropriateness for your company. These actions have been proven by experience, and they really don't cost very much at all.

20

The New Work Democracy

This planning item could be called *perestroika* in the workplace or a new version of industrial democracy. Whatever the label, the last strategic human resources management planning item that I think is important enough to be reported in a separate chapter and which is reasonably certain to occur relates to the work culture. There will be a new openness and greater egalitarianism in most workplaces. I label this "the new work democracy" or "employee partners."

Among other things, this will mean that there will be much more genuine equivalency of treatment throughout a company, workers will be more involved in the direction of the business, and workers will be much more equal in every way. Those who work in a company will be more like partners than hired hands, and there will be a new democracy at work.

Work Culture in the 1990s

This strategic human resources management planning item assumes that the work culture will be very different by the end of the decade than it was at the beginning. It isn't likely that there will be any dramatic changes in the work culture at any point in time, nor will the changes be a single event. Instead, this change in the work culture will evolve through a number of events.

The work culture that is evolving is much more egalitarian and much more open. People at work will be thought of as being equivalent, and people will perceive themselves as being equal to every other person.

Of course, those who work know that some are more equal than others because of pay differences or because there are different benefits or conditions in some cases. But there will be less entitlements and perquisites for a rank or class. Distinctions in status will be considered inappropriate in the evolving work culture.

For a long time there have been efforts in this country to have more equality, more fairness, and greater equivalency of rights. Our history is filled with individuals and groups who struggled in various ways for equal rights at work. There has been a lot of progress, but there are still groups and classes in the workplace.

Unions were the latest group to help in the struggle for equal rights for all working people. Starting in the 1930s, unions brought better conditions and more egalitarianism to the workplace. Many successes can be cited, but on balance, the struggles by the unions have not been successful. Unions are declining because they have largely failed to represent employees and because they did not achieve equality for individual members.

Listed below are the current trends that suggest that this new work culture of more equality and openness at work is evolving.

- There has been a steady decline in production workers or those on hourly pay. This mostly reflects the fact that more operating jobs have a higher technological content, to the point where they are truly technical or administrative in nature. This is breaking down the hourly salary difference.
- With delegative management, many more workers are making substantive decisions about their work, In this sense, all of them are managers. Thus there will be more egalitarianism because work will be more the same.
- As unions decline, there will be less reason to isolate some workers—the union workers—into a different class.
- The work culture that is emerging in the 1990s seems to be one that is freer from bias and preferential treatment. There is more equal opportunity, equal treatment, and high values in working relationships—greater fairness (Chapter 8). Greater fairness will mean more equality at work.
- The average size of companies has been trending downward for some time. Small companies tend to be more open and, at least with respect to conditions of work, more democratic.
- The information the workforce has about their working lives is increasing, in spite of educational deficiency, largely because of the mass media. A well-informed workforce will generally force more openness and create pressure for more equality at work.
- The communications capability is greatly enhanced by technology. As more employees have access to more information, there will be greater openness.

No one of the observable trends seems to be compelling evidence of the emergence of greater democracy at work. However, all of the conditions in combination seem to indicate that there will be at least significantly *more* openness and equality in a majority of companies.

There are many uncertainties about this trend. If future monitoring shows that this was correctly identified as a strategic trend, I suggest that it is worth including as an item and treating as a chapter because the new work democracy would greatly affect the work experience and the nature of the management of personnel.

If these forecasts about the future work culture *are* correct, then there will be a new openness and egalitarianism. Greater openness and egalitarianism at work would surely improve the quality of the working lives of many people. A democratic work environment would also cause some changes in the jobs of the managers of personnel, although not nearly as much as many suggest. Managers would still manage.

The great significance of a work environment characterized by work democracy is the improved conditions of work. Employees are the primary beneficiaries. Greater egalitarianism and openness, however, are also more compatible with a delegative management style and, in my opinion, are essential to achieving high levels of productivity in cases where the employees control the methods and practices of the work.

Employee Partners

Essentially, what must happen, and what I think will happen based upon current observable trends, is that companies will adopt a partnership philosophy toward all employees. Under this philosophy, those who work in a company are not partners in a legalistic sense; the word "partner" is meant in a business sense. A partner is one who works with others in the company as an associate; they work together in a common endeavor.

A partnership philosophy is highly egalitarian. The differences that exist between employees, or employee groups, are related to the nature of work that is done. Where differences in pay, benefits, or conditions of work exist at all, for example, they exist because of legal requirements, because different work requires different pay plans, or because of labor market needs.

Partners are individuals, each with his own skills and talents and each with his own ambitions and objectives. Partners must recognize the need to work effectively, and they must be self-motivated, partly because they work in an environment that involves trust and promotes initiative. They work with others effectively because others are their partners, and each partner recognizes that the effectiveness of each person is important to the results achieved by all.

The partnership philosophy is not permissive. Partners at every level in the organization must adhere to policies and required rules. Partners must be effective in this work.

When a partnership environment is created, employees have a commitment to themselves and to their organization. It makes the difference between doing what one is told to do and doing what one knows needs to be done. It makes the difference between just obeying the rules versus carrying out the work that must be done with commitment and initiative.

To create a partnership philosophy, a company should therefore first examine the work environment it has created. Then the company should consider some affirmative actions.

Above all else, achieving a higher level of democracy at work requires a commitment from executive management. Executives may think of themselves as a separate class or that they *are* the company. However, executive management must be committed to equivalency for all others throughout the company.

An executive commitment to a new work democracy can be achieved only when executives are convinced that they should take some steps toward greater openness and egalitarianism. Then the executives must see clear evidence that each step toward a new work democracy is necessary and that it results in increased productivity and higher levels of a work commitment by the employee-partners.

With a commitment by the executives, there are then a number of specific action steps that would move the organization toward a more democratic environment. Here are some personnel actions that you might consider which relate to this question of work culture. I think that each of these possible actions has great merit in its own right and should be considered regardless of questions about work culture. However, each would move a company toward a more open and egalitarian work culture, and these are presented for your consideration in that context.

No Classes of Employees

Above all else, there should be no classes of employees. This means, for example, no more hourly salary groupings, and no more management and nonmanagement groups. Except for legal reporting purposes, there should be no more exempt and nonexempt.

There should be one class of employees. I think that one class should be called *employees*, because we are all people who work for others for money. Pay methods, conditions, rules, and benefits should be the same for all unless there are compelling reasons for differences based upon work requirements or competitive requirements. Even then there should be just one class of workers-employees.

Be prepared to look hard at your company's rules governing employees. The rules that exist in many companies today don't fit well in an open and egalitarian work environment.

In the past, different rules applied to some employees. Some employees had specific starting and quitting times. Others, such as managers, worked on their own schedules. In the future, with rare exception, the same rules would apply to all worker-partners.

Obviously, some rules might be necessary in some companies in order to conduct the business in an orderly manner, e.g., working hours. In the past, such rules were very broadly applied in operations-level jobs, even when there were no compelling reasons to do so. In the future, there will be fewer rules and more of those that exist will apply to everyone.

Employee Determination

In a democratic work environment, the employees, not the managers, will make decisions about many issues. This will include some personnel policy issues and substantive matters of pay, benefits, and conditions of work.

In some personnel decisions, there are alternatives with approximately equal costs and advantages to the company. In these cases, it is suggested that the employees' views should be determinative as a matter of management practice.

Alternate answers might make no difference to the company, but some of these alternatives might be preferable to the employees. In such cases, the employees should be given an opportunity to express their preferences. Their preferences should be the factor that determines final management decisions.

A Personnel Director

I have long urged companies to have at least one member on the board of directors who has special knowledge and training in the field of human resources management. That seemed to be a sound management practice and was critical to the board in discharging some of its responsibilities.

The director with personnel knowledge would not be an advocate or ombudsman. Rather this person would bring employee considerations to bear in the basic policy and strategic decisions that are made at the board level. This director would also have first-hand knowledge in helping his colleagues on the board review the appropriateness of personnel actions and thinking, which should be an important part of the board's responsibilities if indeed people are important assets.

Open Communications

If there is to be openness, then that would seem to require excellence in communication with employees. Furthermore, if employees are to be more in the mode of employee-partners rather than hired hands, then there must not only be excellence in communications to employees but also open and quick-response answers to their reasonable questions and complaints.

Expect far more open communications with all employees. There may well be a form of an electronic town meeting with all employees. This will probably happen because it can be done.

Top management will be on the company's television network— live and in color. There won't be prepared scripts or playacting; these will be two-way communications with employees.

Grievance Systems

In all operations and at all levels, there will be systems for employees to take questions or complaints to higher levels of management if that is necessary to get satisfactory answers. Appropriate systems for handling questions and complaints would likely be a common practice in a more democratic work environment.

In an employee-partner environment, the grievance systems will be formal only in the sense that they are official, with an expected (but not required) procedure. Detailed and bureaucratic systems, like those in collective bargaining, will not be used. Grievance systems will be simple and designed to get questions answered or complaints resolved—quickly and equitably. Employees will represent themselves, and this will be factored into the system.

Commitment to Employee Success

In a more democratic work environment, it may also be that companies are more committed to the success of employees. No company can guarantee work or jobs, but the type of guarantee that seems appropriate for employee partners would be support in helping the person be as successful and productive as possible.

With great changes in the workplace and rapid increases in technology, human resources management might place more emphasis on activities to help employees become successful in their assigned work. The employer who works for the success of each employee will be promoting more openness and higher productivity.

The success rate of employees in business averages less than 60 percent. That should be increased substantially—and I think the success rates should be more than 90 percent. That will take a much greater employer commitment to employee success in the future than has generally existed in the past.

In a more democratic working environment, companies will want to improve success rates. Those in personnel would have a large role in this work. We have already seen mentoring, counseling, and tutoring programs in some companies that have been directed by human resources management professionals. In the future strategic human resources management planning period, there will likely be more new efforts at supporting employee successes, and many of these will be very successful.

Job Posting

Consider job posting. Post every job opening above entry-level jobs. Make sure the posting, which will probably be done by electronic methods, is available to all employees.

An opportunity to get ahead is part of employee success, and employee success should be an important part of corporate objectives. Few companies have posted job openings except for factory jobs. In the future, more democratic workplaces will post jobs, and that will be an important part of greater openness at work.

Equivalent Pay Packages

In the environment of the new work democracy, all people at work will be treated the same with respect to pay. But there will be different forms of compensation or different types of plans that are particularly needed or appropriate for different categories of work. Examples would be incentive pay for salespersons and long-term income plans for executive managers.

There are special needs for other employees also, and special attention should be paid to such plans. Employee class stock and job protection insurance are two new plans that are of particular value to employee partners below the level of executive management. In other ways, compensation plans for the non-executive group will receive special attention in the future.

Equal Treatment

Most action ideas relating to fairness (Chapter 8) contribute to the new work democracy. If a company provides equal opportunity and equal treatment for all of its employees, then the employees *are* being treated in an egalitarian manner.

This new work democracy is best described by the standards of fairness listed in Chapter 8. More openness and greater egalitarianism at work are fair.

Success Sharing

Success-sharing compensation and employee stock ownership are other actions that a company might consider in a more democratic work environment. When employees share financially in the success of a company, they are being paid like partners. When employees own stock in a company, they *are* partners.

Measures of Employee Success

Companies measure the success of their owners by various financial standards. Companies might consider measuring the success of their employees. Then part of the overall measure of the success of a company will be the success of those who work in the firm and create the success.

Other Practices and Actions

Listed above are eleven specific personnel practices that a company might consider for establishing a more democratic work environment. You can think of others. Then if you want still more items to consider, ask the employees. You will find that they have many suggestions.

21

Eight Additional Planning Items to Consider

The previous sixteen chapters covered the strategic human resources management planning issues that I think are the most important and almost certain to happen. I think that these items will most assuredly impact many companies in some manner.

You might rank these sixteen planning items differently. You might also think of other strategic human resources management planning items, and I would encourage you to do so.

In fact, there are eight items that I considered including as chapters but didn't, mostly because of their relatively low importance or the questionable basis of the prediction, or both. These eight items will be outlined briefly in this chapter and are as follows:

1. The continuing decline of unions
2. Safety at work
3. Reallocation of talent
4. Stress at work
5. Less company loyalty
6. Contract work
7. Privacy-secrecy
8. Executive accountability for employees' welfare

If your company went out of business because of a long union strike, you would not think in terms of a decline in union membership generally, and you would probably rate unions as a major issue. If you had a friend who was raped at work, you would probably consider safety a major issue. In many possible cases like these two illustrations, you would be correct that the item is of high importance in one specific case. But a strategic issue is one that will be of major importance to a broad class of cases in the future, and these have been covered.

Here are brief notes about the eight additional strategic human resources management planning items.

The Decline of Unions

Union membership has been declining for a long time. Information suggests that the decline in unions is not only due to a decline in employment in the traditionally highly unionized industries but also because of an increasing lack of confidence in union activities and some union failures in recent years.

Unions have reacted by trying to organize in new industries. In fact, while union membership has been declining significantly for many years, unions have increased their membership in some areas, such as government employment, health-care institutions, and schools.

As the influence of unions continues to decline, labor relations may become more chaotic in some instances. Faced with a declining membership, union representatives may see a need for dramatic action.

In absolute numbers and as a percentage of the workforce, the decline in union membership in the future will be more gradual than it has been in the past. By the year 2000, union membership will stabilize as a percentage of the workforce.

Unions will be a factor in some industries and in some companies for a very long time. In effect, there will be *pockets* of union influence, and in some instances, unions will be very active and have great power. In the economy overall and as a factor in employee relations, however, unions will have little influence as a strategic factor in human resources management.

Unions are now largely an anachronism. They truly were an institution of an earlier time. As a national force, unions now seem to be playing out a role the best way they know, but they are no longer relevant as a major factor in human resources management.

The diminishing influence and role of unions presents problems. Union demands were used as comparisons in many types of decisions. Furthermore, employers thought that if they didn't provide fair pay, benefits, and proper conditions of work, they would be organized by a union. This reference and this motivation for fairness are now gone.

The leadership of unions is now a minor factor in employee-employer relations. Who or what will take their place in the future?

It may be that new unions are emerging. Associations and worker alliances are often considered to be types of unions, although neither replaces the unions' role with respect to leadership and standards for comparison.

Some employee associations have already started to behave more like unions. What may really make a difference in the next twenty years is the use of communication technology by associations. Associations will use information technology to communicate directly with their members, which could result, as one example, in efforts to influence minimum pay standards in the profession.

Also expect to find associations that provide job counseling advice to their members. In the future, professional associations might also provide training and career-pathing services.

Workplace alliances are small in number and scattered. They are dedicated to fairness in the workplace and are only concerned with a particular workplace—one location in one company. These alliances are few and may or may not become significant.

Most recently, special interest groups have been affecting human resources management matters. It may be that the special interest groups will prove to be another breed of the new unions.

Safety at Work

The traditional view of protection at work is safety. However, employees are increasingly being subjected to dangers other than work-related hazards, and that is the focus of this strategic human resources management planning item. The issue of safety at work now involves protection against work-related and nonwork-related hazards in the workplace.

For example, crime at work is increasing at an alarming rate. Crime at work is increasing less than it is on the streets, but the increased dangers at work are important enough to warrant attention.

Employees increasingly want safer conditions at work. Safety ranges from smoke-free and drug-free workplaces to a workplace with no violence. Companies must increasingly design, locate, and administer facilities to ensure safety at work.

Assaults and robberies by fellow employees or intruders are the most often reported crimes at work. (Note that "at work" includes going to and from work.)

Sexual harassment (not just flirtation) is another major issue of safety at work.

There have been cases where employees have been harmed by demonstrators who were not employees and/or were not demonstrating about anything relating to the workplace.

Every indicator suggests that crime generally and also crime in the workplace will continue to increase. Larger and more militant security forces may be part of the work population. In the future, security at work might rank with job safety in importance.

A special case is when the crime is related to the company's location. If you have a location in a high crime area, the best action is almost always to move. A company cannot change the conditions of a neighborhood.

Strong law and order measures can be taken within a company and its locations, and I certainly recommend that this should be done. Recognize, however, that there will be reactions to crime prevention measures.

Reallocation of Talent

Not long ago, many companies thought they had highly talented people in every section and at every level. Many companies paid premium salaries, offered great job security, and paid for super benefits in their bid to be preferred in labor markets and attract the most talented people.

Now, few companies can afford compensation premiums, the myth of corporate job security has been shattered, and we are in a period of benefit cost containment. Furthermore, there are pockets of labor scarcity. Therefore, all companies have shortages of high talent.

There will be a shortage of talent for the foreseeable future. Companies can't have the highest talent everywhere in their organizations. It is now necessary to allocate talent.

It is a job of management to allocate scarce resources. Now there is a need to allocate scarce *human* resources.

For a long time, the most talented people were in corporate staff jobs, law, finance, and administration. That scarce talent must now be reallocated.

For most companies, the great need for the highest talent is in the operations, particularly in production. The problem is not staff work or even information handling but that we lack the capability to make quality products at a competitive cost. Now the highest talent must be directed—from recruiting through career pathing to top management—into jobs involving making products or service work.

To accomplish this reallocation will require great skills in managing people. Reallocating talent will also require basic changes in our personnel practices. For example, we must pay relatively more in the production areas. This will mean gearing pay more to market pay and less to administrative systems. In addition, highly talented people must be recruited into production rather than corporate staff jobs. Career paths should be through operations and production.

Stress

Stress is now appearing on management agendas, and this is an area of focus in human resources management. It seems that some people have discovered stress at work for the first time. In fact, stress has been part of the work experience since the beginning of time. Now it is becoming center stage in personnel for some reason.

According to one recent study, stress has now (*just* now) "gotten a foothold in the U.S. workforce." According to this study, 70 percent of all workers have health problems because of stress, one-third of all workers may have burnout in the near future, and one-third of all workers are contemplating quitting their jobs because of stress. These findings are fairly typical of a number of studies.

Another study reported that 80 percent of all people thought that there should be employer-paid disability for stress. The company that made this study will sell you stress insurance. More than one insurance company is developing stress disability insurance.

Concerns about stress are largely the cause of counseling activities in some companies. Some are urging major efforts involving substantial costs for dealing with stress at work.

It isn't clear why there has suddenly been so much emphasis on stress at work. In fact, stress is part of work, as it is part of sports, marriage, raising children, and most other activities. There is a lot of evidence to suggest that knowledge work involves *less* stress than the old production jobs.

Whether there is more or less stress, there has been a lot of work, talk, and study about stress. There has been enough activity to think that this could become a strategic personnel planning item in the near future.

Less Company Loyalty

There has been a severe decline in company loyalty. The rate of decline has probably stopped or slowed, but the level of company loyalty is very low, and that may be a significant factor in human resources management throughout the next decade.

Thirty years ago, company loyalty was an important factor in the management of personnel. Company loyalty was an important input to the design of personnel programs and practices. Company loyalty has become a minor factor in human resources management.

The question is whether the absence of loyalty impacts work effectiveness. If you conclude that the absence of company loyalty is important, then you should conclude that some other quality must take its place.

A company can build a strong commitment to excellence. Such a commitment must be mutual, it must be based on reality, and it must be related in large part to each unit. A commitment to work excellence mostly involves bonding to one's associates rather than a faithful obligation to one's employer.

A commitment by workers may increasingly be to their own workplaces, to their careers, and to their close working associates. *Bonding* would then be an important part of working conditions in the future, although it seems unlikely that bonding will be the factor in the future that company loyalty was in the past.

In the past, there was hostility toward companies as well as strong company loyalty. The company that gave to its employees also demanded a lot from them, and those demands often generated hostility. When unions were present, the hostility was accentuated to the point where labor relations resembled a war. With the decline in company loyalty, there has been an equivalent decline in company hostility.

In fact, few have seriously addressed the problems of the decline in company loyalty. That's one reason why I have not rated it highly. But company loyalty has largely disappeared, and practices and thinking in human resources management need to reflect that change.

Contract Workers

The term "contract worker" refers to those who are not regular full-time employees of a company. This represents about a third of the nation's workforce.

There will likely be a continued increase in the number of contract workers. More important, perhaps, is the diversity in the contract work that is emerging.

The different types of contract workers are:

- Part-time, with less than a full schedule each week
- Part-time, with less than a full schedule each year
- Those hired for a specific period of time or for a specific assignment
- Other companies' employees who do work on your premises or in your operation

- Leased workers
- Subcontract workers, including those who work off-site—the "cottage workforce"

It is the last three categories of contract workers that are new. It is in these areas that strategic issues may evolve in the near future.

For example, leased workers have become a major part of the workforce. Leased workers may be an especially important factor in the management of the workforce in small companies or in large companies with small, distant locations.

The management of contract workers is different than the management of regular full-time employees. The ability to manage contract workers is in itself an important human resources management issue.

There are questions about the effectiveness and the quality of work performed by contract workers. Contract workers are often employed to lower payroll costs, but relevant and comparable payroll cost data are often lacking.

Opinions are divided about the future growth and nature of contract work and the nature of the contract workforce. What is clear, however, is that human resources management departments must become knowledgeable about these work groups. Contract work issues will require more attention by human resources management professionals in the future planning period. There are also legal questions as well as issues relating to management and work excellence.

Privacy (Secrecy)

This planning item is properly labeled "privacy" for employees and "secrecy" for employers. In many respects, it is the same issue but the ramifications are quite different and the perceptions are varied, depending upon whether you are looking at the item from an employee's point of view or from an employer's.

Computer technology has generally added to employees' concerns about privacy. Computer-aided personnel may cause the issue of privacy to become a major problem.

In an electronic world, employees will have much less privacy at work and in their lives in general. There will be vast amounts of data about each of us. There will be less privacy because there is more information and it is increasingly accessible to more people. Employers will have access to much of that information.

One issue of privacy will involve what an employer has a right to know about each employee. Employers think they should have the right to know anything that would affect work performance, but that will have to be detailed and will be the basis of some disagreement.

Another issue of privacy will be the wrongful use of personal information by the company or by its employees. The wrongful use of personal information by employees should be a matter for strong discipline. The wrongful use of personal information by the employer will very likely be a matter that is taken to the courts many times in the 1990s.

There will be little secrecy for employers. There won't be enough electronic locks and keys to maintain the level of secrecy of the past. Employers will have to conduct employee relations in the sunshine. This will be a difficult experience for many, and some will have a lot to learn. Many think that employee relations *should* be conducted openly, and I am one of them.

Unless there is wrong-doing, the consequences of both privacy and secrecy are not generally very great. Usually, the worst that could happen is embarrassment, and that is correctable. When there has been wrong-doing, then the privacy-secrecy issue will have major importance.

One of the problems companies will face in dealing with privacy and/or secrecy is one of policy or philosophy. One person sees drug testing as an invasion of privacy; others think it doesn't matter at all and is just a minor inconvenience. Some employers are concerned about employees learning about salary information; others work hard to communicate the same information.

Overall, the strategic significance of privacy (secrecy) is probably not very great. Employees *will* have less privacy in a technological world. Employers *will* have fewer secrets in the area of human resources management. In fact, human resources management practices will be designed with the knowledge that there will be few if any company secrets about employee-employer relations.

Executive Accountability

As a matter of current law, executives have certain accountability for the health, safety, and welfare of employees. Precedents have been set for both wrongful death and negligence.

There are reasons to expect much broader and more specific accountability in the future. The details of greater accountability for employees at work are not yet clear, but you should consider some possibilities.

If a person's career is harmed by a job move or by the fact that the employee was not selected for promotion, the employer and the executives most closely involved might be held responsible. There may be payments to keep the worker whole, with payment for what he might have earned plus damages—and, of course, legal fees.

Workers recruited into a company because of some growth strategy might have legal claims against the company and its executives if the company aborts the project or changes strategies. A change in strategy might be considered a breach of implied contract.

There may be the business equivalent of malpractice suits. If a business does poorly because the executives did not exercise reasonable prudence—or if they made mistakes—then both stockholders and employees might have a claim on the executives for their failures.

Both top executives and members of the board of directors could be held accountable for improper payments to executives, and they might be forced to make restitution. Prior stockholder approval of plans or practices may not be a satisfactory defense in cases of improper and excessive executive pay.

All of these cases of possible future executive accountability were provided by an attorney who specializes in the field. Her predictions are for such conditions not much later than 1995.

Other Issues

Altogether, twenty-four strategic planning issues have been presented in this book; more if you consider planning items that were part of a group of related issues, such as special interest groups. I think that is all of the strategic human resources management issues of any real significance that exist at this time.

Most likely, many who read this book will think of other items, and there are others I might have missed; but I considered more than sixty current observable planning items and evaluated all of them. The twenty-four reported are the ones that truly seemed to be *strategic* planning items of consequence.

There will always be some basis for suggesting that someone's favorite subject should be added. For example, one of my readers suggested that "women in the workforce" was an important item and pointed out that a best-selling trade book on planning devoted an entire chapter to the subject. The chapter was complimentary to women, but women at work is not a strategic human resources management planning issue.

For one thing, it is an error to extrapolate the former growth of women in the workforce into the future. The rate of entry by more women into the workforce has tapered off and the increase in the number of working women is now growing at about the same rate as the workforce overall.

More importantly, with respect to women in the workforce, I ask "So what?" To be a strategic human resources management planning item, the subject has to be more than some form of statistical report or social commentary. To be a strategic planning issue, there must be significance in terms of work results or work conditions.

If you think that women are more talented or less talented, then more women in the workforce would be significant. If you think that women are harder or easier, tougher or softer, more gentle or more harsh, then more women managers might be relevant. But there are no indications that as workers or as managers women show such differences.

Another person who reviewed this manuscript suggested that special treatment for working mothers should be a separate strategic human resources management planning item. No doubt, a company with a first-class day-care center would be a preferred employer for women with young children. But that is a specific tactical employment issue and not a strategic human resources management planning matter. Working mothers would, of course, favor a company with a day-care center.

Another suggestion was to include computer-aided personnel systems as a strategic planning item. This involves general software systems so that personnel information as already recorded is immediately retrievable by the personnel department's PCs. This *was* a strategic human resources management item from 1985 through 1990 but is no longer an issue.

There will probably be readers who think that the special interests of minorities should be a strategic issue in personnel. If this book had been written in the 1960s, the rights of minorities would have been a strategic human resources management planning item. Equal rights has now replaced minority rights and will be a strategic issue for the next three to ten years. Equal rights will be for all groups, and there will be no preferential treatment for any group.

These were the twenty-four strategic human resources management planning items as of June 1991. It just happened to work out to be twenty-four.

If I were asked what the twenty-fifth item would be, I wouldn't know. In fact, I really don't think there are any other items at this time.

The list of strategic human resources management planning items is not fixed. Strategic human resources management planning is a dynamic subject and the list of issues is changing all the time. The twenty-four strategic human resources management planning items presented here are those that existed in June 1991.

As you review these items, remember that they are all based on facts. In selecting these items, I have been a professional analyst and reporter. None of my preferences or opinions have been included. This is what is happening; and my method for collecting, analyzing, and reporting what is happening is described in Chapter 4. If you followed the same process, you would very likely come up with the same items, although not necessarily in the same order of importance.

None of my views or visions of the future are in the identification and weighting of the items that have been reported. The *recommendations* are mine, and reasonable people could, of course, surely come up with different action ideas.

The nature of strategic planning is such that about one-quarter of these items will have run their course within three years. An equivalent number of new strategic issues will almost certainly be added in that same three-year period.

Similarly, by the end of seven years, it is almost certain that more than half of the twenty-four strategic items will have played out in some manner. They will likely be replaced by another ten to twelve items.

The Management of Strategic Human Resources Management Issues

The management of strategic human resources management issues involves:

- Identifying strategic human resources management issues
- Keeping the information up-to-date
- Communicating the strategic human resources management information
- Identifying strategic human resources management issues that have particular relevance to your company
- Taking specific action steps
- Using the strategic information for intelligence and leadership

The identification of the strategic human resources management planning issues has been done in this book. The process for doing this work and the items as of June 16, 1991, have been identified and described.

Because more than half of the items will be played out in seven years or so and because they will be replaced by items that are not now identifiable, it will be necessary to repeat the reporting at least once every seven years—and perhaps as often as every five years. I think that the same process that is described in the first four chapters will be usable five years from now—or fifty years from now.

There is some obsolescence of strategic information every day. There were some changes in information on June 17, 1991. By June 16, 1992, 10 to 20 percent of the information will be obsolete, replaced by new strategic information. Under these conditions, part of the job of managing human resources management information is to keep that information up-to-date.

This is work you must do for yourself, or you must hire someone to do it for you. I can only urge you to do it and describe how I keep the information up-to-date for my own work and my worknetworking clients.

As information is scanned and catalogued for *current* human resources management planning work, we identify information that *might* have a strategic human resources management significance. This is an imperfect system, so we err in the direction of identifying too much, knowing that we can purge information later.

All of this information goes into twenty-five folders. One for each of the twenty-four trends that has been reported plus a folder for potential new items.

Once every six months, all of this information is reviewed, and a report is prepared for networking clients on changes in the strategic items. If there are important events that are clearly affecting a strategic issue, this is reported as soon as possible.

We also have a master disk of strategic human resources management information, mostly containing descriptive information and recommendations. These master disks will be modified every six months. Then if a client wants up-to-date (within six months) information, it can be printed out.

We could send each company a disk and then electronically modify it when there are changes. That is what technology permits, but it is pretty fancy for my relatively small group of worknetworking clients.

This updating is keyed to current human resources management work. If you do this work for yourself, as I have recommended, then you should consider doing the work just described to keep the planning information up-to-date.

With respect to communications, refer to Chapter 2, where I recommend current human resources management information that should be reported to every manager as well as to all employees. Also consider communicating strategic human resources management information to all managers. You could buy them a copy of this book or you could prepare a brief report that includes a list of the strategic planning items that have been described.

You must take the general planning items that have been identified and determine which ones will impact your company. You must be specific about how the planning items will impact your company and when. This is difficult work, requiring a time involvement of top-level people. Typically, at least ten but rarely more than fifteen of the strategic items reported for all companies would impact any one of those companies.

With respect to each of these problems or issues, you need action steps. This is the big payoff from strategic human resources management planning work.

The actions involving decisions, programs, and practices that stem from planning would be very few—but they are generally very important. Actions from strategic planning involve strategic matters and avoiding major mistakes and dealing with strategic issues effectively in a timely and cost-effective manner.

Strategic human resources management planning information provides a level of understanding and a sense of direction that will be helpful to senior managers. This is an example of organizational intelligence. It is a level of understanding that enhances the ability of managers to design new activities and projects that are more relevant and more effective. Organizational intelligence also helps companies avoid mistakes.

Another result of the strategic human resources management process is organizational intelligence and leadership. This is related to visions of the future, which is the subject of the last chapter.

22

Visions of the Future

Strategic planning primarily provides information for action, for operating plans, and for avoiding mistakes. Strategic planning information can also provide inputs for leadership.

Business leaders can greatly affect what actually happens in the future. Basic technology and economic, political, and social factors are the driving forces in our society. But they are steering us in a direction, not to a specific point.

Strategic planning identifies the direction of an issue and describes it sufficiently to ensure a reasonably correct understanding. But forecasting in strategic planning yields a range of possibilities for each planning item. That range of possibilities can be substantial. Leadership can influence where we actually wind up in that range of possibilities.

Leaders cannot influence the future unless they have visions for the future. Visions of the future must be based upon information. Generally speaking, that information should be taken from strategic planning information.

Forecasts, Prophecies, Predictions, and Visions of the Future

In the strategic planning process recommended in this book, the basic system of identifying planning items was *forecasting*. This first involves the identification of current observable events; extrapolating current events into the future on some reasonable basis; and then monitoring the forecasts at least annually against actual events to modify the forecasts. This process is continued for each strategic issue until it becomes a current trend or is no longer a factor in human resources management.

Forecasting is based on facts, starting with observable events. Extrapolations are judgmental, but if done honestly they set a reasonable range of likely possibilities. As the planning item is reviewed each year and the forecasts refined, the range of possibilities becomes more certain and less broad.

Prophecy is very different. Prophecy states what will happen in the future. Prophecies are not provable, and prophets ask that we believe or have faith. In some ways, prophecies are inspired revelations, often presented with great urgency and evangelism.

There have been prophets in business, and some of them have indulged in prophecies about human resources management. In fact, if you read the future-world publications, some are laden with prophecy, often designed to sell an idea or a book. Some of these future-world prophecies are pure fiction, and those who write the books should be classified as novelists.

I don't engage in prophecies. Prophecies can be very entertaining, but they usually lack relevance as well as accuracy. Prophecies can be distractions, and they can be disruptive and destructive, even if well intentioned.

I don't like to give examples of prophecies, but the prediction of guaranteed jobs is a prophecy. The description of work groups who are caring, sensitive, and preoccupied with getting along are prophecies. Workplaces without bosses are prophecies. Prophecies may be interesting, but I have never heard of any that were useful so I avoid them and urge you to do the same.

Predictions foretell the future like prophecies, but they are linked to forecasting. Predictions select one specific condition within the range of possibilities and allege that it will happen. Predictions represent the best guess or most likely condition within the range of possibilities.

Predictions can be very helpful as a way of explaining a strategic planning item, and I did this in some way for almost every strategic human resources management planning issue. If you want to get peoples' attention when you make a prediction within the range of reasonable possibility, make one that is dramatic or unpopular.

I also make predictions about changes outside of the field of personnel that will impact some human resources subjects to illustrate planning items or how a planning item might evolve. For example, it has been predicted that income taxes will never be lower than they were in 1988. This has implications on fair pay.

Predictions can also be a form of shock therapy. The possible consequences of an action—or lack of action—may galvanize people to take proper actions. I didn't use this tactic in this book, but I have used it in client presentations.

Visions are descriptions of the future that are considered desireable but fit into the range of reasonable forecasts. Predictions identify the most likely condition within a reasonable range of forecasts.

Visions are the most desired condition within a reasonable range of forecasts.

Thus visions can be one basis for setting strategic goals and objectives. Visions may sometimes also be an important input to policies.

All visions must be within the range of probable future conditions, so there is reason to think that they can be accomplished. Then visions can be the basis of leadership.

Both in terms of strategic objectives and executive leadership, visions can be very important. Therefore, visions of the future are practical business matters.

I don't think there will be much interest in my visions, but visions of the future are essential for leadership. And some statements about visions at least illustrate what they are and may indicate their importance.

I am not a leader, but I do provide information, including planning information, to leaders and to those who advise leaders. Because of this I have spent some time working on visions. Seven of my visions are briefly described in this chapter. These are:

- A renaissance in education
- A doubling of employee productivity
- A management restructuring
- A performance culture
- Equal treatment at work
- A crime-free workplace
- Employee ownership of stock

A Renaissance in Education

Without a *massive* improvement in education, there can be no significant increase in productivity. Nothing of significance in business can be accomplished without better education. In fact, without great improvement in education, this country will become a second-class economic power.

My vision of the future sees great improvement in education, partly because it can happen and partly because there will be enormous pressure to make it happen. Surely employers can exercise some leadership in this area, and they have every reason for doing so.

It's very likely that employers and parents will be the driving forces that cause the giant leap forward in the public education system. As customers, employers will increasingly demand much greater excellence in education. Parents will see more and more clearly that their children have no future without a better education, and they too will demand massive improvements.

First and foremost, the improvement in education must focus on the public schools. I think that educational excellence should *double* in these institutions.

By the year 2010, we will have free universal education through the tenth grade, plus four years of additional education for qualified students at no cost.

Employers will contribute greatly to this massive improvement in public education. Employment standards will be set to reflect educational requirements in entry-level jobs in this era of technology. Employers will do educational achievement testing, and high school graduates who don't pass the tests will face a lifetime of drudgery; or they will work to get the required education.

Employers will routinely conduct additional educational activities for their employees. Personnel professionals will develop high skills in these areas.

There will be dual educational systems in many areas of the country. Students will be able to choose which public school they attend, and they will have a choice between a public school and a private school. Students going to private schools will be subsidized by government payments. I think that this dual education system is regrettable, but it is probably the only way to get the educational establishment to reform.

The improvement of public education in grades K through 12 will be very great. Today SAT scores average about 900 and GPAs about 2.5 for those who plan to go on to college. By the year 2010, GPAs for this sampling of students will be over 3.5 and SATs will average above 1100.

Students not thinking of going to college have GPAs under 1.5; and that will almost double. A sample testing of those who are not planning to go to college had SATs under 700; and these will rise to about 900. The dropout rate among high school students will be cut in half.

About half of our young people will complete two years of college work. Half of them will go on to get four-year degrees and advanced degrees. The average formal educational level will be sixteen years, including kindergarten.

Colleges as well as employers will be the beneficiaries of a much better public education system. I also see three critical developments at the college level. First, institutions like community colleges will offer a free education to those who qualify, and their curricula will have a very strong technical and para-professional orientation. Second, private colleges will receive the same per-student public subsidy as government-owned colleges and universities. There will also be national minimum standards for grade point averages and standard achievement tests for granting college diplomas.

Reeducation, much of it electronic, will become widespread. Technological advances will make it possible for an individual to choose courses of instruction and access them at low cost. These technologies and the passion for education by people of all ages and following will bring new meaning to the expression "continuing education."

Education will be revered in the twenty-first century. Those who are knowledgeable and intelligent will receive high praise. The educators will be the most respected workers in the society—but they will also be extremely competent, unbelievably competent compared to today's standards.

Productivity Will Double

Productivity will more than double in this country by the year 2010. Throughout the entire period from 1991 through 2010, productivity improvement will average at least 4 percent a year.

Productivity improvement of 4 percent a year or more can happen because of capital substitution. But the capital will be mostly worker controlled, so whether productivity will be increased is a function of employee effectiveness.

I think that productivity *will* increase because of worker effectiveness and capital substitution. It will mostly be the operating managers of people in the various operations in our economy who will bring about the increase in worker effectiveness.

These operating managers will have authority delegated to them that is equivalent to their counterparts in independent firms and managers of business areas in large firms. The management of personnel will be elevated to a level of excellence not contemplated or even understood today. The methods of managing people today will seem crude by the standards of the year 2010.

Operating managers will delegate considerable authority for work methods and work decisions to each individual worker. This will be what is now called empowerment, but I think the degree of delegation will be much greater than the most enthusiastic supporters of empowerment now imagine.

The unprecedented increase in productivity will also be due to a much better educational system. Much better educated workers will have access to vast amounts of information that they will learn to use with great intelligence.

Executive management will, of course, have to direct this extraordinary achievement in productivity. Executive management must set the policies and the new management style. But executive management will have very little involvement in work done in the organization.

A Management Restructuring

Management practices will be very different in the early twenty-first century. Like productivity and education, management excellence throughout the company will more than double. In fact, managers in the year 2001 will look back at practices of 1991 in disbelief and wonder why we did things the way we do them now.

Here are some specifics that have already been covered in some detail in various places in the text:

- Organizational structures will be much less hierarchical. There will only be seven organizational levels in the largest of operations, and the national average will be between three and four organizational levels.
- The span of management will be between ten and twenty. There will be true managers with authority equivalent to that of managers of independent firms of comparable size and type.
- There will be a broad use of organizational unit management practices. The number of organizational units will at least triple, and statistical performance measures will be very good.
- Delegative management will be widespread. There will be high levels of excellence in management at the first levels of operations. In the twenty-first century, the average manager will be better by far than the very best manager is today.
- Empowerment will be widespread. The participative practices of today will be the subject of many jokes.

The Work Culture Will Be Performance-Dominated

A performance culture will evolve. It will replace the entitlement culture that has dominated so much of management's thinking and pay practices for the past fifty years.

The performance culture will run very deep in our social culture. It will be the result of a basic ground swell among the working people.

The performance culture will expect hirings, assignments, promotions, and terminations to be based on capability and performance. Working people are now embarrassed by "plusing" by race, gender, or national origin and will be outraged by even the thought of such a practice in ten years.

Jobs will be paid what they are worth in the marketplace. Artificial pay levels that are in effect for any reason will be regarded as cheating.

People will be paid for their performance. Salary reward for performance and incentive reward systems of all types will be used widely. Million-dollar-a-year incomes will be considered indecent—and, in fact, they will be taxed back to reality.

High performance will be highly respected. High performance will be highly rewarded.

Equal Treatment

Equal treatment will be as much a part of our work culture as one person, one vote is part of our political culture. There will be equal treatment at work; in fact, the trend toward equal treatment started at work some years ago.

There will be little if any preferential treatment in any type at work. Equal opportunity and equal treatment will be thought of as the high moral ground. There will be *no* discrimination or preferential treatment. This will occur because of productivity, fairness, and the law. People will look back to the era of preferential treatment and quotas as a period of injustice.

There will be a much greater egalitarian treatment of workers in their paychecks. High-pay, low-pay ratios will become extreme around the year 1991 and then there will be a great reversal. By 2020, the pay of top executives will rarely be thirty times more than the lowest paid worker (after taxes). A great deal of the egalitarianism in pay will be tax-driven.

There will be a work environment that respects talent and expects effectiveness of work. The only basis for preference will be performance and capability.

In the future, those who choose not to work will not be tolerated. For those who produce the wealth, the ultimate justice is reward for effective work, which will be matched by intolerance for ineffective workers and freeloaders.

A Crime-Free Workplace

The work environment will be almost free from crime. High productivity, accountability for work, and better educated workers will combine to resist crime of all types in the workplace.

There will be no drugs at work and only former drug users, not current users, will be working in private employment. Drug users will be unemployable; or they will be working for government organizations.

Theft, violation of privacy, sexual harassment, and similar crimes will not be tolerated at work in the future. There will be very high values at work, and these will be forced into effect by the workers themselves.

A crime-free workplace with high values may be in sharp contrast to life away from work. We may all have split personalities, but the one at work will avoid crime of any type.

Every employee will be a member of the company's crime-watch program. There won't be anyplace for the criminal at work to hide. Criminals at work will be quickly apprehended, and they will be discharged. Records of criminal behavior of all types will follow people to their next job, and if they continue that behavior at work they will become unemployable.

Employee Stock Ownership

Employees will become the largest single group of stockholders in American business. The conditions for the great growth of stockholdings by American workers now exist. As a group, American workers will own more stock than all the institutional investors (including pension fund managers), and they will own more of America than all of the foreign investors put together.

Employee stock ownership was a strategic human resources management planning item, but it is also a vision of the future. This change can happen at the initiative of business managers, although some simple legislation relating to registration, the use of classes of stocks or bonds, and the tax treatment of dividends would be very helpful.

Both a crime-free workplace and employee stock ownership would be two visions at work which if fulfilled could have enormous impact on the type of society we have. If you could sit with a small group and explore the potential political and social implications of workers being the majority owners of all private companies, you would soon find that the effect is very great and exciting. Employees becoming majority owners of American companies would represent a revolution.

Employee stock ownership would be accomplished by companies for very important and practical business reasons. But those sound business actions would also change the course of history.

Conclusions

Some people write an entire book about visions, predictions, and prophecies. Some have more vision or more imagination than others. As far as human resources management is concerned, the seven visions identified are the only ones I can think of that could be of great importance.

My conclusions about visions are of course my own. There are many visions of how leadership can influence the actual conditions of work life.

Visions only have value if they help leaders direct and energize the work community. Among other things, this means that these visions must be communicated to those in a position of executive leadership—and communicated clearly. This is the only time I have ever publicly presented my visions, and I have only done so here to illustrate why the visions of the future are part of strategic human resources management planning.

I think visions should always be positive. It might be possible to identify negative or gloomy visions, but we don't want anyone to lead us in the direction of negative or gloomy futures. We want leaders to have positive visions of a better work life and then to show us how to get there. Then the leaders should stand aside.

Our vision would not be complete, however, if we did not consider the government and special interest groups. There isn't any reason to hope that the government in Washington or at the state level will be even more effective. There isn't any reason to think that the politicians will have responsibility for much besides getting votes.

There is no reason to think that there will be much leadership in Congress. In fact, working people's respect for members of Congress will be much lower, and by the year 2000, this lack of trust and confidence in Congress may be a major political issue.

Special interest groups will be running out of control, and there will be many of them. They will be in keen competition for favors and for space in the media. They will be the new unions.

Thus planning is of three different types with three different objectives. Planning is current human resources management planning. This is work that must be done. If you don't have information about what is happening currently, you really can't do your job. Strategic human resources management planning involves relatively little extra work because it is based on current planning items that have already been identified. These are then updated each year. The strategic planning items are needed for strategic management; to avoid costly mistakes or unnecessary changes; and to make decisions in an orderly and low-cost manner to achieve a desired result. Visions of the future key off these same strategic planning information items and reasonably represent a prediction that can provide a basis for leadership.

INDEX